D1098133

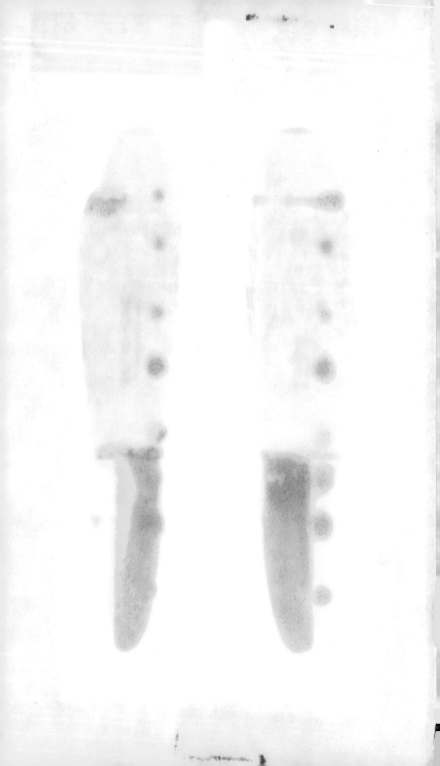

The Decline and

Fall of the New York
YANKEES

by JACK MANN

_____ SIMON AND SCHUSTER, NEW YORK

FIRST PRINTING

LIBRARY OF CONGRESS CATALOG CARD NUMBER: 67–17885
DESIGNED BY EVE METZ
MANUFACTURED IN THE UNITED STATES OF AMERICA
BY H. WOLFF MFG. CO., INC., NEW YORK

The author wishes to express his gratitude to the San Francisco Examiner *for permission to quote from "Casey at the Bat."*

To my Godmother-Aunt, Jane,
who afforded the time, the space
——and me

Contents

Contents

1

... And That Was The House That Ruth Built

IT WAS ONE of those comfortable, embarrassment-of-riches problems that the Yankee management had come to know so well. It wasn't as serious a thing as the periodic dispersal sale, peddling big-leaguers like Joe Beggs and Eddie Miller and Joe Gallagher and Jimmy Gleeson to the other league because the farm system was, alas, becoming too cluttered up with talent again. This problem was merely a bothersome little detail of décor, but no detail was too minute to escape the attention of the *soigné* Yankee management, and something clearly had to be done about it, soon. Stated simply, the problem was this: The Yankee Stadium press room (i.e., the free-load room, where the entrepreneurs of sport honor the birthright of newspapermen to be wined and dined) would have to be enlarged, or the Yankees would have to stop winning championships. They had festooned the wall with pictures of their pennant-winning teams until they had run out of wall.

The presentation began in the front corner of the room, next to the phone booth, with the 1921 American League champions—the team beer baron Jacob Ruppert had bought from

The Decline and Fall of the New York Yankees

Boston, one player at a time, as a man of modest means would buy one golf club at a time until he had a matched set. By 1923 Jacob Ruppert had his matched set and it won the World Championship, beating the haughty Giants, from whom they had humbly subleased the Polo Grounds until Babe Ruth built a new home for them, and vice-versa. The 1921-22-23 pictures were neatly, very properly spaced, about nine inches apart, the way the Yankees always did things. So were those of 1926, '27 and '28. The 1932 group—the one that won shortstop-coach Frank Crosetti the first of his 22 World Series checks—was given a place of its own, but then the pictures started getting closer together because the pennants did. There was 1936-37-38-39, six inches apart. Then 1941-42-43, closer yet. A global war and a change in management gave the 1947 World Champions a little room, but then came the Casey Stengel era and the squeeze was on: 194950515253—pause— 1955565758—pause—1960—pause, but only to fire Stengel —1961626364—whoa. Pause again, not only to fire Yogi Berra for failing, as Stengel had failed, to win a seven-game World Series, but to wonder where the hell to put the 1964 team picture. They were out of wall.

Removing the phone booth helped a little, and there was one expendable picture in the array: the 1954 Yankees were in on a pass. The legend under their picture stated simply, "Won 103 Games," discreetly ignoring the fact that the 1954 Cleveland Indians won 111. Stengel, however, was as proud of that team as he was of any of his 10 pennant winners—and, to hear him pontificate to the tourists over a thousand whiskey-and-waters in a score of hotel bars during a couple of hundred small hours of the morning, he was even prouder of those losers than of any of his winners. It would have been like striking the colors, admitting the Indians had legitimately won that pennant, to take that picture down. It was the missing link in a chain of 10 consecutive pennants. That wouldn't do. Clearly the Yankees were up against the historic problem that the new sociologists have complicated by applying the term "territorial imperative." They had to have more room, or stop winning pennants.

So the Yankees stopped winning pennants, and an era was over, an era that can never come back. The mighty New York Yankees, who bullied baseball for 44 years, winning 29 pennants and 22 World Championships from 1921 through 1964, finished a soggy, convincing 10th in a soggy, unconvincing American League in 1966. And in the final agonized throes of abject failure they made all the thrashing, undignified, desperate moves that losers make. They fired a manager who didn't deserve it, bought players and promoted others who didn't deserve it, gave away bats and then found that when they gave away only baseball they could draw as few as 413 customers to a game at The House That Ruth Built. Then in a final stroke of *lèse-majesté* they fired Red Barber, the dean of that rare breed of tell-the-people-what-happened broadcasters, and for the worst of reasons. There would be four counts to the indictment against Red Barber: (1) an opinion of his own, based on long, hard-earned experience, (2) the integrity, in the afternoon of a life spent substantially in conformity with a system he never really agreed with, to express his opinion, (3) a pride in being a professional reporter, and (4) a contempt for colleagues who find conformity easier, or at least more expedient, than professionalism. All four of these are inimical to what shall be hereafter known as The Corporate Concept, and Red Barber had to go.

The next step after sacking Red, of course, was to hire an-

11

other kind of professional as director of special projects, his principal special project being to relate the New York Yankees to the people in the community in which they function. After 64 years of existence and 44 years of smug dominance, the Yankees are going to try to get to know the people who earn the money to buy the tickets that made them the Yankees. The Yankees are in a hell of a mess.

They are in that mess because of 10 years, and maybe 20 years, of bad management. Not stupid management, but short-sighted management, the failure to recognize that the game of baseball was changing into a system of controlled mediocrity, to which the Yankee method could no longer be superior, or even equal. While the monster television, to which baseball is selling and has almost completely sold its soul, was devouring the minor leagues, which were the source of the Yankees' or any other team's eminence, the owners of baseball were busy legislating excellence out of existence. If you can't lick 'em, enjoin 'em. The sharks kept nibbling at the Yankees' giant tuna until it became a rack of bones, and they got away with it for three principal reasons.

First, the Yankee management helped them. With the minor leagues moribund, bonus boys became baseball's chief crop. During the middle 1950s the kind of money handed out to pimpled youth became ridiculous, if not obscene. The Baltimore Orioles, with general manager Paul Richards as one of the leading heavyweight contenders at the business of spending other people's money, got as silly as anybody. They doled out large sums to such as John Bruce Swango, a pitcher of some presumed ability who found himself unable to pitch in front of large gatherings of people. And to Jim Pyburn, who they say was a pretty good football player.

The Yankees, meanwhile, disdained the vulgar rat race. They did not completely abstain. There were substantial checks given to Tom Carroll and Frank Leja, who, between them, played only 69 games for the Yankees. But George Weiss was still the general manager and he knew that the Yankee method worked. All right, there were 42 minor leagues functioning in 1946, and only 28 in 1956 (including two Mexican leagues), so maybe the farm system was out of style. But kids had always wanted to play for the Yankees because they were the Yankees, and who ever heard of paying a kid a bonus for becoming a Yankee?

So let the Dodgers throw the money around, which they did —and got Ron Fairly, and Frank Howard, for whom they got Claude Osteen and a couple of pennants. Baltimore didn't come up with much except Boog Powell and a few kid pitchers, and they couldn't win a pennant until they dipped into the other league and came up with Frank Robinson in a trade that was the biggest heist since Brink's. But what did they give for Robinson? Milt Pappas, a beardless youth the Tigers—or the Yankees—could have taken out of a Detroit high school graduating class if they'd matched the Orioles' offer.

They didn't, and the parade went on by. It is now stylish among Yankee management to say they knew what was happening, and could see the deterioration coming, but evidently nobody pointed out to George Weiss the error of his intractable ways. One didn't. The Corporate Concept is pyramidal, and Weiss sat at the apex like a buddha. Whatever *is* is right, and George Weiss *was*. Was he ever.

The second reason, or lack of reason, why the Yankees were euchred out of the talent market was the remarkable—you could say spectacular—mistrust baseball executives have for one another. They wrote and rewrote and mangled the bonus rule until it was a bleeding thing, much in the manner of Mel Allen rationalizing a point of Yankee policy. For a while you could give a kid any amount of money but you had to keep him on your bench for two years. Thus Joey Jay, the first of the Little Leaguers to make the big league, sat on the Milwaukee Braves' bench during 1955–56 and didn't get anything but fat. And the Braves blew the pennant in 1956 when the Dodgers' Don Newcombe staggered to victory over the Pirates on the last day of the season, 8–5. A case can be made that the presence of some old pinch-hitter on the Braves' bench, in place of Joey Jay, might have made a vital difference in a 2–1, 14-inning defeat suffered by Warren Spahn on the last Friday night in St. Louis. Or in some other defeat snatched from the jaws of victory along the way. Anyway, a number of the Braves made such a case, and they weren't very happy the next June when a callow youth named Bob (Hawk) Taylor showed up with a $100,000 check and prepared to sit out his two years. He joined another opulently endowed young man named John DeMerit, and the Braves had to win their first pennant with a 23-man team. The Dodgers of 1965, with Mike Kekich and John Purdin not pitching and Willie Crawford occasionally pinch-running, won with 22 full-fledged players, so it could be done. But the Yankees, and especially the Casey Stengel Yankees, preferred to have 25 working men, men who could "execute." They dealt in the present, not in futures, so they not only would not but could not play that self-defeating game.

In another period the rule was that no bonus could exceed $4,000, which in our kind civilization has become no money worth worrying about. And still a number of bemuscled young men who would have been pumping gas somewhere along

Route 66 if they could not hit the curve ball were seen tooling along Route 66 in Lincoln Continentals. There was an ugly rumor that money in excess of $4,000 was being passed out *sub rosa,* and the elders of the National Pastime could not abide that sort of thing. Not because it was dishonest, or because it was hypocritical, but simply because there was no way for one club to know how much money another club was passing under the table. Like, we're all going to chisel, fellas, but let's be fair about it. So more legislation was in order. Men have passed laws against burglary not because they planned to steal from other men, but because they feared being burglarized.

The have-nots struck again, with what Cleveland president Gabe Paul, among others, called "that vicious first-year rule." The rule was vicious only to the haves, of course, but it was another clumsy attempt by baseball executives to keep each other more or less honest. You could sign bonus players for as much money as you wanted or had to give, but you had to keep him on the "parent" roster for the first year or somebody else could draft him. So you'd lose the kid, which to baseball executives is a bad thing; but you'd also lose the money, which to baseball executives is unthinkable. After the first year the player could be optioned out to the minor leagues to learn his trade, the way all players and especially Yankee players had learned their trade for a generation. But he could be optioned for only three years, so that about the time he might be ready to become a bona-fide big-leaguer, somebody could draft him again. "That rule," said Gabe Paul, "precluded a buildup of talent by the Yankees, or by any other club."

That rule also led to some undignified and some downright silly proceedings. The Yankees didn't "protect" Curt Blefary from waivers because they felt they had greater need at the moment for Harry Bright, a career triple-A utility man; and the Baltimore Orioles grabbed him. As a consequence, Blefary's $11,683.04 winner's share made him one of the wealthiest undergraduates at Towson State College when he returned there after the 1966 World Series. He was even wealthier because the Yankees were still paying his college tuition, as part of the bonus deal they had given him. That was pretty funny because it happened to the lordly Yankees. It was even funnier in the unrestricted draft of minor-leaguers in December 1965, when the Yankees, with 190-odd players under contract, could "protect" only 40 of them, and the have-nots could pick them over, at bargain prices. Now, by these various stages of communal confiscation, the lordly Yankees have become have-nots. And when controlled mediocrity has been finally perfected, there will be no haves and no have-nots, and National League president Warren Giles's impossible dream may be realized: a 10-way tie, with everybody finishing with "winning" records of precisely .500. Some maiden-claiming horse races end in photo finishes, and some fights are draws for the same reason: no class. Whatever else the Yankees were—and they were a number of other things—from 1920 through 1964, they were the class of baseball. But they won't be any more, and neither will any other team, because class has been legislated out of existence. Baseball's foreseeable pennant "races" threaten to be a dreary series of slow-motion cavalry charges like the National League's mark-time classic of 1964, when neither the Dodgers nor the Cardinals nor the Reds could win, but the Phillies could lose. The name of the game is overall mediocrity, but baseball has a euphemism for that, too. Call it "balance."

The first thing baseball executives do after they pass a new rule (or in many cases, it seems, *before* they pass a new rule)

16

is to begin calculating ways to violate it. The first-year rule placed all teams in a limbo between piracy and dirty pool, and oh, the shenanigans. The Pirates' almost-great Roberto Clemente still maintains, and of course the Dodgers' management vehemently denies, that he was "covered up" by the Brooklyn organization before Pittsburgh pirated him from Montreal in 1954 for a $4,000 draft price. If he went hitless one day, Clemente says, he'd play the next day. But if he went 3-for-4, he'd sit down for a day or two. Thus a nosy scout would be unlikely to see him at his best two days in a row and suspect that he was too good to be laboring in the minor-league vineyard. The idea of *not* playing Roberto Clemente, for whatever reason, is intriguing. But in those days there were certain restrictions on the minor-league draft. The first-year rule called for more refined hanky-panky, and baseball was ready. The Pirates in 1963 had a young pitcher to whom they had given some money, and they sort of liked him. Not enough to put him on the "big" roster, but enough to hide him from enemy scouts. So they devised a very simple method: They put him on a minor-league roster, to keep him under contract, and they didn't pitch him. Just to be on the safe side, they didn't even put a number on his back. He threw on the sidelines, and pitched batting practice if nobody was watching. But if any scouts, identifiable or otherwise, seemed to be hanging around, he was the bat boy. Get it? Red Murff, the sometime pitcher who scouts for the Mets, got it. And the Mets got the kid in the December draft, cheap. Joe L. Brown, the Pirates' general manager, was furious. In retaliation, he threatened the *reductio ad absurdum:* to sign up a number of singularly uncoordinated youths, put them on minor-league rosters without numbers on their backs and let interloping scouts leap to the conclusion that they were tal-

17

ented enough to not play. Brown's evaluation of the baseball ethic was probably correct, but he was unable to pull off his little caper. The number of places on the number of minor-league teams that have survived the blight of television (and only because the major leagues have subsidized them) is insufficient to permit such a luxurious drollery.

Besides, the baseball structure was too close to *reductio ad absurdum* already to quibble about it. The first-year rule and the unrestricted draft had already rendered the farm system obsolete and, in the process, accomplished the quest of 40 years of losers: Break Up the Yankees. The Yankee management in mid-1965, in mid-second division, was still trying to act as if it weren't so, but they saw the handwriting. "We'll get the edge again, the way we always have," said farm director Johnny Johnson. "With superior scouting." It is indubitably true that astute, well-paid scouts were always the chief ingredient in the success of the Yankee dynasty—next, of course, to the compelling charisma of the Yankees' stupendous success itself, a self-regenerating dynamism. But Johnson knew also that the Yankees' principal tool, scouting, was being taken away from them, that in effect it had already been taken away, by the first-year bonus rule, by the unrestricted draft of minor-leaguers, and now by the third principal contribution to the Yankee downfall, the free-agent draft.

If the basic structure of baseball is of questionable constitutionality, the free-agent draft is almost certainly unconstitutional. For all of this century baseball players have been chattels, bound by the reserve clause to the team with which they sign a contract. The only ways they can change employers are to be sold, traded or discarded outright. And they are not discarded unless they are (a) worthless or (b) overpriced, or, as in the case of Warren Spahn, who was cast adrift by the Mets in mid-1965, a combination of the two. Thus they are never free to seek another job in the open market until they are virtually unemployable. The system is distinct from servitude in two respects. First, baseball players are in most cases well paid. Second, they are free at any time to quit working; if you do not like pitching mop-up relief for the ninth-place team for the amount of money the management sees fit to pay, you may exercise your right of citizenship and go back to pumping gas on Route 66. The mind boggles at the thought of the judicial lightning that would strike if the Metropolitan Life Insurance Company proposed to trade an agent to Equitable Life without bothering to ask him whether he wanted to go, but the right of the National Pastime to hold men in bondage has been sanctified by the Supreme Court of the United States. The Court in 1922 solemnly ruled that baseball is exempt from the nation's antitrust laws, and therefore from its labor laws and a number of other statutes designed to protect free enterprise from itself, on the ground that baseball is not a business but a sport. Despite an occasional cry in the legislative wilderness from such as Representative Emanuel Celler (D.–N.Y.), the agile logic of Chief Justice William Howard Taft and his colleagues has gone unchallenged these 45 years. The only challenge is to *homo sapiens,* who is asked to believe that the Los Angeles Dodgers, who attracted 2,617,029 paying customers in 1966, let out a lucrative radio contract, took their cut of national television revenues, parked a sea of cars at a dollar a copy, conducted a carriage-trade stadium club and operated concessions that sold beer at three times the wholesale price, were doing it all *pour le sport.* The fun-and-games fiction is justified by the reason that it works, that any system that permitted players to drift capriciously from team to team would be chaotic. Sure it would. Teams would lose their communal identity (a feeling baseball's owners like fans to have: "It's *your* team; bring money") as personnel turned over, perhaps 100 percent in some cases, from year to year. The "new" Washington Senators might even have been new that dreary 1961 day in dreary Griffith Stadium, instead of a squad of rejects sent out to do battle against the establishment.

It would be chaotic all right, but what baseball's owners don't mention when they plead for preservation of their own private brand of capitalism is that it would be expensive, too. Does anybody want to bet that Sandy Koufax couldn't have had his $166,666.66 in the spring of 1966 if there had been 20 teams bidding for his services instead of one? The bidding would have opened at about that level. And wouldn't Dodger "policy" have been stretched to give him a contract longer than one year if it had been possible that he could have peddled himself elsewhere? That would have obliged the management to take some of the risk that his arthritic elbow would endure, or that he wouldn't break a leg, catch a line drive in the eye or be run over by a truck. As the system was, Koufax had to take all the risk himself.

The long-range risk on fragile talent is taken by entrepreneurs of other fields. The Columbia Broadcasting System, long before it took a flyer on the Yankees just in time to regret it, watched rival NBC give Milton Berle a 10-year contract, risking the possibility that Uncle Miltie would go out of style. He did, almost immediately, but a contract is a contract. That's show biz. But what about show sport? If William Holden is worth $50,000 a year, well into the 21st century, for his performance in *The Bridge on the River Kwai,* what was Sandy Koufax worth to the Dodgers in 1963, '65 and '66? Possibly another actor or two could have taken Holden's role without turning the picture into a flop, but could the Dodgers' short-ball attack have won any of those championships with anyone but Koufax wearing uniform No. 32? No chance.

So the system worked, in more ways than one, even if it was constitutional only by indulgence. At least, the owners of baseball could argue, a young player had the right to choose which team he would be bound to. And the bidding was competitive. The Garibaldis of Stockton, California, were called upon by 14 big-league scouts and even had a visit from Casey Stengel in June 1962, after their son, Bob, had performed heroically for his Santa Clara team in the College World Series at Omaha. He was a hard-throwing right-handed pitcher and they're the easiest kind to scout. Nobody alive can confidently predict that a kid will ever be a big-league hitter, but when you're scouting a pitcher you can tell whether he has big-league velocity. That won't make him a pitcher, necessarily, but without it he need not apply. Bob Garibaldi seemed to have a big-league fast ball. Among other people he convinced Dolph Camilli, the old Dodger slugger who scouts California for the Yankees. The Yanks dropped out of the bidding at $125,000 and a few days later, in the Candlestick Park office of Giants' owner Horace Stoneham, it was more or less announced that the kid had found it great to be young and a Giant for bounties that added up to about $150,000. That was especially nice for Bob Garibaldi, who turned out not to be a big-league pitcher, but anyway, the owners could point out, it sure as hell was free enterprise. The scouts had nothing up their sleeves but money, and the boy could take his choice of employers.

That prerogative was legislated out of existence in the major-league meeting of December 1964, when the owners voted in the free-agent draft. "Free agent," it must be understood, is another of baseball's euphemisms. A free agent is a player—or a non-player, for that matter—who is not under contract to any professional team. Use of the term suggests that there are mature, ready-to-play athletes standing around in front of drug stores, not employed as big-leaguers only because the idea hasn't occurred to them, or nobody has asked. (Warren Spahn, incidentally, is a free agent because the Giants gave him his outright release. Dominic DiMaggio is not, because he retired voluntarily; if he decided to come out of retirement this spring at age 49, the Red Sox would have first call on him because the Reserve Clause applies in perpetuity.) There are, of course, no such people. The free-agent draft is a draft of college kids and kids just out of high school, which is why it takes place in June. The Yankees this year, for having finished dead last in the American League, have first choice in the draft. They might pick any kind of player because they need every kind of player. Let us say one of their scouts has roamed North Dakota and found that the second baseman of the Wahpeton Science team has exceptionally quick hands. So they select him, which gives them the right to woo him and his parents (which of course they have already done or they wouldn't have selected him). Presumably they offer him a considerable amount of money. The boy doesn't have to accept. He has the alternative of not playing baseball, because the Yankees have selected him and that's that. If he has resisted their blandishments all the way into December, his name goes into a pool. The 20 big-league teams draw lots and it is 19 to 1 that some other team will draw the name of that Wahpeton second baseman. He may like their offer better, and he may not. If he doesn't, he doesn't have to play.

The free-agent draft goes on, in reverse order of finish. The Dodgers, having won the National League pennant last season, have 20th choice this year, so the Yankees have 21st and 41st and 61st, etc. In a banner year, there might be as many as two dozen players really worth signing, or really worth giving the important money the kids, and their parents, insist upon these days. So the Yankees, lucky enough to finish last, might get two of them. So could the Chicago Cubs, who made a nice guy of Leo Durocher. It takes a long time, at this pace, to re-build a dynasty. "The free-agent draft was aimed at us, and the Dodgers," grumbles Yankee farm director Johnny Johnson. "The teams with money. But we'll live with it. We'll get the edge the way we always have: with superior scouting."

There is only one way the Yankees, or anybody, will circumvent the free-agent draft. They will need some help from the father of a bright young prospect, and the father will need only a little help from a lawyer. When baseball owners in effect tell a young man of ability, or assumed ability, that he may not apply for a job he wants merely because they have arbitrarily decided that he cannot, they are in possible violation of the Fourteenth Amendment to the United States Constitution. They are abridging his rights and depriving him of both liberty and property (in the sense of capacity to make money and gain property) without due process of law, or due process of anything except their mistrust of each other. Somebody's daddy will sue, and he'll probably win.

Send not to ask what has happened to the Yankees. It has happened to baseball. There won't be any more dynasties. For all the impression the Baltimore Orioles made on the shoot-from-the-hip reporters in sweeping the 1966 World Series, they are not the kind of team that will win five pennants in a row, and they will have a tough time making it two in a row.

The Decline and Fall of the New York Yankees

Consider for a moment the team the Orioles humiliated in that Series. On the roster of the champion Dodgers were Wes Covington and Dick Stuart, players literally nobody wanted; Jim Gilliam, who couldn't move any more and shouldn't have been expected to at his age; and John Kennedy, a fine glove man who simply cannot hit big-league pitching. And when inadequacy led inevitably to crisis, who was their reinforcement? Dick Schofield, a career spear-carrier who has been the 25th man on most of the teams he has played for in 14 seasons. The Dodgers in the past few years were not even threatening to become a dynasty. They were merely taking advantage of the fact that no team has a chance any longer to build up any real muscle. The Dodgers were a study in applied mediocrity, which is what the game has become.

Nobody makes any more money out of baseball than Dodger president Walter O'Malley, or ever has, and no organization is more shrewd about spending its money. They have the means, and the scouts, to obtain the best players available, and the efficient top-to-bottom organization to get the most out of them. The Dodgers are in far the best position to take charge of baseball, the way the Yankees used to. But they can't either. They can buy the best talent available, but the best talent isn't available. O'Malley can chew on his checkbook in June while other people pick over the top 19 free agents.

"They say this rule is a great leveler," says the Yankees' Johnny Johnson. "We'll see how they like it. We'll see if legislation can win pennants." Legislation can't, of course. But legislation can keep people from winning pennants. It can enforce mediocrity. It hasn't happened only to the Yankees. They simply need a little more time to get used to it.

One other thing has happened, not just to the Yankees and

not just to baseball. It has happened to the nation, and presumably to the world. It is the fetish of security. It is the bright young man, fresh out of Princeton, with the "good" background, with the world by the tail, with a downhill start, who applies for a job and asks, within the first five minutes of the interview, about the retirement plan.

Belief that the strong should help the weak is socialistic. It is also civilized, democratic, Christian and logical. But belief that the strong should have built-in insurance against failure is depressing. Babe Ruth would find it hard to believe, but the new kind of ballplayer talks much more about security than he does about girls. There is a great risk involved in the attempt to become a professional baseball player. Many more fail than succeed. But not quite so many more in this decade, because not quite so many try. It used to take five years, or six, or seven, for a player to learn his trade and make the big league, and now it can be done in three or less. "It has to be," says Johnny Johnson. "If they don't make it in three years, they quit. They get married young, and their wives are putting pressure on them to make more money."

"Everybody is security-conscious," says Joe L. Brown, general manager of the Pittsburgh Pirates. "Five years in the big league and you can get a pension, so that's all they try to do: last five years and get the pension." In addition, the security-conscious young men are being scouted in college by other talent hunters, from business and industry, which offer all kinds of fringe benefits—other forms of built-in security. "We don't have the quality of player we used to have," Johnson reluctantly concedes, "because it just isn't there any more."

And the Yankee dynasty isn't there any more. Forty-six years, almost to the day, after it began with a loud, happy noise, the Yankee Era came to an end in a soggy, awkward silence. Some members of the new-and-different Yankee family still like to tell each other that the era could come back, and of course it could. All they have to do is turn back the clock and re-create the circumstances. Nickel beer could come back, too.

2

Sockdolagers and Haywire

THE YANKEE ERA did not begin in The House That Ruth Built, and neither did it end there. It began on a bright, crisp afternoon in 1920, in the Polo Grounds. It ended on another bright, crisp afternoon in 1966, in a hotel lobby in Cleveland. It began with a shout and ended with a snarl.

The Yankees, conceived as a sort of expansion team in 1903, two years after the American League was formed, were the poor relatives of New York baseball in 1920. Even the Dodgers, out in the wilds of Brooklyn, had won a pennant, and the elite of baseball were the haughty Giants. The Giant management had deigned to rent the Polo Grounds to the up-start Yankees, in the best interests of sport and in the firm belief that the new franchise would never amount to much. Baseball owners have never been reluctant to sublease their playgrounds to unworthy opposition. The Philadelphia Athletics needed the money when they let the Phillies move into Shibe Park in the late 1930s, and they didn't figure to be chased out of town by those National League doormats, who are rivaled only by the Pirates *circa* 1950 and the aboriginal Mets for the title of worst team in big-league history. Walter O'Malley was delighted to allow the Los Angeles Angels to play in the privacy of Chavez Ravine for four years, on his terms. The unwritten terms of such summer rentals are (a) don't win too many games, and (b) more important, don't draw too many paying customers.

The Yankees, as the 1920 season opened, had been perfect tenants, staying in their place in the second division and playing their games to intimate gatherings. The Giants hadn't won a championship in two years, but they had reorganized and, well stocked with talent, were poised to run off a few more pennants to add to the half-dozen they already had in the bank. It would be nice to have the Yankees around, to show by contrast the power and the glory of the Giants, baseball's first dynasty. It would be embarrassing, of course, if the Yankees won the American League pennant and contrived somehow to upset the mighty Giants on their home grounds, but that was highly unlikely. The Boston Red Sox would take care of that contingency. The Sox had played in the first World Series, in 1903, and won it from the Pirates, five games to three. Boston had cut another swath through the new league in 1904, and Giants' manager John McGraw, whether out of contempt or caution, had refused to have his champions meet such a bunch of johnny-come-latelies, so there wasn't any World Series. By 1919, however, the Red Sox were becoming downright dynastic. They had won four more pennants, matching the Giants' total of six, and they had won all four World Series. The only one that was even close was a 4–3 decision, with one tie game, over the Giants in 1912.

The Red Sox did not win the pennant in 1919. The Chicago

White Sox' pitching, defense and Joe Jackson, all presumably trying up to World Series time, had prevailed. But a cloud considerably bigger than a man's hand had materialized on baseball's horizon. The Red Sox had one George Herman Ruth, a reform-school dropout from Baltimore who had established himself as an excellent left-handed pitcher. In those days, however, pitchers went nine innings and came to bat perhaps four times in a game. Once in a while Babe Ruth would hit a ball to places where balls had never been hit before. It occurred to Red Sox manager Ed Barrow that it might be advantageous to have Babe Ruth hit four times every day, and in 1919 he became an outfielder. He hit 29 home runs, which was five more than anybody had ever hit before in either league. If the Red Sox had discovered baseball's ultimate weapon, to complement a pitching staff that included Joe Bush and Sam Jones as well as promising youngsters like Herb Pennock and Waite Hoyt, they might become dangerous. Nobody yet had raised the cry "Break up the Red Sox," but the process had already begun. The Yankees were dismantling the Boston franchise with their own ultimate weapon: money.

The Yankees, *née* Hilltoppers, had come into existence in 1903 when a high-roller named Frank Farrell and Bill Devery, a former New York City police chief, had purchased the Baltimore franchise for $18,000—less than what it takes to buy a Triple-A infielder in the unrestricted draft of minor-leaguers today—and transferred it to New York. Neither Farrell nor Devery had any baseball acumen, other than the intuitive knowledge of the game every fan in every gin mill thinks he has, and it is extremely doubtful that Farrell, whose principal business interest was a large-scale gambling operation, would have been granted a franchise after 1920, when the White Sox' black sox were washed in public. In any case they lost money as the Yankees lost games, and in 1915 they bailed out. And pretty neatly, too, because they found an angel. Braumeister Jacob Ruppert, the Gussie Busch of his time, came up with $460,000 for the franchise. Ruppert had a partner, Tillinghast L'Hommedieu Huston, a soldier who had made his fortune as an engineer, reconstructing Cuba after a tour of duty there in the Spanish-American War. During the First World War he was back in uniform, and on June 26, 1917, when the first wave of the American Expeditionary Force landed in France, Tillinghast L'Hommedieu Huston, still the soldier, was among them.

During 1917, Huston received a "Dear Tillinghast" cable from Ruppert, informing him that he had hired Miller Huggins as manager of the Yankees. Huston was indignant. He was a Wilbert Robinson man, presumably because Uncle Robbie had led Casey Stengel and the other Dodgers to their first pennant the year before. The exchange of opinions between the co-owners became acrimonious but, as many a soldier overseas has discovered to his chagrin and disappointment, Huston found that the greatest advantage in some situations is being *there*. So Ruppert prevailed and established who was minding the store. From then on, they were his Yankees.

Ruppert was once quoted as saying that his idea of a pleasant afternoon at Yankee Stadium was watching the Yankees score seven runs in the first inning, "and then slowly pull away." This may be apocryphal, but Ruppert certainly subscribed to the dictum of Jim Tatum, the late football coach, who said: "Winning isn't the main thing; it's the only thing." Huggins got nowhere with the kind of team he had in 1918, as the Red Sox won everything again, so Ruppert decided he would have to give his man another kind of team. When Ruppert wanted a diamond, he went to Tiffany's (next door, perhaps significantly, to the building that has housed the Yankees' executive offices since 1945). So when he wanted a baseball team, he went to Boston, where they had the best one.

At the end of the 1918 season Ruppert took the rubber band off his bankroll and bought pitchers Ernie Shore and Hub Leonard and outfielder Duffy Lewis. He sent $15,000 and three of the kind of players Huggins couldn't win with. Shore, a very good pitcher, brought one distinction with him that has outlasted even the Yankee dynasty. He pitched the only no-hitter —the only perfect game, in fact—that wasn't. He was called in relief after the starting pitcher, George H. Ruth, walked the leadoff batter and was expelled from the game for sulfurous dissent from the pronouncement of ball four. Shore warmed up hastily and retired the next 27 batters. Duffy Lewis was a cut below Hall of Fame status, but he was the third man in an outfield with Tris Speaker and Harry Hooper, one of the most distinguished outfields of all time and a central reason for the Red Sox' eminence. And Hub Leonard, though he refused to report to the Yankees and was sent to Detroit instead, was a winning pitcher. How, in any time, was it possible to pluck three such plums from somebody else's tree? It was easy. Ruppert may not have known too much about baseball, but he knew all about money.

The Red Sox in 1917 had been taken over by Harry Frazee, and no baseball man he. Frazee was a theatrical producer, with the show-biz tendency to come up short of money from time to time, and the time-to-time intervals were becoming shorter. Just as a banjo player who is "at liberty" may hock his watch, a producer who is in hock may sell his shortstop. Show biz was still a tough racket in 1919, and Frazee sold Carl Mays, the distinguished submarine-ball pitcher, to the Yankees for another $40,000 and two pitchers.

The Yankees finished third in 1920, a performance more remarkable for the fact that it was a tough league. Cleveland, with Stan Coveleskie and Jim Bagby pitching and a strong supporting cast, won the pennant. The White Sox, the only team in big-league history to have four 20-game winners, finished second. (The four were Ed Cicotte, Red Faber, Dickie Kerr and Lefty Williams, all of them still in business because the whistle didn't blow on the Black Sox caper until after the 1920 season ended.) The mighty Red Sox dropped to fifth place, but Frazee still had more assets, and more reasons to liquidate. There wasn't anything wrong with him, he told Ruppert, that a $500,000 loan wouldn't fix. Ruppert didn't throw money around quite that lavishly but he thought about it. Frazee did have this Babe Ruth, who hit the 29 home runs. They negotiated, and on January 3, 1920, they closed the deal. The Yankees bought Ruth for $125,000 and Ruppert extended Frazee a $350,000 loan. Judge Kenesaw Mountain Landis, who would take over as baseball's first commissioner the following year, as ombudsman to insure against another Black Sox scandal, would have thundered in righteous indignation at such a deal, with all its conflict-of-interest implications. But the owners of baseball in those days took the position that the game was their ball and bat, and they ran it pretty much to please themselves—as in fact they still do, although they are much more cautious and much more subtle about it.

During the next three years the one-way railroad from Boston to New York kept running, and faces kept showing up in New York that can be found among the group pictures of the championship teams on the wall of the Yankee Stadium press room: Joe Dugan, Deacon Scott, Wally Schang, Waite Hoyt, Joe Bush, Sam Jones, Mike McNally, Harry Harper, George Pipgras and Herb Pennock. But on May 1, 1920, when the Red Sox showed up at the Polo Grounds, they were still sort of mighty—or at least mighty enough to beat the Yankees. Pennock, the young southpaw, was Boston's starting pitcher, and he looked good—good enough so that Ruppert made a mental note to pick him up the next time he went shopping in Boston. One of Pennock's pitches, however, was too good. Babe Ruth had his first home run in Yankee flannels. The Yanks won, 6–0, and the Yankee Era had begun.

It began with a sockdolager, according to the man from the *Times*. The headline on page 19 read, RUTH DRIVES BALL OVER GRAND STAND. In decades to come, baseballs would be hit over the Polo Grounds roof by people like JoJo Moore and Wilbur Brubaker, but the *Times* man was impressed. "Babe Ruth sneaked a bomb into the park without anybody knowing it," he wrote, "and hid it in his bat. He exploded the weapon in the sixth when he lambasted a home run out over the right field grand stand into Manhattan Field. This was Babe's first home run of the championship season, and it was a sockdolager. The ball flitted out of sight between the third and fourth flagstaffs at the top of the stand."

They may not all have been sockdolagers, but Ruth made 53 more balls flit out of sight that season. He topped himself the next year with 59 and the Yankees had their first pennant. The Giants won, too, and handled their tenants without too much trouble in the Series. But people began coming out to see Ruth, the barrel-chested, spindly-legged phenomenon who was hitting about one of every six home runs hit in the entire league, and hitting them on towering trajectories that made them look even longer than they were. A home run in those days was not a routine thing. The Giant management became uneasy about the Yankees' rising attendance, just as the Yankees would begin worrying about the Mets' popularity 40 years later, and early in 1922 they suggested to Ruppert that his team find somewhere else to play. Ruppert responded by decreeing the erection of Yankee Stadium, a pleasure dome the likes of which American sport had never seen. He built it directly across the Harlem River, where the Giant management could watch it rise from the windows of their executive offices. And he built it to the specifications of Babe Ruth (and, it was to turn out, to the specifications of Lou Gehrig, Tommy Henrich, Yogi Berra, Roger Maris and Joe Pepitone). Ruth could hit a ball over everything but Ruppert didn't want that to be necessary. The right-field fence would be close, 296 feet, and, for good measure, it would be low, 43 inches high. The fans had shown that they liked home runs, and they would have them.

The Yankees won again in 1922, their last year in the Polo Grounds. So did the Giants, and swept the Yanks in the Series. But in 1923 the juggernaut gained momentum. The Yankees opened the season in Yankee Stadium and Ruth showed the logic of the architecture by hitting a home run. The Yankees —aided by 21 victories by the now mature Herb Pennock, newly ransomed from Boston—won the pennant and beat the Giants in the World Series, four games to two. And they beat the Giants in paid attendance by almost 200,000. The Yankee Era was in full flower. In the next 20 years the Giants would enjoy moderate success, winning four pennants. The Yankees would win 11, and nine World Championships. It had all begun with one swing by a funny-looking man on May Day, 1920, and where would it ever end?

It would be easy to say the Yankees' suzerainty over baseball ended on October 16, 1964, the day lovable Yogi Berra walked the plank. A seven-game World Series is as convincing as a tie, but the Yanks had been beaten by the ragged Cardinals, who had staggered home on the last day in a slow-motion National League race, very nearly snatching defeat from the jaws of victory in a final weekend with the Mets, of all people. The Yankees, or any team worthy of championship status, should have eaten them alive. The Yankees, though, had been in trouble in their own league, bailed out only by the late acquisition of Pete Ramos to rescue a faltering pitching staff. Mickey Mantle, like an old thoroughbred going on class and guts, had played winning baseball despite enough painful ailments to populate an orthopedic ward, but he was turning 33 and looking 37. Tony Kubek was beginning to suspect that his physical debilities were chronic, and Whitey Ford had finished the Series with a useless left arm and a frightened look on his face.

Worse, there were no new stars on the horizon. Yankee brass talked bravely of Roger Repoz and Bobby Murcer, but the farm system had dried up, and they knew it. Any competent critic, if unhindered by a life-long experience that made Yankee superiority an unquestioned fact of life, could have confidently predicted that the 1964 pennant would be the last the Yanks would win for a considerable time; that they would slide into the second division the next season, and deeper the next; and that neither Yogi Berra nor Johnny Keane nor even the charismatic Ralph Houk would be able to do very much about it. There was, of course, no critic so free of mind. For 45 years, most of the life-span of most of the men alive who had played for the Yankees, or against them, or covered them, or managed their affairs, or just watched them, they had been the Yankees, and certainly they would be all right. Sometimes they *didn't* win the pennant, but when they didn't the very idea of it could make the book for a long-run Broadway musical.

Ironically, the reporters who chronicled the Yankees' wonders were least competent of all to judge what was happening to them, or actually what had already happened. Because of the habit of sports editors of assigning "writers" on a day-in, day-out, year-after-year "beat" basis, the men who should be most objective about a baseball team generally become least objective, spending too much time too close to their subject to see what it really is, making assumptions that things will be simply because they always have been. It is difficult to assess the work of a 34-year-old shortstop when you have gotten drunk with him and/or met his wife and kids. Reporters who had lived with the great Brooklyn Dodgers for a decade or more watched them get old right under their noses during the 1957 season, and didn't even realize what was happening until September. The Dodgers limped home third that year, and it figured, in retrospect, that they would fall to seventh place in their first season in Los Angeles. But nobody figured it ahead of time. Similarly, the beginning of the end of the Milwaukee franchise was their failure in 1959, a failure occasioned by nothing more sinister than age. The naïve Milwaukee fans thought the Joe Adcocks and Johnny Logans and Andy Pafkos would go on forever, and nobody told them they wouldn't because nobody really thought about it. Nobody thought about the Yankees, either.

The Yankees flopped into the second division in 1965, for the first time in 40 years. The seventh-place finish of 1925 could be explained away as a phenomenon occasioned by Babe Ruth's celebrated "bellyache," but the Yankees of 1965, as strange as it seemed, appeared simply to be a bad baseball team. They suffered a series of crippling injuries, but injuries had not stopped Yankee teams before. Arthur E. (Red) Patterson, resident explainer for the Dodgers, was Yankee publicist in 1949, and he made a season-long saga of their daily sick call; yet the Yankees won the pennant and needed only five games to polish off a good Brooklyn team in the Series. But in those days, when the Yankee manager pushed the button marked "bench," up popped Johnny Mize, or Johnny Hopp, or a little later Bob Cerv or Enos Slaughter. When 1965 manager Johnny Keane called for help, he could pick only from among such non-stalwarts as Horace Clarke, Ray Barker and Doc Edwards. The Yankees, in sickness or in health, were in trouble. And, since the trouble began under Berra's leadership and threatens to go on and on, it is easy to conclude that his sacrifice to the angry gods was the end of the Yankee Era.

But it is too easy. Yogi's disgrace was not a deviation from the Yankee pattern of doing things, or what used to be the Yankee pattern of doing things. There was nothing hysterical, or even panicky, about the way they cut him loose. It was a quiet, decorous, dispassionate proceeding, served with coffee in the executive suite on the 29th floor of the Squibb Building, overlooking Fifth Avenue. It was a cool, calculating executive decision, as much in keeping with The Corporate Concept as the rude dismissal of Stengel as manager and George Weiss as general manager four years earlier, with a mealymouthed explanation that seemed to say they were too old, and with the cool, calculating implication that the Yankees felt no obligation, really, to explain anything they did. Whatever they had done, ever since Ruppert made an arbitrary decision and presented Miller Huggins to his partner as a *fait accompli* 47 years earlier, had turned out to be the right thing to do, so only an arrogant fool would suggest that they were doing anything wrong. And the arrogant fool would be made to feel like Oliver Twist asking for seconds on the porridge; all he would get for his trouble would be a supercilious look and an even more mealymouthed answer.

The day Yogi walked the plank was the end of Yogi (the Mets would hire him as window-dressing, but nobody would ever again take him seriously as a manager, any more than the Yankee brass had really taken him seriously), but it wasn't the end of the Yankee Era. The Yankees were still, supremely, an organization and what's the point of being an organization if you don't have somebody's head rolling around on the floor once in a while? A real organization can't be defeated by anything but disorganization, and there wasn't any panic, or any confusion, about sacking Berra. That would come later.

Firing Mel Allen that fall without giving him anything but the standard mealymouthed explanation, and gumming up the announcement of his firing, was a pretty good symptom. And making Dan Topping, Jr., general manager when his experience was limited to peddling hot dogs wasn't too bad either. But the disintegration of the Yankee organization became manifest in the lobby of the Sheraton-Cleveland Hotel on the afternoon of April 19, 1966.

It was a Tuesday, and the Yankees were scheduled to play the Indians a night game. They were going against Sam McDowell, the flaky flamethrower, and that doesn't make any team especially happy, but they had Mel Stottlemyre ready, so it might not be too bad. It was midafternoon and some of the players were standing around the lobby, as players do, belaboring the obvious. At one end of the lobby Elston Howard and Roger Maris were discussing McDowell. "Sam," Howard said, "can *bring* it."

About then a silly woman, with an embarrassed husband trailing along, approached the group. She was about 50, and she giggled. "You're going to lose tonight, you know," she informed the players.

"That right?" said Maris, and moved his toothpick a little.

"You know the Indians have a better team," the woman said.

"We'll show up," Howard promised. "We been here before."

The woman giggled, and needled, some more. Then she asked the players for their autographs, "for my little boy," and was dragged away by her husband. It is a tableau guaranteed to be enacted in any hotel where a baseball team is billeted.

"Stupid broad," Maris said as the woman's plaid, pleated skirt disappeared down the steps. " 'You're gonna lose,' " he mimicked.

"Always, we're gonna lose," said Howard. "Every year, they're gonna knock off the Yankees. And every year they don't. What would they do without the Yankees?"

"Bush town," concluded Maris. These were the sixth-place Yankees, acting like World Champions. With three Most Valuable Player awards, one American League batting championship and the cosmic record for home runs between them, they were second-division ballplayers, and they couldn't believe it.

At the other end of the lobby sat Johnny Keane, the manager, his lips characteristically pursed but with no real expression on his leathery, wrinkled face. The day before had been an off day, and Keane and Red Barber had been sent ahead as a token force to attend the luncheon meeting of the Wahoo Club, a chamber-of-commerce kind of gathering of Indians' fans. The Cleveland players were obliged to attend, with the exception of one who called to say that he had to take his wife to a doctor because she had suffered a nasty fall. Manager

Birdie Tebbetts tentatively accepted the excuse but instructed a functionary to check the story. "I think he may be a ducker," Tebbetts said.

Keane sat on the dais with a thin, polite smile as Tebbetts introduced his players, one by one, and said funny things about them. Then the meeting was over and Cleveland reporters, with the tedious problem of the off-day story, approached Keane. They knew he had a problem, and a problem is a story—especially in Cleveland, and more especially if the problem is the Yankees'. In a game in New York the day before, shortstop Ruben Amaro had smashed up his knee and would be out of action for a long time, probably for the season. The Yankees had traded Phil Linz to the Phillies for Amaro when it was discovered that Kubek's physical problem was not only chronic but quite dangerous, and that he could not play any more. So now Keane had no shortstop, or did he? Bobby Murcer, a little man with a creditable but unimpressive record in the minor leagues, was on the roster. His big-league credentials were completely untested and the pennant race—which is what you call it if you're the Yankee manager—was on, so it was no time for on-the-job training. On the other hand, he had had a good spring, as they say. So the Cleveland reporters asked questions and Keane, as always, answered.

"The kid has earned a shot," was the way the morning paper had quoted the manager of the New York Yankees. "It's his job until he loses it." Murcer, it seemed, could begin losing his job right away. He was a left-handed hitter and McDowell was a left-handed pitcher, certainly the best southpaw this side of Sandy Koufax and possibly the hardest thrower in the game. The alternative plan would have been to play Cletis Boyer at short, which he had long ago proved he could handle, and bring

Tom Tresh in from the outfield to play third base, at least temporarily—at least until McDowell's turn was past, and Murcer could break into a more reasonable situation. But Keane, clearly, was throwing the kid into the deep water to see if he could swim.

Conversation must be made in a hotel lobby, to avert ennui at best and madness at worst, so conversation was made. "I see you're going to play the kid," a reporter said.

"Where did you get that idea?" Keane asked.

"I read the paper," the reporter said.

"No, I'm not going to play the kid," Keane said, and took a puff on his cigar. "Boyer will play short and Tresh will play third."

"Just for tonight."

"Until we change it," Keane said.

"When did you change your mind?" the reporter asked.

Johnny Keane had endured that depressing, frustrating 1965 season without losing his cool. He had weathered the second-guessing of the press about his ability to handle men without blowing up at any of the man-handlers who had questioned his knowledge in that area. He had been understanding toward Joe Pepitone, who could test any man's patience. He was normally a placid man, but now he fairly snarled: "I didn't change my mind." End of conversation in hotel lobby.

But another characteristic of the late John Keane was that he told the truth. If he did not change his mind, there was only one other possibility: Somebody changed it for him. Somebody at 745 Fifth Avenue must have picked up the phone and told him it was not a time to play Murcer. A cool, calculating executive decision must have been passed down through the organization, in such a way that each functionary would be

41

given to understand the fact that Murcer must not play, and the reasons therefor.

"I wonder how that kid feels right now," said a reporter, taking his evening meal in the press room of Municipal Stadium, a half-hour before game time.

"Oh, I don't think he really feels so bad," a colleague said. "Down deep, he's probably glad."

"Glad to go up against McDowell?" the reporter asked.

"No," the colleague said. "Glad not to. That would be a hell of a way to break in."

There was a confused pause. "Don't you know," the colleague asked, "that Boyer is playing short and Tresh third?"

Robert O. Fishel, the Yankees' publicity director, was sitting at the table. If his hair weren't so black and kinky, Fishel would look even more like Hume Cronyn, the actor. His complexion is rather swarthy, but at this point it turned white. "Murcer *isn't* playing?" he asked.

No, Murcer wasn't. Bob Fishel, given the limitations of working for an organization that made a habit for years of presenting things as they really weren't, is in the top five of sports publicity men, and he ranks high among human beings in general. He does too much work because he takes his job very seriously—and not, as in the case of most publicity men, only people who can do them or their organization some good. There was this sports editor who was fired a few years ago, and to a PR man there is nothing quite as out of style as an unfrocked sports editor: What good can he do you? This sports editor in his period of unemployment received about 10 phone calls from publicity people and four or five invitations to lunch. They were all from Bob Fishel.

Fishel, that evening in Cleveland, rushed out of the press room. A few minutes later he returned and apologized personally to each reporter covering the Yankees. He was humiliated. A command decision had been made in his organization and he, the man in charge of disseminating information, had not been informed. Reporters, for lack of information, had written uninformed stories. There was disorganization in the organization.

Keane was by no means the first manager ever to be second-guessed from upstairs. Casey Stengel will never get over the time they traded Tommy Byrne to the St. Louis Browns for Stubby Overmire, just before the midnight trading deadline, after he had told reporters there wouldn't be any trades. Cincinnati Reds president Bill DeWitt almost drove manager Dick Sisler out of his mind with phone calls from upstairs to the dugout, in the middle of a game, advising him to do such things as "get that pitcher the hell out of there." (DeWitt later proved his perspicacity in two ways: by firing Sisler when the Reds didn't win the 1965 pennant, and by trading Frank Robinson to Baltimore.) Other owners, notably Horace Stoneham of the Giants and Tom Yawkey of the Red Sox, have developed crushes on certain players and required that they be played.

But such cross-purpose maneuvers simply are not supposed to happen in the Yankee organization, and the obvious confusion indicated that finally, almost a half-century after Ruppert hired a manager behind his partner's back, the panic was on. Murcer was at Toledo within a couple of days, and Keane was back home in Houston after a couple of weeks, but those are details.

It had been, or should have been, evident the year before

that there was little left of The Yankee Dynasty except its dignity. But now, with two key executives made to look like fools in a situation that could have been handled by a simple telephone call, the dignity was gone, too.

3

The Luck of the Lion

No, Mr. Stogel said, he was not going to drive anybody all the way down to the Bronx to see a silly baseball game.

"But, Poppa," Philip said, "it's a doubleheader."

"So that's two silly baseball games," Mr. Stogel said.

"Poppa," said Sanford, the elder brother, "I'll mind the the store. It's Ruffing and Gomez against Feller and Harder. You could never see that again. Let them go."

"So take the boys," Mrs. Stogel said with an air of finality. "Philip is 15. He could learn the business some other day."

Mr. Stogel compromised. He drove Philip and his friend down to Woodlawn Road at 233rd Street, the terminus of the Jerome Avenue El, grumbling and snorting every mile of the way. He didn't say a discernible word until he stopped the car at the subway station and the boys tumbled out of the car like sailors answering general quarters. Then he said: "Philip! You got money?"

"We got a dollar-fifty each, Poppa, and Momma made us chicken sandwiches. The tickets are a dollar-ten, so we got

45

subway and Momma said we could have a soda."

"So take a dollar," Mr. Stogel said. "You might get hungry later." He ground the gears as he started away. *"Two* silly baseball games!"

It was 10:30 A.M. when the boys raced down the steps of the El at 161st Street and dashed along Jerome Avenue to the general-admission gate on the first-base side of Yankee Stadium. The gates would open at 11 A.M. The boys were pressed against the iron grating by other boys, most of them gripping brown paper bags in one hand and a dollar-ten in the other. When the gate opened the man couldn't take the money fast enough, as a horde of teen-agers sprinted up the ramp into the lower deck, streaming into the front row of the general admission section, just inches away from the reserved seats that sold for a dollar-sixty-five. Mr. Stogel hadn't understood why anybody would leave home at 9:30 in the morning to witness an event that would not take place until 2 o'clock in the afternoon, and the boys had tried to explain. There were only so many seats in the first row of general admission, with their dollar-sixty-five command of the proceedings. And, too, there was batting practice.

A few minutes before 12 the Yankees came out. The year was 1939 and they came out of the third-base dugout in those days. Paul Schreiber, then the only professional batting-practice pitcher in the world—and who but the Yankees would think of hiring a man to feed himself to the other animals?— warmed up briefly and began throwing lollipops. One of the first hitters was Steve Sundra, a big, moon-faced right-handed pitcher who might have been of use to some other team but was strictly surplus to the Yankees. He would win only 21 games in his Yankee career and bow out with a 4.22 earned-run average, but this was batting practice. Sundra batted left-handed, and Schreiber, true to his trade, threw where big Steve was swinging. In five swings he clouted three "home runs," two of them towering rockets into the third deck in right field. The 15-year-olds had never seen a ball hit into the third deck. One of them, in fact, had never seen the third deck, and he would never forget Steve Sundra, who surely must have been the strongest man alive. Years later he would see that broad, pinstriped back when the New York *Times* reported briefly that Steve Sundra, a former Yankee pitcher, had died of cancer at the age of 42. At the time of his death, the dispatch reported, he weighed less than 100 pounds.

Then the varsity came out, in batting-order succession: Crosetti, Rolfe, Henrich, and then the great, graceful, dead-panned DiMaggio. Philip Stogel, a Yankee fan, stood and applauded each of them in his turn, and he kept standing and applauding through DiMaggio's turn as the great one swung easily, languidly, flawlessly. After several sharp line drives he concluded with a rain-maker into the left-field bullpen and trotted easily, languidly, flawlessly past first base and into the outfield, where he would stand with feet spread wide, arms folded over his chest.

Philip stood and applauded DiMaggio every step of the way, and so did most of the front row of the general admission, but Philip's companion slumped low in his seat. He glanced furtively over his shoulder from time to time, scanning the other general-admission seats, which were filling rapidly now. The "crucial" doubleheader, with its confrontation of perhaps the league's best four pitchers (Bobo Newsom would have argued the point), had been publicized for a week, and by two o'clock there would be almost 77,000 paid admissions, the biggest crowd since they began enforcing the fire laws. Philip's companion feared that some one of the 77,000 would see him, and he would be found out.

Philip's companion was a Giant fan, and he was miserable with the guilty pangs of disloyalty. Bringing his dollar-ten to Yankee Stadium he was bringing aid and comfort to a hated enemy. For a votary of Ott and Hubbell to applaud DiMaggio would be a treasonable act. There was dire peril in even *being* in Yankee Stadium, the danger of exposure to fact, of facing reality. If you had never seen Bill Dickey, you could argue on faith that he couldn't carry Harry Danning's mask for him. It was the all-hit, no-pitch, no-brains American League, wasn't it, or how could a big glom like Rudy York hit all those home runs? Sure, the Yankees had won three World Series in a row, but they were lucky stiffs. How about that ground ball off Freddie Fitzsimmons' glove in the 1936 Series (when Philip's companion was 11 and had no really clear idea who Freddie Fitzsimmons was). Henny, the paperboy, saw that game, or anyway he said he had, and Henny said Burgess Whitehead would have gobbled it up if Fitzsimmons hadn't deflected it away from him. Then the Giants would have won it easy. And take the '38 Series. Dizzy Dean, who didn't have any arm left, had the Yankees beaten with that junk he was throwing, until Frank Crosetti hit one out of left field. Crosetti, with nine home runs all year in that cheesy American League, and he hits one over everything. That had to be some kind of luck, too.

(Philip's companion didn't know it then, but he had at least some authentic support for the latter theory. Dan Daniel, the elder statesman of the baseball writers, sat in the press box in Wrigley Field twenty years later and, without doing anything as undignified as pointing, indicated the yellow-brick building behind left field. "I still find it difficult to believe," he said, "that Mr. Crosetti hit that building. But he did." Dan's hallmark phrase in the face of the unexpected always was "It came as no surprise to the writer," but apparently Crosetti's home run was an exception to the rule.)

Yankee luck was an article of faith for a votary of Ott and Hubbell. And that was why Philip's companion, peering nervously over his shoulder, knew he had made a mistake. He could have maintained his faith unshaken simply by staying away from Yankee Stadium. It is an uneasy feeling that one's fundamental beliefs are about to be cluttered up with facts.

But you don't go to the zoo because you love the lion. The lion is powerful and cruel and swift and lithe and terrifying and fascinating. You don't root for the lion, because you can tell at first glance that he doesn't need support, moral or otherwise. And very few people ever *rooted* for the Yankees, in the die-a-little sense that characterized the hysterical, wait-till-next-year Dodger fan of the 1930s, or the solemn, long-suffering Giant fan of the '40s; the Yankees have had many, many followers and very, very few fans. You root for Xerox and you follow AT&T. And you come to see the lion because he *is*. Philip's companion had come to see the lion, and he was.

Bob Feller started the first game, against Lefty Gomez. Feller was 21 years old. Later he would become a great pitcher, but he was then at the peak of his physical power as a thrower. And that was it, the sophisticated National League fan told Philip: he could throw through a wall if he could hit the wall. A year earlier he had set a big-league record, striking out 18. Big deal. He got beat, 4–1, didn't he? A thrower. But today Bob Feller was hitting the wall. Others may have thrown harder, but it seems safe to say nobody ever threw *much* harder than Feller at 21. Later a cursory study of physics would show that the "hop" on a fast ball is an impossibility, another of baseball's superstitious illusions. A ball thrown very fast (*real* fast, as baseball people put it) seems to resist the pull of gravity to a greater degree than a ball thrown fast because it does not have as much time to descend, and thus, by contrast, it seems to rise. On the other hand, the physicists also insist that a curve ball is an optical illusion, and their theory was authenticated a quarter-century ago by a stroboscopic study in *Life* magazine of Carl Hubbell's screwball: straight as a string. Had the scientists been applying scientific skepticism it might have occurred to them that they had discovered another kind of illusion, because nobody can throw a ball perfectly straight in the earth's atmosphere. And had the scientist ever played baseball, they might have concluded that a screwball was hardly an appropriate subject for an objective study of a curve ball, which is something else. In any case, pragmatic curve-baller Curt Davis, then with the Dodgers, suggested an empirical approach of his own. If those photographers say there's no such thing as a curve ball, he said, let one of them stand behind a tree and I'll stand 60 feet, 6 inches away with a baseball, and we'll see.

Sir Isaac Newton to the contrary, Bob Feller's fast ball hopped that day. It jumped. When the white ball passed the light pin-striped shirt of a right-handed Yankee batter, it blurred. By the end of the first inning Feller had made at least one more believer, one who began to wonder how anyone ever beat him. Philip, the Yankee fan, clapped his hands when the great DiMaggio came up for his second turn at bat, and Philip's companion needled as Feller got two strikes over. It could have been, then, that Feller challenged DiMaggio, a bravado in which a pitcher says in effect: "This is my best shot; let's see you hit it." It is more likely that Feller, still only 21, made a mistake and made the pitch too good. In any case the fast ball blurred as it came in, about waist high. And it blurred as it went out. It was a classic collision of baseball's two fundamental strengths: the power pitcher and the power hitter. The line drive never rose more than 15 feet high on the way to the left-field seats, and it was a home run when it left the bat. The power-to-power clash of bat and ball had imparted a spin that sent the drive in a curve to the left, like a hooked tee shot. It went around the foul pole, fair, and landed 20 rows back, in foul ground.

Power hitting had by 1939 become baseball's staple, and in the generation to follow, the 15-year-old doubter would see titanic home runs fall like rain from the bats of Kiner and Mize and Mays and Mathews and Kluszewski and Killebrew, but it would be 23 years before he would see the raw, stark-naked power explosion of a best-to-best matching like DiMaggio-Feller that day. It would be a 4-wood shot into the Dodger Stadium bleachers (please to call it a "pavilion") off Sandy Koufax, the next of the very great power pitchers, in the fourth and final game of the 1963 World Series. And of course it would be hit by Mickey Mantle, the next of the very great Yankee hitters after DiMaggio.

A couple of innings later Joe Gordon, poured out of the Yankees' cornucopia of talent when Tony Lazzeri lost a step to advancing age and became just a good baseball player, matched his wiry, remarkably coordinated muscles against Feller and hit another home run. But Lefty Gomez wasn't 21 any longer, and the Indians pecked away at him until they beat him for Feller, 5–4. In the second game, after Feller had slicked his hair and taken a seat behind the Cleveland dugout —not many rows in front of the kids in the front row of general admission—the Indians' Mel Harder took the mound against the Yanks' Bump Hadley. No, not Ruffing. As often happens, the New York publicity department and Yankee manager Joe McCarthy had not seen eye-to-eye on the pitching rotation; promise them Ruffing, to get 77,000 people in the ball park, but give them anything.

The 15-year-olds learned something right there. In the theater, when you go to see Anne Bancroft and the lead is going to be played by her understudy, Tondelayo Schwartzkopf, some veteran spear-carrier is given the unpleasant task of coming out in front of the curtain a few minutes before post time and announcing that Miss Bancroft unfortunately slipped on a rug in her dressing room the night before and feels that she could not, under the circumstances, give her best performance. You may then check Miss Schwartzkopf's credits in the Playbill and decide whether you want to exchange your tickets for another night. Even used-car dealers can't sell you a Cadillac and deliver a Rambler. But in baseball it was *caveat emptor* in 1939, and it still is. The Dodgers in the 1950s tried to stimulate Ebbets Field attendance by conducting a series of "nights" for Long Island communities. On Baldwin night, for example, anybody from Baldwin was invited to come to see the Dodgers play on a certain date, and they could hire a bus and come in a group if they wanted to. Tickets for the game were made available in sporting-goods stores in Baldwin, and the Baldwin fans weren't charged any more than anyone else. Such an occasion, a game against the Philadelphia Phillies, was promoted for June 19, 1956, and it was

52

proclaimed on posters for a month in advance that Robin Roberts, winner of 138 games in the previous six seasons, would pitch for Philadelphia. Predicting that a pitcher will work on a particular day a month hence is as risky a proposition as predicting the weather, and in fact it involves predicting the weather, because one day's rain can knock the rotation askew. The Baldwin fans came and saw Stu Miller, who had won 15 big-league games, between trips to the minors, in the previous six seasons.

In 1961, the day after Roger Maris had hit his 60th home run, a father took a day off from work and took his two small sons to Yankee Stadium, for their first view of the new Babe Ruth. Maris didn't even take batting practice, and All Those Wonderful Fans who had supported the Yankees in their pennant drive saw a lineup that demonstrated the Yanks' great bench strength—Bobby Hale, for instance. The fans booed disloyally, but a championship game was played, so there were no refunds. Many San Francisco fans bought tickets in 1966 for what figured to be Juan Marichal's first turn against the Dodgers since he had clobbered John Roseboro with a bat the preceding season. The Giants' management didn't promise that Marichal would pitch, but it also didn't say he wouldn't. San Francisco fans are sophisticated, and can read. It figured that you use your best pitcher against your strongest opposition, or at least the opposition of which you have the strongest fear. So manager Herman Franks used up Marichal in the final game of a series in Houston, and he missed the Dodger series. "Suppose I had used somebody else in Houston," Franks argued, "and lost the game. I've got that game won now, haven't I?" And the management has the money. That's show sport.

The Decline and Fall of the New York Yankees

One of the peripheral reasons McCarthy might have decided to save Ruffing for another day during that double-header back in 1939 was that Harder, a consistent winner, had the distinction of being the pitcher DiMaggio, by his own testimony, least liked to hit against. Harder had never overpowered anybody, but he could put the ball where he wanted it, and where DiMaggio didn't. In that second game he put the ball where nobody wanted it and won, 7–1. The Indians dispatched the journeyman Hadley and the *coup de grâce* was a home run inside the park by Bruce Campbell.

But another play stands out in memory. First base was being minded by Ellsworth (Babe) Dahlgren, a right-handed fielder and a good one. Some Indian ripped a ground ball through or past Dahlgren, and it had two-base hit written all over it. But from nowhere came the agile Gordon, an acrobat figuratively and literally. He dove across the grass, caught the ball near the foul line and, from a sitting position, lobbed the ball to Dahlgren for the out. The 15-year-old Giant fan grudgingly conceded that Gordon was a better fielder than Alex Kampouris, or Bill Cissell, or any of the people the Giants had been using at second base lately. Gordon might, he thought secretly, even be as good as Burgess Whitehead. The Giant fan was deeply disturbed. He had seen the lion, and he *was*. Or at least he seemed to be. The Yankees won the pennant that year and humiliated the Reds in The World Series.

The lucky-Yankees theory was rekindled when 1940 turned out to be The Year the Yankees Didn't Win the Pennant. They won 88 games, but they finished third. Creaking noises were audible from the Yankee machine, followed by what sounded very much like alibis: "We just never got started." Gomez seemed to have had it. Crosetti really never got started, and wound up with a .194 average. There were evident weaknesses, and something had to be done. So the Yankees did something. Bushy-browed Ed Barrow had been the field manager of the dynastic Red Sox during the teens, and was then and on through the 1930s the shrewdest baseball man alive if Branch Rickey wasn't. In 1921 Jacob Ruppert had asked him to come to work as Yankee business manager, and Barrow, inasmuch as Ruppert had already stripped his organization of talent, agreed. Combining his acumen and Ruppert's money, Barrow had by 1938, if not earlier, established the strongest organization baseball had ever known. "The Little World Series" of 1938, between the International League and the American Association, was between Newark and Kansas City, both Yankee-owned teams, and naturally it went seven games. With notable exceptions like Charley Keller and Joe Gordon, the Yankees hadn't been able to promote anybody to the big league because they didn't need anybody. But now, after the disaster of 1940, it was time to move. Barrow plucked eclectically among the plums on the farm and came up with Phil Rizzuto and Ernie Bonham.

Rizzuto, the runt the Giants hadn't been able to see when he placed himself right under their noses, would have as much a claim to baseball's "Mr. Shortstop" title in the next 15 years as Marty Marion, PeeWee Reese or anybody. Bonham, known as Tiny because he was big and chubby, wouldn't last very long—like Sundra, he wouldn't live very long, either—but he would make a remarkable record. He would win only 79 games, but he would make a career earned-run average of 2.73, lower than any Yankee pitcher except two who ever won as many as 20 games, lifetime. Bonham finished .03 lower than the average through 1966 of the great Edward Charles Ford.

55

The Decline and Fall of the New York Yankees

Bonham's ERA was tied by Bobby Shantz, who won only 30 games as a Yankee, and beaten by the current Steve Hamilton (2.63), who had won only 23 games going into the 1967 season.*

Bonham would also pitch the Yankees to the 1941 pennant, winning 21 of their 101 victories, and to triumph over the Dodgers in the World Series. But again, they would have to be lucky.

Mickey Owen, the Dodger catcher in that World Series, has had to live with it, and he has done so gracefully. The Yankees led the series, two games to one, but the Dodgers led that fourth game in Ebbets Field, 4–3. Relief pitcher Hugh Casey had two outs, none on, in the ninth, and two strikes on Tommy Henrich. The pitch was a curve, down and in to the left-handed hitter. (Owen does not substantiate the latter-day theory that it was a spitball, and Casey is dead, a suicide. Henrich isn't sure.) Henrich missed the ball and so did Owen. It skittered off his mitt, back to the screen, and rolled dead at the feet of the public-address announcer, seated on a camp chair. The announcer was Charlie Clark, now a reporter-editor in the sports department of *Newsday*, the opulent Long Island tabloid, and for a second he was tempted to pick it up. "I wish I had now," Charlie says. "There would have been hell to pay, but I'd have been famous."

It was Owen, a fine catcher, who became famous. Henrich got to first base and the Yankees won the game. But even after Owen's fabled boo-boo, what was the situation? The

* Anyone who wishes to make anything of the fact that the four low-est career ERAs for a Yankee since 1920 were made by left-handers (see Appendix) may feel welcome. The Ruthian architecture of the Stadium could be the first clue.

Yanks had the tying run at first base with two out in the ninth. No team is an odds-on favorite in such a situation, because there is a lot of work to be done. With an experienced, gutsy pitcher like Casey going, and with the Dodgers having last licks no matter what happened, who would have bet the Yankees' chances? You could have found a bet, because people had come to expect the late-inning *coup de foudre* from the Yankees. By 1941 the word *blitzkrieg* was part of the language, and that was the way the Yankees seemed to strike: give them a small opening and they drove massively through it. Cincinnati shortstop Billy Myers had erred in the 10th inning of the final game of the 1939 Series, and the Yankees had gone around and around the bases for three runs before the inning was over. Only one other team in baseball history has ever given fans, and their opponents, the feeling that they were not really in deep trouble if they came to the eighth inning "only" two runs behind, or to the ninth "only" a run behind. That was the Brooklyn Dodgers of 1952–56. The Robinson-Snider-Campanella-Hodges gang, which on occasion made a No. 8 hitter out of Carl Furillo, would have been a nice kind of team to have in any ball park, and would have won a couple of pennants. But in cozy Ebbets Field they were murder. Given their home geography, they were probably the most menacing team ever assembled. It hurt Warren Spahn's considerable pride that he was almost always sure to be the starting pitcher the day after the Milwaukee Braves left Brooklyn, but only a tinkerer like Bobby Bragan would start a left-hander in Ebbets Field.

The Yankees, however, had horses for all the courses. When Henrich reached first base, they struck like Ray Robinson, sensing the kill. Hitting in baseball, like hitting in boxing, must be done in combinations to be effective, and the Yankees launched a flurry: right-left-left-right. DiMaggio singled, Keller doubled. Dickey walked. Gordon doubled, and forget it. The score was 7–4. The Dodgers' turn at bat in the bottom of the ninth was perfunctory, a mere detail, and so was the fifth game. An even-up Series had been turned into a 4–1 rout, with one swing—that missed.

Yankee luck? "Luck," Branch Rickey said, "is the residue of design." "God is on the side of the stronger battalions"— so the weaker battalions blame God. God was in deepest trouble from Giant fans in 1951, the year Bobby Thomson hit The Home Run. The Giants, exhausted from their "Miracle" of 37 victories in their last 44 games—and maybe in some cases a little hung over—showed up on the Thursday morning after to meet the Yankees in a Series that was, from their point of view, as anticlimactic as a Series can ever be. The rested Yankees had Allie Reynolds ready and Leo Durocher had decided to pitch Dave Koslo, a journeyman southpaw. Actually, Durocher hadn't decided anything; he had no choice. Sal Maglie had started and Larry Jansen had finished the third game of the playoff with the Dodgers the day before. Sheldon Jones had been bombed, 10–0, the day before that. Durocher could have pitched Jim Hearn with two days' rest, but that seemed a waste against Reynolds, a clutch performer who seemed, with two no-hitters that season, at his peak.

But lo, the Giants got to Reynolds for three runs in the first inning, with Monte Irvin putting the whipped cream on top with a steal of home. Alvin Dark hit a home run later and the Giants won, 5–1. The Yanks won the second game, but the Giants stayed loose, with everything to gain. On Saturday,

Hearn started and went far enough to win, 6–2, when Eddie Stanky slid into second and kicked the ball out of Rizzuto's glove. Now the Giants had the theoretical edge, since Maglie was ready for the Sunday game (he wanted three days' rest and didn't want four). Casey Stengel would have to use Bob Kuzava or Tom Morgan, neither of whom he wanted to use.

So it rained on Sunday. That made Reynolds ready for Monday, and the Giants didn't win another game. They "almost" won the sixth, however. The last out, with the Yankees leading, 4–3, was a line drive to right field by Sal Yvars. It was sinking, and Hank Bauer had to slide on the seat of his pants to catch it and prevent the tying run. He slid accordingly and caught the ball. Another Yankee had done what he had to do, which was what most of the teams in the 1949–60 era of Casey Stengel did. They beat you just a little bit. They never (except in 1958, when the rest of the American League fell apart) ran away and hid like Joe McCarthy's 19½-game winners of 1936. They did what they had to do for Stengel (or, in the case of Bauer and a number of others, in spite of him). "They executed," in Stengel's words, and left another two baseball generations moaning about Yankee luck—and about Stengel's maddening conjurations.

The Yankee Dynasty was already in decline in the 1950s, because the have-nots had legislated to cut their supply line. But class doesn't die easily, and the Yankees executed. They were still better than everybody else. From 1920 through 1964 the Yankees won more games than anybody in the American League, marking up an almost incredible .619 winning percentage over a 45-year period. And they did what they had to do in one other respect: They murdered the second-division teams. There is a hoary baseball theory, based on the old 154-

game season, that there are 50 games you will lose no matter what you do, 50 you will win almost automatically, and 50 to worry about. Corollary to this is the necessity to make the most of the schedule against the weak teams in the games you should win. For those 45 years the Yankees had a .666 winning percentage against the second division—two victories out of every three games. In 13 seasons they had a winning percentage higher than .700 against the second division, and in 10 of those seasons they won the pennant. The modern history of baseball abounds with the sad tales of runners-up who could say, "We'd have won the pennant if we could have taken the season series from Washington." Or done better against Houston or the Mets. Beating the hell out of the weak is to some extent a function of killer instinct. It is also a matter of paying attention, and Yankee teams always paid attention. They did in one respect that makes perhaps the most spectacular statistic of their era.

The Yankees scored more runs than any American League team in their 45-year era, which is no surprise. And they allowed fewer, which shouldn't be a surprise because tight defense was a major factor in the success of even their Murderer's Row aggregation. They hit vastly more home runs (6,463 to runner-up Cleveland's 4,526) and had a higher team batting average (.276) than anybody. Of course they made the fewest errors (400 fewer than next-best Cleveland) and their pitching staff's cumulative earned-run average for 25 years was the lowest. It was 3.56, precisely half an earned run lower than the overall league average, including the expansion teams.*

* The Yankee ERA for their 45-year domination is probably lower, because team earned-run averages were not kept before the 1930 season and the Yankees had some rather good pitching in the 1920s.

The most spectacular statistic, in a way, is that the Yankees from 1920 through 1964 made the most double plays, 7,143. The clue here is that the runners-up are the Red Sox, who won just one pennant in all that time; the Minnesota Twins, who were the Washington Senators for 41 of those years and won twice; and the Baltimore Orioles, who were the St. Louis Browns for 34 years and won a pennant once, in the middle of World War II. The team that leads the league in double plays is either very good or very bad. You can't make a double play if there isn't anybody on base. When a shortstop with a last-place team comes up with a ground ball, he can throw it to second with reasonable assurance that there will be a force play, because he is conditioned by experience to assume that the opposition will have men on base very much of the time. The second baseman, it follows, can blow the pivot a number of times and still complete a large number of double plays. Thus bad teams lead leagues in double plays.*

It is difficult for a "real" good team to lead a league in double plays. Real good pitching does not put so many runners

---

* A team can be a combination of very good and very bad and still lead in DPs, and the Pittsburgh Pirates of 1966 were a fine example. Their pitching was bad. "Do you realize," said Gene Mauch, manager of the Phillies, when the season had about two weeks to go, "that this team can win the pennant without a legitimate starting pitcher?" On the other hand, at shortstop the Pirates had Gene Alley, the best shortstop in baseball and the *de facto* Most Valuable Player of the National League, although he received not a single first-place vote. The Baseball Writers' classic question about an MVP candidate is: "Where would they have finished without him?" In Alley's case the answer is that the Pirates would have finished in the second division without him, and the only qualification is how deep in the second division. Alley and Bill Mazeroski, the nonpareil second baseman, spent all year masking the fact that the Pirates' pitching was not of big-league caliber, and they succeeded, often by making double plays on base hits, almost to the end.

on base. Real good teams have confidence that they will score some runs, so they do not as often have to give an intentional pass to set up the double play in the middle innings; they can let you have the run, and see you later. Real good teams do not get so many double plays on steals, or advances after fly balls, because they are more often two or three or four runs ahead and the opposition cannot play for one run. Real good teams also do not make so many "accidental" double plays, on line drives hit right at somebody, because not so many line drives are hit off real good pitching. Yet the Yankees, scoring the most runs and having the real good pitching, consistently led in double plays. This means that while the bad teams were cashing in only some of their many double-play chances, the Yankees were taking advantage of almost all of theirs. This was good baseball. This was the Yankees, who could execute.

More important, the Yankees, 1920–64, made not only the fans but the opposition *believe* that they could execute, and expect that they would. If some of the opposition chose to remain unconvinced and grumble about "Yankee luck," that was all right with the Yankees. The pressure in the eighth and ninth innings, whether from feared execution or impending luck, would have the same effect. Anyway, the Yankees never considered luck a factor. Miller Huggins wouldn't let them think they were lucky, and neither would Joe McCarthy. Only Casey Stengel ever made luck a part of his toolkit. A master psychologist, Stengel didn't invent the expression but he would use it frequently, after pulling off an occult maneuver that resulted in victory: "I'd rather be lucky than good anytime." Stengel knew he had men who could execute, but if the opposition wanted to grumble about luck . . . well, that just gave them something else to think about.

"We had the feeling we were good," says Johnny Murphy, the relief pitcher who picked up the pieces from some of Gomez' incomplete victories in the late '30s and formed half of baseball's first noted "two-headed" pitching combination. "Joe McCarthy gave us the feeling," says Murphy, now head of the Mets' player-development program. "He'd say, 'What the hell are you doing? Those clowns don't belong on the same field with you.' And we'd believe it."

Roger Maris and Elston Howard still were trying to believe it, listening to the needling from the silly woman in the Sheraton-Cleveland Hotel lobby early in the 1966 season. But they couldn't. They had always interpreted the accusation "lucky" to mean they were good. And now they couldn't even get lucky any more. So maybe, just maybe, they weren't good?

4

Pride in Pinstripes

THE SECOND MOST successful baseball organization of modern times, artistically and fiscally, has been the Dodgers. Has been, because that was exactly what Walter O'Malley's small-arms platoon became with the retirement of Sandy Koufax. A vertical graph of the Brooklyn–Los Angeles success in their era, which lasted little more than half the length of the Yankees' span of supremacy, would show many peaks, like a radar picture of an invasion fleet. Three of the peaks would be flat on top, representing the back-to-back successes of 1952–53, 1955–56 and 1965–66 and reflecting how very difficult it has become, in this age of controlled mediocrity, for the cream to stay on top. Other than the Yankees and Dodgers, the only repeat winner in either league since World War II has been the Milwaukee Braves of 1957–58, and they quickly hit the skids.

A similar graph of the Yankees' success in their era would show only two sharp peaks, and seven plateaus. There is a marked human tendency to live life on plateaus because they are comfortable. They give a feeling of equilibrium, stability, security. For every man who has climbed to the top and slipped to the bottom in some field of human endeavor—Richard Nixon, Bobo Olson, Fabian—there are thousands who have found themselves a leveling-off place and just stayed there. Now, the dangerous thing about life on a plateau is that it gives one the idea that there isn't anyplace else. The Yankees found their plateau—a very high one, where the atmosphere was thin—and stayed there almost incessantly from the advent of Casey Stengel in 1949 through the banishment of Yogi Berra in 1964. That is why the roller-coaster ride is making them a little dizzy, from the back room of the clubhouse, where the players hide from reporters, to the front office, where the executives used to hide from reporters.*

The Yankee problem of adjustment to new plateaus, whatever they may be, is something like trying to live somewhere else after you've been a Texan. It can be done, but not gracefully. One complication is that Yankee World Champions, like the United States Senate, have been a continuing body. It is inevitable, when a "new" team wins a pennant, that the wire services will put out a story enumerating the members of the team who have any World Series experience. Which four Milwaukee Braves of 1957 had had prior Series workouts made an intriguing quiz question. Everybody knew about Red

---

* "Used to," because Michael Burke, the sharp and personable CBS executive who became president of the Yankees last fall when Dan Topping cashed in his last stack of chips, has so far made himself eminently available and proposes that his open-door policy will filter down through his chilly organization. If the thaw ever permeates the rubbing room, the *sanctum sanctorum* where Yankee heroes have long enjoyed diplomatic immunity from the questions of their image-builders, Burke will have gone a long way toward his goal of "changing the climate" of the Yankees.

Schoendienst and Andy Pafko, but who were the other two? Answer: Del Rice and Nippy Jones (who would get hit on the shoeshine by a pitch and set up Eddie Mathews' game-winning home run as "Yankee luck" turned bad), who were Cardinals in 1946. The Baltimore Orioles in '65 had Frank Robinson, Luis Aparicio and . . . ? Stu Miller, who was with the 1962 Giants. There are no such guessing games with the Yankees. Since 1923, they have not sent any team into a World Series that has not included several—usually a dozen or more, and always a half-dozen—players who not only have been in a World Series before, but have been on the winning end of it.

Thus any young player who has carried his duffle into the Yankee camp since Coolidge was President has had it quickly impressed upon his psyche not that he is to aspire to victory, but to *assume* it. We win, kid. Pawn shops have always abounded with the personal effects of people who thought positively, and the psychological factor in sports has always been arrantly overrated. Knute Rockne, as well as God, was almost always on the side of the stronger battalions, and whichever Notre Dame team finally won one for the Gipper was probably a two-touchdown favorite. But horses with any kind of class usually run just a little better in good company than they do against platers who offer them no challenge, and the average golfer tends to come home a stroke or two better in a good foursome than when he plays with hackers. Not enough horses have been to head-shrinkers to determine by what equine e.s.p. or osmosis the tranference of class occurs, but in the case of a man in competition the process is fairly obvious. He tries harder in fast company, and pays more assiduous attention, because it is expected of him, and because failure would be embarrassing. This very simple, very human motivation could be the basis in fact, if there is any, of the

Doctrine ("myth," says Birdie Tebbetts, who had a good rear view of the Yankees for most of his 30 years in the game) of Transvestitism: put a Yankee uniform on a player and he becomes a better player. It sometimes worked, if only marginally. There were no magical metamorphoses, like Clark Kent doing his quick change in a phone booth and coming out as Superman, but there did sometimes seem to be perceptible differences between a player's performance in the Yankee pinstripes and in somebody else's flannels. The difference, principally, between being a winning player and a losing player, and there are both kinds. There are finely coordinated athletes—pitchers, in particular—who seem able to do everything, and lose. And there is the Jim Gilliam variety, who can't do much of anything, really, except beat you.

Whether or not it is reasonable that there can be such a thing as a winning attitude, the Yankees in their era believed there was. "All this stuff up to now," said Whitey Ford, watching a game from the press box in San Juan, Puerto Rico, as the Yankees' 1965 spring training entered its final week, "is nonsense. It doesn't mean a thing. But now it's time to get into the winning habit." Whitey then went on in an attempt to explain the winning habit, the assumption of success that gave him his fabulous .696 winning percentage, and the Yankees 13 pennants, in his 17-year career. He spoke of the spirit as if it were a benign virus, contagious and incurable. No such epidemic struck the Yankees in 1965, which was strange to Ford. It had always worked, even in that bad 1959 season, when the Yankees came off the floor to finish third, and Ford in a mediocre year went 16–10. The virus infected just about all the Yankees, just about all the time. Look what it did to Billy Martin.

No Yankee ever had a more severe case. It is not an insult

to Billy Martin to say that he was one of the most overrated players in baseball history. (Southpaw Jim Brewer would testify that it is dangerous, having had his jaw shattered by Martin's one-punch assault while pitching for the Cubs a few years ago.) He wasn't bad. He fielded adequately as a second baseman, and hit enough to justify his existence. And he hustled as much as anyone ever hustled. But he simply couldn't have been as good as Casey Stengel thought "that fresh kid" was. When Martin came out of the Army, late in the 1955 season, Stengel put him in the lineup as a shortstop, which he patently wasn't, and batted him *third* for the New York Yankees. Stengel as well as everybody was charmed by Martin's performance in the 1953 World Series, when he made a record 12 hits, batted .500, drove in eight runs and saved a game with a desperation catch of Jackie Robinson's pop fly near the pitcher's mound as Dodger runners circled the bases with two out. Stengel, as well as everybody, forgot that Martin went into that 1953 World Series as a .257 hitter. So he batted him third and Martin batted .300, about three miles over his head. Then he played all seven games of the Series and hit .320. Playing regularly again during the 1956 season— a little more regularly than most marginal players played for Stengel —Martin found his level again, at .264. So Stengel played him every day in the World Series and he hit .296. In 527 regular-season games as a Yankee, Billy Martin batted .262 and hit 30 home runs. In 28 World Series games as a Yankee, he batted .333 and hit five home runs. In those 28 World Series games he handled the ball in the field 131 times. Martin, who had led the Pacific Coast League in errors the year before he became a Yankee, made one (1) error in World Series play. Many good players have melted in the crucible of the

World Series, but it cooled Billy Martin. Whether it was the Yankee uniform or the Yankee motivation, being a Yankee made Martin a better player than he would have been anywhere else, or would ever be anywhere else.

After Billy's birthday party at the Copacabana in New York on May 16, 1957, somebody had to go. The brawl in the men's room, according to Hank Bauer, wasn't the fault of anybody but the bad-mouthed drunk who started it. In any case it wasn't Martin's fault. But it was terribly undignified, and the Yankee management knew immediately that somebody had to go. It wouldn't be Bauer, who had hit 26 home runs and batted in 84 runs the year before, to establish his pride as "the best .250 hitter in baseball." It certainly wouldn't be Yogi Berra, the three-time Most Valuable Player who had driven the Dodgers' MVP, Don Newcombe, into ignominious retreat with three home runs in the previous World Series. It would have to be Martin, no matter what Stengel thought. Martin, along with the unseasoned Ralph Terry (who would come back to the Yankees when he was seasoned), the almost-good-enough Woody Held and the not-good-enough Bob Martyn, were shipped to Kansas City. On the return jaunt the shuttle brought Ryne Duren, Jim Pisoni and Harry Simpson.

Martin played out the season in Kansas City and hit .251. He knew he had been sold down the river, but it wasn't the end of the world. That had been only his 29th birthday, and he had a few years of productivity—maybe, as ballplayers go, his best years—ahead of him. The following year, sent to Detroit in the miscellaneous kind of 13-man trade that doesn't really accomplish anything except to show the fans you've Done Something, Martin batted .255. In 1959, shunted to Cleveland in another deal, he hit .260. At the end of the year he was thrown into a deal with Cincinnati for Johnny Temple. The biggest impression he made there was on Jim Brewer's jaw. He wound up in Milwaukee. In each town, in each uniform, Billy Martin hustled. And in each town they waited for him to provide that Promethean spark they'd read and heard so much about. But somehow it wasn't the same. Not only was Martin no longer inspirational, but he wasn't particularly helpful. Whether it was the uniform or the motivation, it wasn't the same. He was playing for people who tolerated failure, or at least mediocrity, and it wasn't like being a Yankee.

Fear of failure was part of the Yankee attitude, too, and it could give the uniform a negative effect. Produce, it was understood in those 1950s, or you'll be on the next shipment to Kansas City. (Jack Lang, of the Long Island *Press,* suggested at about that time that the New York and Kansas City teams be designated as 1 and 1A in future American League races, inasmuch as their shuttle trades seemed to indicate an interlocking directorate.) Such pressure could be the spur to greater achievement, or it could be just too much pressure. Players generally exult when they are traded to the Yankees, but Harry Simpson didn't when they told him he was a part of the deal for Billy Martin. First of all, Simpson was a Negro, and the Yankees had made it fairly evident, between Jackie Robinson in 1947 and Elston Howard in 1955, that they had no great zeal to be avant-garde in the integration of baseball. Second, Simpson had experienced enough trouble just trying to be a ballplayer. In Cleveland he tried to tell them he just wasn't a pull hitter, and the management insisted he was. Third, he was recovering from personal tragedy, the death of a young child, and he and his wife had found a home in

Kansas City where things were friendly and peaceful. Harry Simpson had found his plateau, and he wanted to stay there. Had he remained with the Yankees long enough, Simpson would have seen, on September 14, 1958, how tranquil the upper plateau can be.

It was one of those great-moments-in-sports days. The Yankees had arrived in Kansas City at about 7:30 that Sunday morning, as rested and refreshed as people usually are after on overnight train ride. There had been a day game in Chicago the day before, and plenty of time to go to the stockyards for dinner before train time. About six hours, in fact, because the train didn't leave until 11-something. The Yankees were even farther behind in conversion to air travel than they were in availing themselves of the rich sources of Negro and Latin-American playing talent, and as far as anyone could figure it at the time, the only reason was that crotchety Bill ("The only way to fly is by plane") McCorry, the traveling secretary, didn't like to fly. The first jet-age World Series—a rat race of the first magnitude—wouldn't come until the next year, but other teams were already flying and Walter O'Malley, always two or three moves ahead, had bought a Convair to transport his Dodgers. But the Yankees rode the rails. They rode into Kansas City that Sunday morning and the troops proceeded to the Muehlebach Hotel. They would have only "lounging" rooms because they would have to be at the ball park by 11 o'clock and they were leaving—on a train, of course—after the doubleheader. Long after the doubleheader.

It was one of those days to test the theory that sports "writing" is an enchanting way to make a living. But at least it would be a good story. The Yankees were about 14 games ahead and the magic number was one. If they won either game (and what was the price on 1A sweeping a doubleheader from 1?) they would clinch their fourth-straight pennant. They had won five straight before—nobody else had ever won four in a row—so this would be Casey Stengel's ninth winner in 10 years. How could it be a bad story? Stick around. The Yankees won the first game, 5–3, for Duke Maas, and more history had been made. The players made their way through the picnicking fans on the grassy left-field slope, into the clubhouse, where the television cameras had been set up to record the celebration.

Celebration? They didn't even shake hands. They strode in orderly fashion to the stools in front of their lockers, some stopping to pick up a sandwich from the table in the middle of the room. As they passed, Mel Allen tried frantically to flag down somebody to speak into the microphone he was holding, but nobody was interested. He almost snared Bobby Shantz, but Bobby made one of his quick moves and escaped into the shower room. In one corner Enos Slaughter displayed the box of rifle ammunition he had bought in town to carry on those Carolina hunting jaunts that kept his aging legs in youthful shape. He showed the bullets to Andy Carey, who at age 26 had already cashed four World Series checks, three of them winner's shares, in five years in the big league. Frank Crosetti, the dour coach who had cashed 17 Series checks and who had walked off the bus and into the clubhouse that day studying an oil-stock prospectus without stumbling a step, sat in another corner, taking inventory of the bag full of slightly soiled batting practice balls. Stengel, with the world's most highly developed public-relations sense, finally rescued Mel Allen. He filibustered before the television camera for perhaps 10 minutes, and in the soliloquy he delivered himself of one of his truly classic lines: "I couldn't of done it without the players." A five-foot shelf of apocrypha has been attributed to Stengel, who never minded being misquoted as long as it read good, but he really did utter that one.

There was a celebration of sorts back at the hotel. There was steak and champagne in a party room while waiting for train time. Johnny Kucks got smashed, and he had a pretty good reason. Kucks in 1956, at age 23, had won 18 games for the Yankees. He had also pitched the 9–0 shutout that beat the Dodgers in the seventh game of the World Series, and he had done it all with a sinking fast ball. "I don't know why it sinks, or how," Kucks had said in answer to a question early in the 1958 season. "I'm just glad it does." And about then it stopped sinking. In the spring of 1959, when Yankee management decided it was about time to bring Ralph Terry back from the Kansas City "farm," Kucks would have to go, and he was pretty sure about that. And he was right. Ryne Duren got smashed, too. He was going to achieve a certain degree of fame in the 1958 Series, winning a game and losing another, striking out 14 batters in nine and a third innings and infuriating an umpire by putting his hand to the throat in baseball's "choke-up" gesture. But Duren became most famous on the train that night. Whether it was the champagne or the fact that Yankee coach Ralph Houk had been his manager at Denver the year before, Duren decided it was in order to shove Houk's cigar down his throat, and there was a scene.

Duren almost was cheated of his fame for that caper, because the journalists on the train, whether from the champagne or out of loyalty to the Yankees, entered into a conspiracy of silence. The world knew nothing of the incident until Leonard Shecter of the New York *Post,* who had been made a member of the conspiracy without being asked whether he wanted to be, called his office to report that a cigar had been smashed by a man who got smashed. An eager rewrite man, one who wouldn't ever have to look Duren, Houk or any other Yankee in the eye, then took typewriter in hand and made much more of the silly incident than it really was. That's Journalism, U.S.A., another form of show sport. The Yankees didn't ship Duren to Kansas City. They wanted to ship Shecter, though, for telling the people what happened.

Among Shecter's proudest trophies is Roger Maris' designation of him, the year the surly Maris hit all the home runs and was constitutionally incapable of handling his eminence, as the chief ripper. To rip, in the patois of the never-never land of professional sport, is to report any fact about a man that his clergyman would not include in a funeral eulogy to his family and friends. If a $40,000-a-year outfielder hits a ground ball to the second baseman and does not run it out, to point out his nonfeasance in the public prints is a rip, and is rewarded by the player's righteous indignation or, more often, his sullen silence. A nine-game hitting streak should be duly recorded, but call attention to the fact that Ike Ozark, the cleanup hitter, has not batted in a run since Bastille Day and you are a ripper. Of the athlete, as of the dead, speak nothing but good. The most heinous kind of rip is the personal rip. Bobby Richardson's devout Christianity was a topic fit for fair comment, but the suggestion that his traditionally South Carolinian attitude toward Negroes seems at variance with the teachings of Christ was quite unethical—a rip. Call attention, as Shecter once did, to the curious fact that a player lends his name to a cigar advertisement when in fact he does not

74

smoke cigars, and he will refuse thereafter to tell you what time it is.

When ballplayers discuss what they call "the good writers," the conversation is a roll call of the nonworking press, the drones who blandly report the news that the pitcher believes the home run was hit off a slider that got up a little high, and don't bother to ask him what the hell he was thinking about to throw Harmon Killebrew a strike with an 0–2 count and two men on base. These are the writers—and they are in no valid sense of the term reporters—who "get along." "I like old Jim," a $22,000 infielder with a .211 batting average will say, "because if he doesn't have anything good to write about you, he doesn't write anything. He doesn't rip." It is generally conceded, outside of Los Angeles, that Dick Young of the New York *Daily News* is the most competent and accomplished baseball reporter of our time, and the players of both leagues generally recognize his excellence, grudgingly. "He's good," they say, "but he'll rip you."

Playwrights sit in Sardi's in the small hours in cognition of the fact that a few trenchant paragraphs by Walter Kerr may destroy a work that is the product of two years' effort and a lifetime of experience. Almost none of them thinks the critic system fair, but almost all of them gloomily accept it as a fact of their professional lives. High courts of the land have decreed that "the widest latitude is to be allowed" in journalistic appraisal of public (not simply political) figures, and politicians adopt the attitude "Say anything you want, but spell my name right." They do, or they don't remain politicians very long. Strangely, among all the fields of endeavor that depend on publicity and public opinion for their success, and indeed their survival, only professional athletes cry for the *nil nisi bonum* treatment from the press. Baseball owners would have to empty their treasure trove of television revenue to buy the free advertising given them annually by newspapers. Yet, almost without exception, they act as if they are doing a newspaperman a favor when they allow him to watch their game.

The attitude is endemic in baseball, but nowhere has it been as refined, and defined, as by the Yankees of the past generation. The most important organization in baseball was consistently the least accessible to the press, which is by any definition the surrogate of the public, which paid the overhead on The House That Ruth Built. Mike Burke, the new president of the "new" Yankees, believes that the "haughty, cold, remote climate" (and the adjectives are his) can be changed because it filtered down from the top, and there's a new man, and a new climate, at the top. Maybe he is right, but there is a supportable theory that the attitude filtered up. There could have been no more complacency, and no more arrogance, in the executive suite overlooking Fifth Avenue that day in 1958 than there was in the visiting clubhouse in Kansas City, where Enos Slaughter showed Andy Carey his bullets and Frank Crosetti counted the used baseballs. If the-press-be-damned has been an attitude in baseball, especially since television came along and brought money, it was a policy with the Yankees.

Presumably nobody in the Yankee management told Al Downing, the shy young pitcher, to flee into the asylum of the rubbing room after he'd been knocked out of the box. And presumably nobody in the Yankee management told him not to, either, since complaints to the management did not make Downing any more available. Downing didn't come along until Ralph Houk had become manager and propounded a theory that winning championships and having fun were not mutually exclusive. And by then the ultra-businesslike George Weiss had been turned out to his Connecticut pasture and replaced as general manager by the easygoing—too easygoing—Roy Hamey. So probably it never happened to Downing. But there was a time, a long time, when new Yankees were briefed, officially and unofficially, to beware of the rip. "They tell me what to say," a young Yankee was heard to say a decade ago, "and what can I do?" He could invent a gambit, like the young Mickey Mantle. Asked what he had in mind when he overthrew the cutoff man in the third inning, Mantle would say, "What difference does it make?"

What difference, indeed, it would occur to the reporter, whether the New York Yankees won or lost, or whether they played baseball at all. And the reporter would think of the many, many ways there were to make a living besides playing Boswell to potential gas-pumpers on Route 66. But then he would think of what the doctors and dentists at the cocktail parties always said about what a great job he had, getting to see all those games and talk to all those guys, and he would think about the kids to be fed, and he would think of a question to ask Yogi Berra, who was always so eminently quotable in Arthur Daley's column in the New York *Times*. "Heard Around the Batting Cage" always read like a conclave of stand-up comedians, with Yogi as top banana. Certainly Yogi would have something interesting, and probably something funny, to say. Just ask him. "Huh," Yogi would say. "How the hell would I know?"

Elston Howard would answer questions, but that didn't help much for his first few years. The lone Negro on the team, like the lone Jewish member a country club keeps as a pet to show it isn't restricted, Howard was the Yankees' answer to the NAACP pickets who marched around Yankee Stadium, protesting a lily-white policy. He played it cool and his answers hewed strictly to the company line. He never said anything that he wasn't pretty sure the manager would say, or had already said. Almost all of the writers "wrote Stengel" in those days. The fact that Casey was consistently, spectacularly quotable was only one reason why he got more "ink" than Eisenhower in the 1950s. The auxiliary, equal reason was that almost none of his troops—Whitey Ford being the singular exception—was very quotable at all.

Elston Howard became a regular in 1960, the Most Valuable Player in 1963 and thereafter, like Jackie Robinson after the MVP ended his ordeal of silence in 1949, his own man, with no particular concern about what he could or couldn't say. Mantle matured, and perhaps mellowed, in his later years and a personality emerged, like a butterfly from a cocoon. The shy, introverted country kid would never develop drawing-room suavity, which on him would look silly, but he became a man of wit and humor. Tony Kubek, given veteran status, a less attentive front office and the awareness of a latent intellectuality that baseball was not the only way of life, spoke his mind—to nonrippers. Even Maris relaxed a little—just a little—when he stopped hitting home runs. The Yankees of the early 1960s, whether because of Houk's have-fun policy or not, seemed capable of having fun, and seemed to be having it.

Besides, the clowns had arrived.

There was a time, and it wasn't so long ago, when talent was not the sole criterion for becoming a Yankee. There was a certain standard of decorum, of dignity, of deportment, that was requisite. Vic Power, rather than Elston Howard, might have been the first Negro Yankee (Power is a Puerto Rican, but his pigmentation is dark and baseball's racial quota system does not quibble about the fine distinction) if he had measured up. Power was a very fine baseball player. At Kansas City in 1953, the last year it was a Yankee farm, he made 217 hits and led the league in batting, at .349. He also was the most dexterous right-handed first baseman this side of Gil Hodges, who must have been the best of all time. (Speaking of the 3–6–3 double play, Stengel used to say: "No right-handed first baseman can make that play except the big guy in Brooklyn.") But Power was a hot dog, which as closely as it can be translated to English is baseball language for show-off. He would catch the ball with one hand. He also would talk, about anything, to anybody, and say what he thought. And he generally did not have the humility, the in-his-place attitude, that would be becoming to the first dark-complected Yankee. So he was thrown into a trade that brought the Yankees pitcher Harry Byrd, who lasted a year. Power didn't make the Hall of Fame, but he went on to become the best one-handed first baseman in history, hit .300 in a couple of towns and did things, like stealing home twice in one game, that might have made life more interesting in Yankee Stadium.

But the Yankees didn't want to be interesting. They wanted to win. If there ever was a high priest of that fundamental precept of the Yankee Era, it was not Miller Huggins, nor Joe McCarthy, nor Billy Martin, nor George Weiss. Not even Jake Ruppert. It was Jim Turner, the sometime pitcher and two-time pitching coach. Turner is a Tennesseean, but he is living proof that the New England ideal of common-sense conservatism is more a state of mind than a matter of geography. He was past his 30th birthday by the time he got to the big league, and in his rookie year, 1937, he won 20 games for the Boston Braves, a .500 ball club. Turner pitched for the Yankees only briefly, during the war years, but he helped them win a pennant in 1943 and the pinstripes were indelibly imposed upon his psyche.

They were visible through his Italian silk suit one afternoon in May 1959. It was a Year the Yankees Didn't Win the Pennant, and it was becoming painfully evident, even at that early stage, that they wouldn't. Frank Lary of the Tigers, their nemesis, had beaten them that afternon and crammed them into the cellar, the first time a Yankee team had touched bottom since 1925. Turner stopped in the Stadium press room after the game for the one tall scotch-and-water he allowed himself after a game, win or lose, and a newspaperman made what was supposed to be a facetious remark to him. Losing couldn't be all bad, the reporter said, because attendance was perceptibly up from 1958, when the Yankees had breezed, almost wire-to-wire, to the pennant. Jim Turner was outraged. "Do you actually believe," he demanded, "that people come out to see the Yankees lose?" The reporter thought it was obvious that many people did. Did Turner expect them to draw more with a 14-game lead than when they were in a race, or what could conceivably be a race? "Certainly," he said. "People want to see the Yankees because they're the best. That's what this country is built on: You make more money than the other people because you make the best product. Yes, if the Yankees won every game, even more people would want to see them, because they're the best. That's what American people want." Turner paused, sipped his drink and smiled a knowing smile. "If you think people come out to see the Yankees lose," he said, "well, all I can tell you is that that's Communist thinking."

It is just as well for Turner's peace of mind that it dawned on somebody upstairs, shortly after the Communist infiltration of Yankee Stadium in 1959, that the price on a vote of confidence for him by his pitchers would have been 6–5 and pick 'em. Because he was replaced by Johnny Sain, he wasn't around when the clowns arrived. Then, when he returned in 1966, nothing was funny any more, even to the clowns. Turner's sense of free enterprise could not have abided, for example, the dictum of young Jim Bouton on the inflated salaries of ballplayers. Bouton had been a 21-game winner and he was still trying to get the Yankees to reward him with his idea of a 21-win salary—or, more accurately, baseball's idea. Bouton's self-interest was enlightened. "Teachers, and doctors, should be paid that kind of money," he said. "Not ballplayers. But since that money comes into the ball park, it should go someplace. It might as well go to the players."

Only in the traditionalist Yankee context could Bouton be termed a clown. He would pull a floppy fedora over his ears and do a convincing imitation of Crazy Guggenheim, and sing the themes of radio serials of his childhood, like "Little Orphan Annie," on the team bus. Things like that. But he is a thoughtful, sensitive man, with a philosophy undeveloped by formal education but bolstered by innate logic. He had given more consideration to Appalachia than to kid Kentuckian Steve Hamilton about the poverty program, and he knew a backlash was something besides the follow-through of a bat that occasionally crowns a catcher. The Yankee traditionalists did not mind so much that Bouton had ideas. What was alarming was that he expressed them to other players, or to those who would listen, and to reporters. "When I came here," Bouton said, "some of the players took me aside and told me to watch out for certain writers. I decided to make up my own mind, and I can honestly say no writer has ever written anything malicious about me." Had any reporter wanted to rip him, Bouton had given them all the tools for the job. Candidly and matter-of-factly, he gave them just about all the information about himself that he knew, negative as well as positive, often more information than their questions merited. Other players, notably Maris, grumbled as the newspapermen gravitated naturally toward Bouton's locker after a game, whether he had been in it or not. For years before they had tended to converge on Whitey Ford, the crudely gracious oasis in a desert of hostility, and the other players never marched past him—as some did to Bouton—opening and closing their fingers in the internationally understood sign that means "You talk too much." Nobody ever tried to enforce on Ford the unwritten law that Bouton already understood, and ignored.

"A lot of players feel," Bouton said, "that if they have something personal between themselves and a writer, they can expect the other players to refuse to talk to him. I don't believe in that. Their [the players'] resentment embarrassed me at first. I was on the team and I wanted to be a member of it. But now I don't care what they say. The older guys wanted to set the pace for me when I was a rookie, and I suppose that was right. But now I have as much right to set it as anyone. I don't get on them for not talking to reporters, so it's none of their business if I do talk to them. A lot of guys stay in this game a long time without learning that the writer is their PR man. They should be considerate to him for selfish reasons, if no other."

For whatever reason, Bouton consistently practiced what he preached. Even when a sore arm rendered him almost useless and plunged him into quiet desperation about his future, he met what he considered his ethical obligations. Pitching carefully in relief in a game against Detroit in 1964, Bouton threw a home-run ball to Al Kaline and was beaten. It was a galling, frustrating experience, but for almost a half-hour after the game he sat in front of his locker and discussed the game, and his tortured feelings, with reporters. There was a class, almost a gallantry, about the way Bouton handled himself, clinging to his principles as a career that should have been approaching high noon seemed to darken into twilight.

Across the Yankee dressing room coach Frank Crosetti, a lifetime .245 hitter who had banked more Yankee World Series checks than Babe Ruth and Lou Gehrig combined (21–14), still could not tolerate the concept of being considerate to reporters, even for selfish reasons. "Look at that," Crosetti growled, combing the peripheral hair around the shiny dome that led him, on many opening days, to be busy in the dugout runway while the rest of the champions were lining up on the foul lines and baring their heads for the flag-raisings. "You'd think he won the damn game."

If Bouton was a clown only to the Crosetti mentality, at least two members of the new wave of the early 1960s were comedians by any definition: Phil Linz naturally, and Joe Pepitone unnaturally. Pepitone was endowed with considerable talents and Linz was not. "Pepitone," manager Johnny Keane said, about the time he was slapping him with a fine for being late for work again, "ought to be a $100,000 ballplayer." The estimate may have been slightly generous. (Keane in his patient alarm about the way the 1965 Yankees were going, or weren't going, may have been playing the Stengel game of building a player up, or tearing him down, in the press.) But Pepitone was a sure-handed first baseman and played better than adequate center field. For all that and the "Stadium Stroke" that makes him a home-run hitter in New York, however, Pepitone wouldn't have survived one spring training as a Yankee in the days when the three Ds—decorum, dignity and deportment—were as significant marks on the report card as RBIs.

Flaky, flamboyant, eccentric—call it what you will, this dizzy kid out of Brooklyn (and Joe Pepitone will be a kid when he comes back to the Stadium for the Old Timers' Game) could not be decorous if the Yankees hired Angier Biddle Duke and Amy Vanderbilt as his tutors. He also traded in his dignity for popularity. In an overweening attempt to be one of the boys, and without the wit to make the boys laugh with him, he settled for having them laugh at him. Mickey Mantle can deliver himself of a remark as bawdy as any ever heard on a troopship, and in all-male company it comes off legitimately funny, funny enough to justify its earthiness. The Rabelaisian capers Pepitone puts himself through are degrading. But the guys laugh, so the price is right. Pepitone's deportment, at least until a marriage that "gave him incentive and straightened him out," was a constant concern of Yankee management. He made an open joke about the number of years he'd have to play to pay back the money he'd been advanced to solve financial problems. And Wally Moses, the batting coach, felt constrained on more than one occasion to lecture Pepitone about getting enough sleep to get him to the ball park on time. "Now, you hit today," Moses said after one game, having taken Pepitone out for early batting practice to talk him back into his undercut swing, a bad habit to almost any other hitter

84

but one with Pepitone's style. "So don't go staying out all night and louse yourself up. You got to play two tomorrow, you know."

"He's not a bad boy," Keane said of Pepitone, and he wasn't. He was no more of a headache to the Yankees than Bo Belinsky to the Los Angeles Angels, Van Lingle Mungo to the old Brooklyn Dodgers (who once had to be flown out of Cuba under cover of darkness in order, the Dodger management believed, to preserve his life), Babe Ruth, or any number of traveling athletes who, like Rudyard Kipling's single men in barracks, did not grow into plaster saints. Pepitone was, in a word, colorful. But a few years earlier, when the legislative machinations of the have-nots were cutting off their sources of decorous, dignified talent and the Yankee management was not facing the facts, Pepitone need not have applied. The Yankees were selling baseball, not color—pure, simple, unexcelled and unadorned baseball. They didn't need any characters, so Pete Ramos need not have applied, either.

Ramos first attracted the Yankees' attention in the middle 1950s, when he was losing games for the sorry Washington Senators and serving up home runs. Robin Roberts had set a major-league record for gopher balls in 1956, giving 46 homers. Ramos almost matched that the following year, with 43. He came back with 38 more in 1958. To the Yankee management, however, Pedro Ramos was something else. He was that nutty Cuban who kept challenging Mickey Mantle to a foot race.

The Sporting News had timed Mantle in 3.1 seconds getting to first base, and the only other big-leaguer who matched that figure was Bill White, then of the New York Giants. But nobody had asked Pete Ramos, and he wanted to prove something. He never got the chance. The Yankees kept saying it was too dangerous to Mantle's fragile legs but that was patent nonsense because the Yankees didn't stop Mantle from stealing bases in situations where stolen bases weren't really needed. "I can't stop him," Stengel would say. The real reason was that it would have been undignified. The Yankees sold baseball, not track meets, and Ramos need not apply.

He applied anyway. In spring training each year he would visit Casey Stengel on the Yankee bench in an attempt to convince him how much he could help a pennant contender. Stengel wasn't sure Ramos couldn't help his team, but he never got him. "They traded off Vic Power because they didn't think he was their kind of Negro," wrote Leonard Shecter of the New York *Post*. "They probably felt Ramos wasn't their kind of Spanish-speaking ballplayer." Except for a brief peek at little Willie Miranda, the good-field, no-hit sprite who gave them a few laughs in 1953, there wasn't a kind of Spanish-speaking ballplayer the Yankees were looking for until 1959, when they decided it was time to bring Ralph Terry back from the Kansas City "farm," and took Hector Lopez in the package deal. But certainly Ramos was not the Yankee type, for a number of reasons.

It was remarkable, and it should have been indicative of the Yankee decline, when they took Ramos—nay, sought and embraced him—in September 1964, when things got really tough. He was with Cleveland then, and still being different. For one thing, he had balked all the previous season as Indians' manager Birdie Tebbetts had tried to sell him the wisdom of becoming a relief pitcher. "I don't be happy in the bullpen," he told Tebbetts. For another, Ramos was still too gregarious to submit to the disciplines of baseball. Just as he had always visited Stengel, he would sit and talk in the Yankee dugout when they came to Cleveland (though apparently even Ramos did not have the audacity to visit the enemy camp when the Indians played in Yankee Stadium). In lip service to the rule on fraternization (everybody does it, but don't let the people see it), Tebbetts had fined Ramos $50 for being too obviously chummy with Camilo Pascual of the Minnesota Twins, a fellow Cuban with whom he had suffered long in Washington. And his clothes. Ye gods, those clothes!

In gratitude, perhaps, to the Yankee for bringing him to New York to save their 1964 pennant, Ramos made a concession. He gave up the five-gallon Stetson that had crowned his neo-Western sartorial splendor. "Yogi don't tell me not to wear my hat," Ramos said, "but I want to be nice. I don't want to break no rules." The sombrero was about all Pete gave up. Not quite. He wore his tight black cowboy pants outside the ornate boots, rather than tucking them in the top. The black shirt was like a newly discovered constellation, with shining mother-of-pearl buttons everywhere necessary, and almost everywhere else, too. The ensemble was topped by an almost incandescent orange sweater. And that was only one ensemble.

And only one symptom that the Yankees were functioning on a new plateau. Ramos' Cuban palm ball ("You call it a spitball, it's illegal") saved the pennant, and Yankee décor, if not decorum, was changed, perhaps forevermore. Even Linz, a legitimately funny man (the worst of all possible kinds to an organization that is trying to be terribly serious when it is becoming ridiculous) wasn't banished immediately, even after the high crime of playing his harmonica on the team bus out of Chicago after a losing game. Manager Berra chewed him out and fined him, and Linz's response was that he gave 100 percent all the time.

He had something there. All of Phil Linz wasn't an appreciable fraction of Mickey Mantle, but the Yankees got all he had, and they knew it. Whether he was sincere or not when he issued his pronunciamento about winning and having fun not being irreconcilable, General Manager Ralph Houk had created a Frankenstein monster. The modestly talented Linz was it, a man who could take baseball completely seriously on the field and be almost completely frivolous about it between games. "Play me or trade me" has been the ultimatum of all the Don Zimmers riding all the benches, but Linz, as a Yankee utility man, gave Houk a variation on the theme: "Play me or keep me." He knew his limitations, better than anybody knew them. But when Tony Kubek was injured during the '64 season, Linz filled in at shortstop well enough to keep the leaking ship on keel. And in the World Series his home run off Bob Gibson in the final game kept the Yankees alive until the final inning.

When Kubek retired and there was no shortstop in sight, Linz had to go to Philadelphia for Ruben Amaro. Linz didn't play in Philadelphia, and what talent he had rusted during the 1966 season. Meanwhile he was demonstrating how to have fun though making a lot of money, operating his "Mr. Laffs" bistro, with its wall-to-wall airline stewardesses, on First Avenue in New York. On the good nights at Mr. Laffs they line up seven deep at the bar. The main attraction is the girls, and many of them were acquaintances Linz made in the days when he was demonstrating how to have fun though a Yankee. Phil was only a peripheral Yankee, but the organization will never be quite the same after him. Even if there is always a

Frank Crosetti or a Jim Turner, it can't be quite the same.

To what extent Crosetti and Turner are effects of the Yankee syndrome of stuffiness and to what extent they have been its cause is moot because it is immeasurable. In any case they are its manifestations, gray-flanneled functionaries who gain about as much enjoyment out of the delightful occupation of participating in a game as bank tellers derive from cashing checks. The fact that Crosetti lives in a modest apartment on Walton Avenue, not far from Yankee Stadium, and walks to work is his own business. Andrew Carnegie was thrifty, too, we are told. It is nevertheless melancholy that Crosetti denies himself the chief pleasure of playing baseball, managing it, coaching it, writing about it or simply watching it: he doesn't enjoy the second guess. In a game in Cleveland on a night in 1959, Hector Lopez attempted to score from second base on a single and was thrown out. It was difficult to tell whether Lopez had run through third-base coach Crosetti's stop sign or whether Crosetti had sent him home. But that fact had to be ascertained in order to write an intelligent account of the game for All Those Wonderful Fans. Subsequent events indicated that, had Lopez stopped at third, the Yankees might have won. The press corps, well aware of the fury of Crosetti questioned, huddled in a group in the Yankee clubhouse, advising each other that somebody, sooner or later, was going to have to address Crosetti. Finally, furtively, somebody did. "Frank," the reporter began, "I—"

"Don't ask me any bleeding questions," Crosetti ranted. "You bleeding guys write any bleeding thing you want, but don't ask me any bleeding questions." Check. No questions. But in the corner of the room, not nearly dressed, sat Lopez. He must have some idea whether Crosetti's light was red or green. The reporter approached Lopez. "Leave him the bleed alone," Crosetti roared. "Don't ask him any bleeding questions. You bleeding guys can blame it on me. Yeah, I sent him in. It's my fault, okay? Write it that way. But leave him alone." End of interview.

It is not especially important that a few low-priced reporters —"the bread-and-butter guys," television pundit Howard Cosell calls them in his double play of one-upmanship, demonstrating both his magnificence and his munificence in one phrase—were frustrated in their attempts to write adequate accounts of the game. It is a little sad, however, that All Those Wonderful Fans were denied an explanation of what happened. They surely wouldn't find out from television, because television works for the management. In one of the Yankee-Dodger World Series in the '50s, Carl Furillo hit a ball up the alley in right-center in Yankee Stadium. It would have been a stand-up double for Furillo's mother, but he went for third and was thrown out, easily. It was a late inning and the Dodgers were three runs down. A high school coach would have bawled the hell out of Furillo. Vin Scully, the best of the TV announcers now that Red Barber has been muted (and because he studied under Red Barber), was at the mike and it was evident he wanted to tell the people Furillo had made a dumb play. "Well, Carl Furillo," Scully said when the noise subsided, "well, I guess you could say Carl gambled." Going for an extra base when you're three runs down in a late inning is a gamble, of course. So is Russian roulette. If a Yankee, or anybody else, pulls that kind of rock when you're watching TV this summer, don't expect an indictment by the telecasters. They work not for the network and not for the sponsor but for the ball club; would you expect them to rip?

Turner was never as sulfuric as Crosetti, but he was often very logical. There was the day—it happens every day in every major-league park—when a kid draped himself across the top of the Yankee dugout and said, "Mr. Turner, could I get an autographed baseball?" Mr. Turner turned and looked at the boy, about 12 years old, and smiled that thin smile. His attitude was almost avuncular, and quite logical. "Now, son," Turner said, "I'll tell you what I would do if I wanted an autographed baseball. Now, you must understand I don't want an autographed baseball, but I'm just telling you what I would do if I wanted one. I would go to a sporting-goods store and buy an American League baseball. It would cost you about three dollars, and it comes in a box. I would send that baseball to the New York Yankees, 161st Street and River Avenue, and I would send a letter with it asking to have the players autograph it. I would include my address and the return postage. Now, I'm not telling you what to do, but that's what I would do if I wanted an autographed baseball." The kid looked puzzled, and withdrew. Kids who lean over the dugout and ask for autographed baseballs may not expect to get them. They certainly don't expect to get a lecture on postal procedure.

The Yankees is dead, and to some degree they have bored themselves to death.

5

"Run, Sheep, Run"

THE YANKEES, two runs behind, had runners at first and second and nobody out. The batter was Bob Turley, who never hit a baseball as hard as he could throw it. The situation cried out for a bunt, and the defenses inched toward the plate as the pitch was delivered. Turley swung and the ball bounced softly to the right side. And softly through the right side. One run scored, and before the inning was over the Yankees had three runs and one more of the 4,292 victories they scored in the Yankee Era, 1920–64. (During the same period the Yankees lost 2,643 times, for a winning percentage of .619 —85 points higher than the next-best Cleveland Indians.)

What, manager Casey Stengel was asked later, inspired him to have the weak-hitting, slow-footed Turley swing away under such conditions, risking a double play that would take the Yankees right out of the game? Well, he might have said, Turley is not a real good bunter, and the way they defense against the bunt these days, only a real good bunter is fairly sure to advance the runner. In addition, the ball is so resilient these days, in order to ensure the home runs that All Those Wonderful

Fans are supposed to want, that an inexpert bunter could not only force a runner at third but bunt into a double play—in the air or, in the case of a slow runner like Turley, on the ground. One must also consider that the opposition, in defending against the bunt, has its second baseman in motion to cover first, the shortstop moving toward second and the first baseman and pitcher rushing the plate. The alternate procedure, in an attempt to get the front man, would have the third baseman charging, too, and the shortstop going to cover third. In any case a number of infielders would be in motion, committed by inertia to left or right, and any kind of ground ball would have a fighting chance to go through and lead to a big, decisive inning; a double play would be highly unlikely under such conditions and a force at second, or a play at first, would advance at least one runner and possibly both, thereby accomplishing the purpose of a sacrifice bunt. Adding the element of surprise, hitting away seemed better percentage than the bunt, which many fans feel is automatic because they haven't tried to bunt a rabbit ball thrown by a big-league pitcher.

Casey Stengel didn't say any of that, but he said all of it. He put it this way:

"Because it's run, sheep, run, and you can't bunt with the lively ball."

There is not even trivial tragedy in the fact that the Yankees' reticence/hostility toward the press deprived a generation of "bread-and-butter" reporters of what would have been some of the best sports stories of the century. Pity them not. If they had had any ambition, they would have quit chronicling a game for a pittance and gone to work, making important money by writing doggerel to prove the merits of one detergent over another. The rather melancholy fact is that several generations of

93

The Decline and Fall of the New York Yankees

Yankees (a baseball generation being approximately five years, and you could look it up) were presented to the kids and the grownup kids who were their followers and might have become their fans as some magnificent kind of robots with numbers on their backs. When some of them loosened up over a cup of cheer and stopped parroting the company line, they had personalities: beliefs, hopes, doubts, fears, jealousies—all of them off the record, "because if they found out upstairs that I said that, I'd have my ass in a sling." The Yankees, or most of them, were people. If you pricked them, they bled, and if you tickled them (most of them), they would laugh.

But on the Yankees' loftiest, headiest plateau, 1949–60, very few of their Boswells bothered either to prick or tickle, because Casey Stengel took care of all that. He very often would prick his players, with criticism that ranged from trenchant and sarcastic to downright nasty, little valentines of vitriol to be read with morning coffee. And he tickled the press with just about every *obiter dictum* he issued. They called Joe McCarthy "The Pushbutton Manager" in the 1930s because of his unimaginative system, by which he wrote the names of his best nine players on the lineup card and then found himself a good seat to watch them win. The outstanding characteristic of McCarthy's managing technique was the button he didn't push, the one marked "panic." Miller Huggins, on the "Murderers' Row" plateau of the 1920s, had made it a cliché that you don't break up a winning combination. McCarthy projected the thesis further and never broke up a losing combination, the few times he had one, because he knew it would soon be a winning combination again. "He was a hell of a manager," says Lefty Gomez, who won 189 games for the Yankees and, like Billy Martin, exceeded himself in World Series competition. "He made us believe we were good," says Johnny Murphy, now director of the Mets' player-procurement program. "Sure, he got nasty once in a while, when he'd been drinking too much," says Murphy, who won 93 games for the Yankees, almost exclusively as a relief pitcher, and picked up the pieces of many others, notably for Gomez when that fine left arm began to go bad. "But it was McCarthy who made us believe in ourselves. 'Look at those clowns,' he'd say. 'You going to let them beat you? They don't belong on the same field with you.' Sure, it's natural to have doubts about yourself, no matter how good you are. But Joe didn't let us have many."

The all-time chief manipulator, though, not only of the Yankees but of all baseball, all sport, was Stengel. It wasn't only that he handled his players like marionettes, getting them up and sitting them down like end men in a minstrel show, using them and not using them in capricious patterns most managers (Gene Mauch of the Phillies is one exception) would consider inadvisable because of the deleterious effect it might have on the morale of sensitive stars, or would-be stars. Stengel was the master manipulator because he had one other button that he pushed every day he managed the Yankees and later the Mets. It was the button marked "Press."

"Run, sheep, run, and you can't bunt with the lively ball" is probably the most Stengelesque quote that ever actually got quoted. (The same journalists who improved on the drolleries of Yogi Berra, who needed it, did a lot of lily-gilding on Stengel. There is a serious question, for example, whether Stengel ever really said, "Can't anybody here play this game?" But what the hell. Stengel would appreciate fully that only a chump lets facts stand in the way of a good line. You think James Boswell didn't improve on some of Dr. Johnson's wisecracks?)

There is something essential, something definitive, about "run, sheep, run." It is the kind of thing Stengel would say to change a dull, analytical story into a laugher, by changing a logical tactical maneuver into a cutie-pie caper. It's so *writable*.

But a duplicate prize for 14-karat Stengelese might have been awarded to that "I couldn't have done it without the players." There was a sad song in the 1930s, the lament of a bandleader: "I Got Those Oh-What-an-Easy-Job-You-Got-All-You-Do-Is-Wave-a-Stick Blues." Stengel never had such blues. The men executed, but Stengel won. All the "I Am" medals of recent times in baseball were pinned on the late Charley Dressen ("No matter where the Braves finish," it was said of him, "Charley will be five games ahead of them"), and Dressen was pretty fast with the vertical pronoun. But a Stengel soliloquy often sounded like a pitch from a jockey's agent, one of those lovable rascals who make their living cajoling and conning horse trainers to give their clients a ride, without mentioning their clients' names. "I ride your filly the last time, and I do 109 [pounds]," says a 205-pound agent, "and I win the National Stallion for you last spring. I think I fit your filly pretty good." It was a point of pride to Stengel that "I win the season series from every club in the league." In a post-mortem of a game he might play four or five positions: "If I come up with that ground ball in the seventh I don't have to pitch to that big ape, and then I get the ball up in his eyes, the only place he can hit it. And that other pitcher was throwing me grounders all night, anyway, but the umpire don't bend over far enough to see them." They were "my" owners. And they were "my" writers. With certain notable exceptions, they really were.

"Mr. Terry threw them lollipops again," Stengel might say, "so they handed me the vaseline pot." This was in the time when Ralph Terry, having been reclaimed by the Yankees after his apprenticeship in Kansas City was completed and showing promise of becoming a very important pitcher, threatened to be instead what old-line baseball people, in their scorn for things intellectual, call an "Einstein." This means that, instead of persevering with his basic tools, fast balls, curves, sliders and an occasional change of pace, he began experimenting. Ultimately, if briefly, Terry would become an important pitcher, winning 78 games for the Yankees. But in this period he "fooled around" with things like slow curves, and he wasn't winning. This was a time for a reporter to question Ralph Terry, an articulate young man and a psychology major in college. He was tampering with himself, changing his basic style, and his elders were saying he was making a mistake. Was he, out of stubbornness or out of some abstruse theory of his own, taking the risk of throwing away a bright career? It couldn't be a bad story, and all they had to do was ask Terry a few questions.

Some of "my writers" did, and some didn't. Some "wrote Stengel," because it was easier. First of all, although Ralph Terry was one of the most accessible, least hostile of the Yankees, a man does not like to be asked how it came to pass that he just had the hell knocked out of him out there, in front of television and everybody. The manager had issued his pronunciamento on the subject, and it was far more quotable than anything the pitcher, in his depression, was likely to say about himself.

Besides: "They handed me the vaseline pot." That was almost as good as "run, sheep, run," and it had an extra merit. One of the frustrations of covering sports is that most of the most colorful statements uttered in dressing rooms are so colorful as to cost any newspaper its mailing privileges if they were

97

written as uttered. When you read, after a team has been shut out by a powerful pitching performance, the observation of one of the vanquished that "he stuck the bats down our throats," that is not where the man said the pitcher stuck the bats. When the batter says the pitch he hit for the home run was not quite waist-high, realize that he had a much more specific anatomical designation for the level of the pitch. When a timid batter shies away from a curve ball, they say his tail is in the dugout, and they don't say tail.

Many sports reporters strive to convey this sort of realism, not only out of devotion to truth but for the sheer devilment of slipping obscenity, or the strongest possible suggestion of obscenity, past the copy desk. It brings the roguish kind of kicks Arthur Godfrey has enjoyed for years, slipping veiled punch lines of slightly off-color jokes into the badinage of his morning radio program. Stan Hochman of the Philadelphia *News* merited some kind of journalistic mischief award after the All-Star game in San Francisco in 1961, the one in which Stu Miller was blown off the pitcher's mound. The only reasonable time of day to play baseball in ill-conceived Candlestick Park is 11 A.M., when the weather is usually calm and sometimes balmy. Games would then be over before the winds rose and changed direction, or directions, which is in about the third inning of games begun at 1 P.M. "That," Hochman wrote, "was when the shift hit the fans." Such a line is the publishable ideal of naughtiness: to a reader who knows the original line, it is not only funny but makes him feel "in"; to a reader who doesn't recognize it, the line can be understood literally, or not at all, and in either case it leaves him unsullied.

"The vaseline pot" was cited again and again as reporters "wrote Stengel," and precious few readers understood its significance. In Stengel's context it meant something unkind and unfair had been done to him. If nobody understood it, everybody understood that Casey Stengel was supposed to be inscrutable; nobody minded and "my writers" had their fun. Similarly, only Stengel's contemporaries ("most people my age are dead") and the few remaining farmers of the nation understood what Stengel meant by "road apples." It was his graphic suggestion of horse manure, which in its adjectival form is baseball's most useful, or most utilized, descriptive. Very loosely translated, it most closely expresses the concept of inferiority. "What the hell do you think happened?" the losing pitcher will snarl. "I threw him a horse-manure pitch, that's what happened." Hochman, who gives you 100 percent, all the time, once tried to paraphrase horse-manure fielding by the Phillies as "cowpasturish"; it was not one of his nobler efforts.

One good quote is the cornerstone of a sports story, especially in an afternoon newspaper story, and many a story has been a collection of pedestrian facts, or observations, built around a one-line gag. Stengel dispensed one-liners like a one-man team of gag writers, and he did everything but mimeograph them. Breathes there a man with soul so dead that he could go back to his typewriter and *not* write "run, sheep, run"? If there ever was one, he probably turned in his baseball writer's card and went to work writing speeches for William Knowland. And, in his zeal to get "the vaseline pot" on paper, might a journalist not forget to ask Ralph Terry to explain the logic behind his pitching pattern, or forget what Terry had to say, even if he bothered to ask him? Another day, another Stengel story. And another mass-circulation message to another Yankee, to the effect that he had better begin to execute in the manner his manager prescribed, or else.

The Decline and Fall of the New York Yankees

Of every $10 a man is paid to manage a big-league team, about $3 is for "handling" the press. Some managers, like the loquacious Birdie Tebbetts, overdo the public-relations aspect; others, like Herman Franks of the Giants, never get the idea at all. But nobody ever approached and nobody ever will approach the virtuosity of Stengel, who was a genius at management of the news. Casals' cello was never manipulated with more subtle delicacy than Stengel's carrot-and-stick inducement of newspapers to do his bidding. If you mentioned the name of Ivan Petrovich Pavlov, the Old Professor would ask what league he played in, yet he managed to establish a remarkable set of conditioned reflexes among "my writers." First, he understood the functions and limitations of various newspapers, and the differences between them, which many high-priced public-relations pundits patently do not. A story that would call for a five-column headline in the New York *Post* would be virtually useless to The Man from the *Times,* and Stengel knew that. He also knew which men were from which papers, though he consistently pretended not to by using no proper names.

"I'll talk to these guys first," he said in St. Petersburg one spring day, referring to the morning-paper reporters, "because I know you guys [the afternoon-paper reporters] can't write the box score." Then, after a quick briefing sufficient unto the purposes of A.M. publication, Stengel would hand out an all-but-mimeographed "angle" for the afternoons. Instead of force-feeding a story that would be acceptable only to the company house organ, as so many public-relations slickers try to do, Casey tailored his handouts to the needs, or at least the wants, of all. And the dosage was emulsified, like cod-liver oil in orange juice.

100

"Let me ask you a question," the seminar would begin, and journalists would be flattered that the resident genius of the World Champions was about to draw on their acumen. They would be until they found out that Stengel's "question" was only an opening gambit, a preamble to a lecture. Anyone who took it literally and tried to answer would likely hear another Stengel standard: "You're full of ——, and I'll tell you why." In the course of his address Stengel would, at some point, lower his gravel voice, look over his shoulder and say, "I shouldn't tell you this, but . . ." That was the signal to take out paper and pencil. The Professor was about to drop a story.

Sometimes he dropped them subtly, but heavily. Subtly, because he allowed his remarks to be overheard, rather than delivering them directly. Heavily, because his constructive criticisms of his players were frequently as benevolent as indictments. Bobby Richardson made 1,432 hits in his foreshortened career as a Yankee and was one of the dwindling few major-leaguers of the home-run-happy 1960s to make more than 200 in a season. He finished with a lifetime average of .266, highly respectable for a second baseman of his fielding dexterity. The Yankees won the pennant in 1962 and Mickey Mantle was made the Most Valuable Player for the third time, but that winter the Mantles' Christmas card to the Richardsons of Sumter, South Carolina, was addressed to the Most Valuable Player. In his early years as a Yankee, however, Richardson did not threaten to rattle the doors of the Hall of Fame, and his hitting—especially his aversion to taking a base on balls—scared nobody except himself and Stengel. The manager was leaning on the batting cage in Yankee Stadium one day in 1958 (a posture he did not normally assume, preferring to hold court in the dugout) when Richardson took his swings. The swings didn't produce much. "Maybe," Stengel said loudly and sarcastically, "someday he'll hit the way I tell him to." Richardson heard the crack, but if he hadn't he could have read it. It was duly recorded by several reporters within earshot.

Jerry Lumpe came to the Yankees in the latter part of the 1957 season, batted a part-time .340 the rest of the way and made himself quite useful in the losing World Series. The next year he was a disappointment, however, or at least Stengel thought he was. It is questionable whether Lumpe ever would have been more than a journeyman ballplayer, but what was Heard Around the Batting Cage one day in 1958 didn't help. Stengel made another of his unwonted visits to the cage and watched Lumpe spray a few line drives. Lumpe, a reporter observed, had a nice swing.* "Yeah," Stengel remarked loudly. "He looks like the greatest hitter in the world, until you play him." The remark was recorded for posterity, and for Lumpe, who has never forgotten it. Another Stengelism, after a road-apple performance, was the threat to "back up the moving van," i.e., ship a player or players to Kansas City, or some other oblivion. The following May, Lumpe was in the van, en route to Kansas City.

Stengel dropped most of his stories to "my writers" on a

---

* This is meaningless, or almost. Henry Aaron, by his own observation after watching the movies, has a bad swing, with a number of technical defects. So does Roberto Clemente. Willie Mays doesn't always look like poetry in motion either, and Bill Skowron, who hit .294 and 165 home runs in 1,087 games as a Yankee, may have been the worst-looking good hitter who ever lived. A right-handed hitter, he would go after outside pitches with his head turned so far his gaze would be fixed on the third-base boxes—and hit them into the right-center bleachers.

group plan, but occasionally he could be more selective. In mid-1959 the Yankees were going badly, and among the reasons was the fact that Don Larsen, the pluperfect pitcher, wasn't getting many batters out. Larsen had been one of Stengel's favorites ("The world," wrote Munro Leaf, creator of *Ferdinand the Bull*, "will always have a soft spot in its heart for the guy who just doesn't give a damn") even before he got everybody out in Yankee Stadium that day, October 8, 1956. If Larsen couldn't execute as a pitcher, Stengel reasoned, what would be wrong with making him a left fielder? He always could hit, which was more than most of the Yankees were doing at the time. So on a Saturday in Detroit he sent Larsen out to left field to shag flies during batting practice. "Look at the big ox," Stengel said in the dugout. "I told him to go out there, so he went. But he ain't shagging, is he?"

This casual remark was dropped before a number of "my writers," but Sunday was another day. There was, for some reason, only one writer in the dugout with Stengel as the Yankees rehearsed. "I shouldn't tell you this, but . . ." Stengel began. The ears perked up. "I got a pitcher on my team that don't tell his infielders when he's going to throw the slow ball." In modern, terribly specialized baseball, part of the business of "defensing" (a barbarism borrowed from professional football) is stationing one's infielders not only according to the propensities of individual hitters, but according to the abilities of one's own pitcher—and, refining the matter one more degree, according to the particular pitch the pitcher has selected for delivery. If the pitcher has determined to throw a change-of-pace, an offering slow in contrast to the other arrows in his quiver, to get the batter's timing off, he is expected to wiggle his fingers behind his back or go through some other gesture to advise the

103

fielders what is going to happen. This is essential because, if the change-of-pace does not succeed in upsetting the hitter's timing, he will pull the ball, and it would be advisable for the shortstop to take a subtle step to his right (or, if the hitter is left-handed, the second baseman to his left). And Stengel had a pitcher who was neglecting this basic nuance—a *Yankee* pitcher. "And do you think it's one of these dumb kids?" he asked rhetorically. "Well, it's Mr. Ford, of Glen Cove, Long Island. I shouldn't tell you, but that's who it is."

Mr. Stengel was exclusively addressing a reporter whose name he had never indicated he knew. But the reporter was from *Newsday*, the principal Long Island daily. Mr. Ford had in fact moved a few miles from Glen Cove to Lake Success, Long Island (taking with him a dog whose name was Casey, whatever significance may be drawn from that). But Mr. Ford every afternoon had a copy of *Newsday* delivered to his front porch, and Mr. Stengel somehow knew that. The previous day's press release had been for the benefit of any newspaper Mr. Larsen might read, presuming Mr. Larsen read any newspaper, but today's announcement was supposed to go special-delivery to Mr. Ford. Stengel selected his media like Jack Nicklaus picking a golf club.

From time to time Stengel would issue a sort of oral white paper, not picking on any single player or clique of players, but sketching an outline of the pattern of conduct he expected of his men. Casey, who has closed as many hotel bars as any man alive, had no illusions about the fact that some ballplayers are as disposed to take an occasional dram of cheering liquid as some shipping clerks or account executives, and the thought did not particularly disturb him. "It ain't what you do that matters so much," he often said. "It's staying up all night doing it." The man who could execute was free to keep the most demanding social schedule without feeling the lash of Stengelian oratory.

But during that 1959 season, when Yankee management was casting about for explanations of the strange decline of a team that had run through the American League the previous year, Stengel seemed to recognize a closer correlation between clean living and execution. The management even went to the extent of hiring private eyes to observe their employees' peregrinations during all those dangerous leisure hours on the road, and the snoops they hired obviously weren't—no pun intended—Yankee followers. One of them tailed Bobby Shantz and Bobby Richardson, both of whose idea of high living is an extra scoop of ice cream. The trail led to the YMCA, where Shantz and Richardson shamelessly played ping-pong, far into the evening.

During a series in Detroit, late in July, Stengel gave up on the Yankees' pennant chances. The day before a transient Tiger infielder named Coot Veal hit a ground ball and was out, except that the throw was off line, into the runner. The first baseman, of course, was the accident-prone Bill Skowron. The Moose was always one of Stengel's favorites and might have realized Casey's visions for him had he not been plagued by crippling injuries. Early in his career Skowron used his great strength to move an air conditioner in his New Jersey home, and his back was never really the same again. This time Skowron, a right-handed fielder, reached for the throw and Veal ran into his left wrist as he fled across the bag, bending it backward and breaking it. "If you had him," Casey said mournfully when the news came that Skowron had been shipped home for the rest of the season, "you could even think about winning it. You'd like to see him play and make some money, because he always takes care of himself."

Stengel added another curious observation: "And he ain't a bolshevik on the club." Stengel did not encourage individualism among his troops any more strongly than the rest of the baseball establishment, which sees dark portents in the intellectual curiosity of such eggheads as Jim Brosnan, who not only read books but wrote them. A man who contemplates the system in which he works might arrive at the conclusion that it is not the best of all possible systems, and the boat might rock. If there was a bolshevik in the Yankee camp while it was on the Stengelian plateau, however, his identity was one of those truths known only to Stengel in his infinite, inscrutable wisdom.

There was a suspect for a few minutes in 1959. Mark Freeman, six-feet-six and 220 pounds, looked like pitcher. But he thought like what he was, a psychology major out of Louisiana State University. In the 1960 Baseball Register, under "Hobbies," where it usually says "hunting and fishing" or "golf, hunting and fishing" or simply "watching television," it was reported that Freeman was disposed toward "psychology and vocabulary." *Vocabulary?* Despite a tendency toward wildness, Freeman won 35 games in three years at Denver. When he emerged from the vineyards he was traded—to Kansas City, of course. The Yankees took him back in exchange for ageing Murry Dickson, then peddled him to the Cubs. He didn't turn up again. He wasn't a good pitcher, and that was too bad. It would have been interesting to hear him explain to the boys in the back of the bus how "vocabulary" can be a hobby.

After the 1959 season Stengel established that "my owners" owned him. There was a midwinter press conference in the suite over Fifth Avenue. The coffee was fresh and hot, and the little sandwiches were tasty, but for a while there didn't seem to be any purpose to the meeting, especially having Stengel present. Then Casey said, "Let me ask you a question." He was thinking about backing up the moving van again. The Yankees had staggered home third. Berra, 34 years old, and Mantle, with a damaged shoulder (from taking Red Schoendienst out of a play at second base during the previous World Series) added to his several leg problems, had put in mediocre—for them—seasons. Whitey Ford had won only 16 games. All three were at the stage where, in baseball's strange economic system, the pay raises come as much for seniority and past performance as for what a player has done lately.

But the Yankees had not won the pennant. They had drawn pretty well during the season, Turner's Law (excellence equals prosperity) notwithstanding, but they had missed that beautiful bonanza, three World Series games in the large and ludicrous Los Angeles Coliseum, and somebody was damned well going to pay for that. It is Americana, however, that bank clerks who support families on $97.34 a week become righteously indignant when they read that management is trying to sign Roger Maris for a pittance of $65,000 instead of the $72,000 he wants and so richly deserves. At pact-inking time, All Those Wonderful Fans almost invariably identify with labor, so management must be quite delicate when it gets to budget-trimming. How to swing public opinion against its own heroes? Expecting Yankee followers to root for Dan Topping and Del Webb would be as reasonable as expecting them to send a Christmas card to the finance company. Yet there might be a way: give management a personality *hoi polloi can* identify with. Humanize the image. Who else?

"I got these players," Stengel began, "who got the bad watches, that they can't tell midnight from noon." He went on and on, and he was very funny. His remarks were duly recorded, and duly read. "So *that's* why they didn't win the pennant," thinks Fred Fan. "I knew there had to be something wrong. These bums have been playing around."

It is interesting to consider how enthusiastically Stengel would have joined the attempt to put a "hold" on the Yankee payroll level, had he foreseen that just about a year later, in the same executive suite, with essentially the same personnel present, "my owners" were going to give him, figuratively speaking, his gold watch. The Corporate Concept is a two-edged sword, but Stengel tried to live with it to the end. He was hurt, deeply, by his rude dismissal, but he held still while management went through the mealymouthed routine about how they felt that it was time for a change. "My writers" strove mightily to get Stengel to say, in as plain English as he could muster, that he had been fired, and he talked around and around the point, inviting the reporters to draw their own conclusions, with reasonable assurance of what those conclusions would be.

Finally Joe Reichler of the Associated Press, now factotum to the new commissioner of baseball, came back from the phone booth and threw the gauntlet. "Casey," he said, "I want you to know that the AP is saying you were fired."

Stengel had never been "Ned in the Third Reader" (his expression for colossal naiveté) about communications media before, and he wasn't going to be now. "What does the UP say?" he asked.

Stengel used, amused and bemused "my writers," but he did not strive consciously to ingratiate himself with the press, as some managers do. His eminence was a product of Turner's Law: He got the most ink simply because he offered a better product. It was not merely easier to "write Stengel" than to probe the psyches of his more sensitive athletes, but artistically more profitable. Generally speaking, Casey treated all reporters equally, but he sometimes made distinctions between their works and managed to convey the message if their reportage displeased him. One night in Cleveland, after a Yankee victory, the door to the visitors' dressing room remained locked for more than ten minutes. Stengel's writers railed at the attendant, advising him that Casey Stengel never, never locked out the press, even in defeat. Finally Stengel himself appeared at the door and beckoned the reporters in. Yes, he said, he had ordered the door closed, "because there are some writers in this town who do not interest me."

Some whiskey was poured on the evening of Stengel's 69th birthday, which took place in a hotel on the road. In fact, a lot of whiskey was poured, and after a while Stengel began to deliver himself of a critique of the manner in which some of his writers had been treating him. "And that," he said, "includes Mr. Trimble." Joe Trimble of the New York *Daily News* was present, and he was puzzled. His coverage of the Yankees had been gentle, if not benign, and he hadn't been accused of a rip since 1945, when Nick Etten, a large first baseman, pursued him through several cars of a moving train. ("They were playing a game," colleague Dick Young wrote of the event, "called 'Throw Trimble From the Train.'") Trimble had always evinced due reverence for The Corporate Concept, and in time he would exceed himself in that regard by composing a midwinter essay that suggested that Mickey Mantle was selfish for asking for a raise. But on this occasion he had done something wrong. He never figured out what it was, but Stengel's ranting on the subject broke up his birthday party.

Stengel made himself not merely available to the press but inescapable.* He liked to talk baseball to newspapermen be-

* There is the eerie suggestion in the architecture of Yankee Stadium that the aloofness of the players was built in. It is the only stadium in

cause he liked to talk baseball to anybody. With a background of experience in the game that he considered unparalleled, he wanted to be listened to. At the Del Prado Hotel in Chicago his listener would be Al Lopez, White Sox manager, with whom he had much in common. Stengel had been Lopez' manager in Brooklyn in 1934–35. An undistinguished outfielder named Randy Moore had touted them on oil stock, and as a consequence they were the only two financially independent managers in baseball. At the Muehlebach Hotel in Kansas City his listeners, gathered around his bar stool like students at the Acropolis sitting at Socrates' knee, would be tourists from Topeka who didn't know a squeeze play from a sacrifice fly. "Let me ask you a question," he would say, and they would listen, all the way to closing time. They wouldn't have even a vague idea what he was talking about most of the time, but he would take them all the way back to Kankakee in the Northern Association in 1910, describe the two home runs he hit against the Yankees in the 1923 World Series (he had hit five all season for the Giants), and tell about being paid $15,000 not to manage the Dodgers in 1937. "You're full of soup," he would

---

baseball where the reporters enter the clubhouse not through the front door, to the players' habitat, but through a side door, to the manager's office. Not can, but *must*. If you go to the main door, the guard—do the Yankees sign them or trap them?—stares at you as if you're some kind of nut and gestures with his thumb toward the side entrance. A reporter who doesn't especially want to talk to the manager can, of course, proceed through his office to the players' area. Few do, because such effrontery involves a baleful look from the manager, followed by a some-kind-of-nut attitude from the players, who are accustomed to getting all the funny, angry or otherwise interesting things said before the image-builders arrive. The Stadium, we are told, was tailored to the measurements of Babe Ruth, but refinements have been added from time to time since then, and maybe the side door was one.

say to some pot-and-pan salesman from Ponca City, Oklahoma, who offered the observation that people don't bunt enough any more, "and I'll tell you why." Casey Stengel, like all the hams from Julius Caesar to Jackie Gleason, never had to be turned on.

One of the darkest hours of Stengel's career occurred on a Saturday night in June 1962. The Mets were playing their first series in Dodger Stadium, and they faced Sandy Koufax, the young left-hander who had begun to get the ball in the strike zone the year before and looked as if he might be some kind of pitcher after all. Koufax threw nine pitches in the first inning, all strikes. Frank Thomas, leading off the second inning, bounced a ball to Maury Wills in the hole, spun his wheels getting out of the batter's box and was thrown out by a step and a half. That was as close as the Mets would come to making a hit all night.

In a middle inning Richie Ashburn, who had been to bat more than 10,000 times in the National League, watched a fast ball go by for strike one, turned around and took a little walk. "Either my eyes are going bad," Ashburn said later, "or that was the fastest goddamn pitch I ever saw."

In the ninth inning Stengel tapped Gene Woodling on the shoulder. Woodling had been at bat about 6,000 times (he batted .285 in 698 games as a Yankee) in the American League, but never before in the National. "Go up there and hit," Stengel said. "It'll be a new experience for you." It was one of Stengel's must-write lines, but it would go to waste. The first pitch from Koufax was that big, cruel curve that came in at Adam's-apple level and careened sharply down and away until the catcher got it at the knees, on the outside corner. Woodling, as Ashburn had done earlier, left the batter's box and took

111

a contemplative stroll for himself. He thought about his farm, outside Cleveland, where he took his teammates for cookouts when his recent employers, the Baltimore Orioles, were in town. Woodling was 39 years old and baseball wasn't much fun anymore. "That," he said the next morning, "is the kind of pitch that sends you back to the farm."

Another era had begun, one in which a no-hitter by Sandy Koufax would be unlikely to push a raid on a topless pizza parlor (there is, or was, one near the Los Angeles airport) off page one. But this was his first one, and it was news. Sandy sat long after the game, in discourse about the other discouraging, desperate days, when Dixie Howell, the old catcher, used to warm him up with shinguards on because his legs were black and blue from fielding fast balls on the bounce. He told them about the times he'd considered quitting, because he doubted he ever should have been a baseball player and had already wasted too much of his life at it. It was the kind of story a man could write without asking Casey Stengel what he thought about the game, and men did.

"I stayed in my office until one o'clock," Stengel said sadly the next morning, "and nobody showed up."

There was very little that could have been said about Koufax' pitching that night. (Some Philistines, of course, knocked the game by innuendo, lamenting that it was too bad the opposition was "just the Mets.") Stengel would have had something to say, however, and it might have been constructive. He introduced a number of fresh ideas to baseball, ideas others may have thought of but nobody had tried. Casey tried them because he was a rare kind of man: one who did not, despite advanced age, subscribe to the tedious theory that a thing can be done only one way simply because it has always been done that one way (and that, in a capsule, is the kind of thinking that is done by almost all of the guiding minds of baseball). Because of his incantations and machinations, Stengel has taken his place in baseball's annals as, first, a character, and second, an innovator. He was both, but it seems unfortunate that the buffoon-and-platoon elements of his being have obscured the shriekingly obvious fact that he must have been a fairly capable manager. In a dozen years with the Yankees, Stengel won ten pennants and eight World Series, something no manager will ever, ever do again unless the structure of baseball is radically altered, and how could anybody knock a record like that?

A lot of somebodies could. He was a tinkerer, some said, and the Yankees could have won more easily if he'd left them alone, instead of overmanaging. Why shouldn't he win, others asked, when he always had the best horses in a bad league? And who did Joe Louis ever beat, or Kelso? They beat everybody there was to beat, and so did Stengel. The American League was in truth not much for most of the years of Stengel's plateau, partly because it lagged far behind the National in racial integration, but for all of those years the Yankees figured to face the good pitching in every town they entered— or every town that had any good pitching. A .500 pitcher could make a big name and a little money for himself by beating the Yankees a couple of times a year. It is incalculable how much money the Yankees made for "Yankee-killers" like Frank Lary and Don Mossi.*

---

* As feeble as the Yanks were in 1965–66, the myth was still operative. Fred Whitfield of the Indians is a quite handy ballplayer to have around, but he just about became a household word in Cleveland by doing a disproportionate share of his hitting against the Yankees.

113

The Decline and Fall of the New York Yankees

You never make a better target than when you're on top, and Stengel for all the kindnesses of "my writers" heard the potshots all the way. Howard Cosell, the radio-TV pundit, seemed to make a project of deprecating Casey—not while he was managing the Yankees to all those championships, but later, when he was being amazed by the Mets. Cosell's motivation was transparent. If you want to be a big guy, the most direct way is to whip the biggest kid on the block. Stengel, by volume of newsprint or any other measurement, was the biggest name in American sports, ever. Besides, saddled with a helpless team, Stengel was defenseless against criticisms of his managing acumen. The Mets were so bad that nobody could prove they were being managed ineptly; they were so bad that nobody could prove they weren't, either. It was a perfect setup. If anyone in Stengel's defense pointed to his record with the Yankees, Cosell could say he was younger then. Didn't the Yankees dump him because he was too old? Cosell's aggravated assault on his reputation was, from a point of view, the highest compliment Casey was ever paid. Or it would have been, if Cosell hadn't carried it to an absurd extreme.

In the press room of Yankee Stadium, during the 1964 World Series, Cosell was pushing his Stengel-must-go program on Leonard Koppett of the New York *Times*. Koppett, who is analytical about things, had a question to ask. "Howard," he said, "how many more games do you think the Mets would have won this year if they'd had a good manager instead of Casey?"

Cosell fired from the hip. "Forty," he said.

A slow-thinking reporter of the bread-and-butter class masticated his free food and ruminated on the proposition for a few minutes. "The Mets won 53 games this year," he said finally. "And you say they'd have won 40 more for another manager. Fifty-three and 40 is 93. You are about to go out and watch a World Series involving the St. Louis Cardinals, who won 93 games this year. Are you suggesting there is a manager somewhere who would have won the pennant with the *Mets?*" Cosell thought about it awhile and ultimately decided that "anybody" could have managed the Mets to 20 more victories than Stengel had.

Without "the men who can execute," Stengel wasn't too much help to the Mets—no more than any other human could have been. Despite a persistent emphasis on ultra-fundamental points of play and frequent urgings to even established players to adjust their styles to "my way," Casey was not an effective teacher. For one thing, there was the communication problem. To some extent Stengel's arcane delivery was part of the act, as much as the little dance step when he demonstrated how Yogi Berra "gave it the howja-do" in his adventures under fly balls as a neo-outfielder. The quaint obscurantism amused people, and in one of his finest hours Stengel delighted a Senate investigating committee with a fractured-syntax filibuster of circumlocution that was like nothing they'd ever entered in *The Congressional Record*. He could speak in painfully direct English when he was indignant or otherwise chagrined, and more concerned with the substance than the form of his remarks. But the regulation spiel was often lost on young players. He did not bore them to death, as many of baseball's elders do in their attempts to impart their wisdom. (One could almost hear the mental valves snapping shut as the late Rogers Hornsby exhorted them to hit the way nobody but the great Rogers Hornsby could ever hit.) The young men simply didn't have any clear idea

115

what Stengel was talking about. In time they came to understand, but if they stayed around that long they were Yankees, and could execute beyond tutoring.

Very few Yankees hated or even strongly disliked Stengel, but a majority of them were happy when Ralph Houk succeeded him after the 1960 season. Some of the reasons were personal: a vague idea of "not feeling close" to Casey, or the memory of some stinging critique he had visited upon them in the past. Gene Woodling, a mature and basically placid man, is far from manic about it, but he has not forgotten the knock Stengel put on him for a fielding play he made, or didn't make, in the Yankees' sweep of the Phillies in 1950—a World Series in which Woodling batted .429. A few of the reasons for Houk's popularity, however, were tactical; Stengel was about as close to senility at the end of three score and ten as Winston Churchill was, but he was not up to the minute in every respect. Under Houk, Tony Kubek and Bobby Richardson said, they learned to apply refinements of modern "defensing" that they had never known before.

Stengel was not omniscient and his teaching powers were limited. But, given players who could execute, he could win. His first pennant in 1949, his first year as Yankee manager, was as remarkable as any of his accomplishments. The Yankees had gone through a demoralizing season in 1948. Opening as World Champions (victors over the Dodgers in a seven-game series that was as wild as any, except perhaps the 1960 tug-of-war with the Pirates), the team spun its wheels. Relief pitcher Joe Page, the toast of 1947, was ineffective. Joe DiMaggio showed signs of wearing out, and Mickey Mantle was in high school in Commerce, Oklahoma; for the first time since Ruth's home run off Herb Pennock on May Day, 1920, the Yankees stood in jeopardy of facing life without a Big Guy, the superstar who could rally them by the sheer example of his excellence. Joe Gordon was gone, helping Cleveland to the pennant with his most productive season, and Charley Keller had had it. Whether it was the players or the management who first lost faith in Bucky Harris as manager, he had to go at the end of the season. The Yankees had finished third, two games behind Boston and Cleveland, who tied.* The Yankees had come close, but that wasn't good enough, and general manager George Weiss surveyed the field of managing talent. He finally came up with . . .

. . . *who?* That clown? Casey Stengel, who had managed Brooklyn for three years and the Boston Braves (sometimes Bees) for six years and never got either of them out of the second division? Stengel had his claims to fame, of course. He had thumbed his nose at the Yankee dugout after hitting a home run for the Giants in the 1923 World Series. He had once raised his cap and a sparrow flew out. In 1943 he had his leg broken when he was struck by a Boston taxicab, and Dave Egan, the late sports columnist, had suggested the driver be made Boston's Man of the Year. So he had won the Pacific Coast League pennant with Oakland in 1948: That made him a Yankee manager? What ever happened to the standards of decorum and dignity? Weiss had to be kidding.

Weiss wasn't kidding. Hiring Stengel was probably the most imaginative move he ever made, but Weiss didn't pull it out of a hat. He knew something about Casey Stengel. Back in

* In the silly one-game playoff—would you believe Red Sox manager Joe McCarthy started Denny Galehouse?—young Lou Boudreau demonstrated his acumen as a manager by hitting two home runs and a double as the Indians won, 8–3.

1925, young (31) George Weiss was running the New Haven franchise in the Eastern League, having euchred the owners out of the property for $5,000. On May 22 the Braves, motivated as much by civic uplift as by self-interest, bought the Worcester, Massachusetts, team, which was in eighth place. They needed a manager, so they offered the job to Casey Stengel, a 35-year-old Boston outfielder with an average of .077 whom they were about to dismiss anyway. They asked him to take over Worcester as playing manager, and as an added inducement told him he could double as president. Stengel took the job. One of the brighter things he did was to hit .320 for the rest of the season, but in any case Worcester finished third and Weiss had a chance to observe Stengel's work. George Weiss doesn't forget.

Stengel, with almost nobody taking him seriously, took charge of the 1949 Yankees. Some good things happened. Berra, the improbable young catcher, proved he was for real, and Page came back to have a good year, his last one. A rookie outfielder named Hank Bauer made himself quite useful. Ed Lopat, taken from the Chicago White Sox a year earlier for non-Yankee-type catcher Aaron Robinson, teamed with Allie Reynolds (with Page finishing his games) and Vic Raschi to give the Yankees a pitching nucleus that matched anybody's. A good-looking young second baseman named Jerry Coleman materialized, and Yankee dollars ransomed Johnny Mize, an old first baseman who could still execute with his bat, from the Giants. But some bad things happened, too. The Yankees suffered a succession of injuries, making it necessary for Stengel to improvise all the way.

True, the Yankees had many legitimate injuries. But the Yankee publicist at the time was Red Patterson, now master of all he purveys about the Dodgers. Red was a baseball writer for the late, lamented New York *Herald Tribune* in the 1930s and he was probably born about a decade too late, because he has never been lacking in imagination. Some dispute the claim, but it was probably he who originated the term "tape-measure home run" in his last years with the Yankees, which were Mickey Mantle's first years. His measurement of that alleged 565-foot home run Mantle hit off Chuck Stobbs in Washington might not survive the exacting inquisition of geodetic scientists, but it was a hell of an idea. So was the Casualty List of 1949. Red in midseason issued a daily communiqué that enumerated the misfortunes that had befallen the Yankees. Before season's end he had run the list of injuries past 70, which, as he would say, "may be a record." But to get it there Patterson had to broaden his definition of an injury to a degree unprecedented in war or peace. He swears that not a single shaving cut made the list, but one suspects a hangnail or two might have been included.

Not only were there few dry eyes in the gin mills where Yankee followers gathered (some of them even became fans, but they soon got over it), but the impact of Patterson's pathos was felt in very high places. Ernest Hemingway, whose *Across the River and into the Trees* had been greeted with about as much enthusiasm as Bucky Harris' managing the year before, was at work, broodingly, on *The Old Man and the Sea*. He polished and honed the little novel, striving toward perfection, eliminating all that was superfluous. One of the elements Hemingway presumably considered pertinent, because it went unhoned, was the self-edifying thought of the wretched old fisherman as the taut line slowly sawed the flesh from his wrist. If the Great DiMaggio could play, enduring the pain of the bone spur on his heel, certainly he, the fisherman, could stand a little excoriation. The faith sustained him.* However grave a public issue the Yankees' misfortunes of 1949 amounted to, the clown manager plotted, improvised and prevailed. The Yankees had to go all the way to the wire with the well-endowed Red Sox, and they met them head-on and beat them on the last day to win Stengel's first pennant. The Yankees disposed of the Dodgers in five games in the World Series, and some people began to take Stengel seriously.

The Casualty List was actually a blessing in disguise. That's a cliché, but so is "Necessity is the mother of invention." Stengel might have evolved his platoon system anyway, but in 1949, with somebody in sick bay almost every day, he had to. If you had to play Joe Collins, a first baseman, in right field in order to get another left-handed hitter in the lineup—well, how did you know he couldn't play until you played him? Collins could. Not every day, but who played every day? You could even get away with playing a spectacularly slow-footed man like Elston Howard in left field—that Yankee Stadium

---

* A minority interpretation was that Hemingway was being ironical, equating faith in a god with faith in a demigod, thereby pointing up the misdirected idolatry of our times. If we do not revere or admire Joe Willie Namath, most of us at least envy him for being the athletic object of adulation, wealthy, a Lothario and a to-hell-with-it-all citizen— all the things most of us would like to be, while teaching our children that none of them is of true value. It seemed that Hemingway, who had conveyed some memorable ideas on the true values in life, might have been ridiculing the overweening interest we lavish on people who are paid very important money to play very unimportant games. But few readers have agreed, so maybe it was misinterpreting Hemingway to ascribe to him a sense of the ridiculous. Maybe he felt the same kind of empathy for the Great DiMaggio as his Old Man—the same kind he felt for the brave bulls.

120

left field that has been the humiliation of so many men who really were left fielders. But in a World Series, in October, when the early shadows turn it into a clown's den? Stengel played Howard in left field against Milwaukee in 1958, when he was 29 years old and even slower. So he saved a game with a diving catch of a sinking line drive. And the Yankees, down three games to one, went on to win another World Championship.

It began of necessity in 1949, but it was policy thereafter. Almost every Yankee, except Mantle when he was healthy, would have to read the lineup card each day to find out whether he was playing. The system endeared Stengel to nobody but marginal Yankees, who knew they would be unlikely to get into a starting lineup at all if they played for another manager. It infuriated others. Hank Bauer still can become livid when he remembers being replaced frequently by men who, in his opinion, couldn't carry his bat. One game, early in a season early in Stengel's plateau, stands out in memory. Bauer was off to a fast start, with a dozen or so home runs before the end of May, so he started a game against Cleveland in Yankee Stadium, despite the fact that the Indians' starter was Early Wynn, a tough right-hander at the peak of his powers. In the third inning, with the game scoreless, the Yankees got two runners on base and the hitter was Bauer. But it wasn't. A funny thing happened to him on the way up to the plate. Stengel called him back and sent up Joe Collins, who hadn't hit a home run since opening day. So Joe Collins hit a three-run homer off Early Wynn and the Yankees won, 3–0.

Things like that happened, and kept happening, annoying Casey's players, exasperating the opposition, satisfying "my

121

owners" and delighting "my writers." He had the men who could execute and he was lucky. Stengel, like Harry Truman, bridled under the belittling kind of criticism he received. But, like Harry Truman, he had a profound sense of history and an abiding sense of security that his place in that history was being established.

The Yankees trailed the Pittsburgh Pirates, three games to two, in the 1960 World Series, and Stengel was sending Mr. Ford out to pitch the sixth game in Forbes Field. One of "my writers" had a certain sense of history, too, and asked Casey if he would save him his lineup card as a souvenir. Stengel was 70 years old and there had been speculation that he would retire at the end of the season. Therefore, if the Pirates won today and Stengel did retire, that lineup card would be the last he ever filled out—a collector's item. Mr. Ford did not give the Pirates any runs that day and the Series had to go to a seventh game.

As the crowd flowed onto the field and the Yankees battled their way from the third-base dugout toward first base (both dressing rooms are behind first base in ancient Forbes Field), Stengel was observed, hobbling along with the little gimp the Boston cab driver had left him with. Suddenly he did a rear march and struggled back through the crowd, fending off autograph hunters and enduring the jeers of Pittsburgh fans with "Beat 'em, Bucs" hats on. At length Casey reached the Yankee dugout and ripped down the lineup card, adhesive-taped to the concrete wall. Then he resumed his march toward the dressing room, through the milling mob. The writer, watching from the auxiliary press box in the upper deck, had a warm feeling. That's nice, he thought. He remembered what I asked him, and he went to all that trouble to go back and get me that lineup card. That's class.

When the crowd of newspapermen, cameras and tape recorders thinned a little in the Yankee clubhouse, an hour or so later, Stengel saw the historically minded writer. He grinned, reached back in his locker and came up with the lineup card. "I almost forgot," he said. The card he handed the writer was the first carbon copy. The original was visible in Casey's left hip pocket.

Casey Stengel knew a collector's item when he saw one, too. He wasn't Ned in the Third Reader.

6

Superball

We'd put up even money now,
   With Casey at the bat.

Not Casey Stengel. Casey, the fictional long-ball hitter of the short-ball days. The ultimate weapon, the guy who could make everything all right with one swing. Ernest L. Thayer, in his primeval baseball poem, made a classic by DeWolf Hopper's reiteration, manifested no acute knowledge of the game, even as it was played in those days. But many an unskilled literary work has justified its existence by the inclusion of an element of universality, a valid statement of conditions that would apply in any time. Thayer's limping epic, which John Milton would have said used rhyme as "a device to set off wretched matter and lame meter," had a universality.

The Mudville nine, one gathers, was a pretty bad ball club. It had all the problems the Yankees now have, less one. The personnel, as Thayer describes that ninth inning, seemed to consist of a singular collection of road apples. But they had a

124

Big Guy, the kind the Yankees always used to have, a Ruth, Gehrig, DiMaggio, Mantle, who could make everything all right with one swing, or one "big" play, that could rally the supporting cast, by inspiration, to emulation and excessive effort.

The Mudville nine's problem that day, as they went to the bottom of the ninth inning trailing New York, 4–2, was starkly simple. They had to stay alive. Two of the first four men had to get on base, somehow, to assure that mighty Casey would have one more swing at that arrogant New York pitcher. Had there been no Casey, presumably, the Mudville hitters would have skulked to the plate, assumed a tail-in-the-dugout posture and gone away quietly. No noise from the gathering of 5,000 would have rattled in the dell or recoiled upon the flat, because they had no faith at all in Flynn and Blake and they should have had none in Cooney and Barrows, and I'll tell you why. But there was a Casey, which was a special reason to get on base, and they all did.

When Cooney died at second,
  And Barrows did the same,
A sickly silence fell upon
  The patrons of the game.

The patrons of the game should have asked for their money back. Cooney and Barrows, in their zeal to get Casey "one more whack at that," had died at *second,* one after the other. One must believe this was poetic license; "died at first" would have rendered Thayer's meter even more lame.* One *must*

* Poetry was sacrificed to plausibility in later published forms. In *The Fireside Book of Baseball,* Cooney and Barrows died at first. However,

believe this, because the several other possibilities are too dreadful to contemplate. Did Cooney double and then get himself picked off second, like Joe Gordon in the last inning of the 1942 World Series? Or did he walk and go out stealing? Did Barrows "do the same," whatever it was, or did he single and get thrown out stretching? Are we asked to believe that two hitters, back-to-back, tried for the extra base with their team two runs down in the ninth? Unlikely, because such heads-down play would have brought a more animated response than silence, however sickly. This was a crowd which, minutes later, would be yelling "Kill him! Kill the umpire!" because he called a strike on Casey, who himself didn't beef about the call. It is not unlikely that such a gathering would have entertained the idea of lynching Cooney and Barrows, or at least tarring and feathering them, in the fashion of the day. In any case, there were two out and Mudville was in bad trouble:

> But Flynn preceded Casey,
>   As did also Jimmy Blake,
> And the former was a puddin'
>   And the latter was a fake.

The functional definition of a puddin' is lost in antiquity, but it does not seem to have a positive connotation. Flynn must have been an out man. Fakes we have yet with us, so we understand that Blake was masquerading as a ballplayer. Pause here to give Mudville's anonymous manager a vote

---

this rewrite of history is not bolstered in credibility by the fact that the epithet for the next batter, Flynn, is changed from "puddin'" to "lulu."

of confidence—the classic antecedent to stripping off his buttons. Howard Cosell would have to admit that even Casey Stengel could make up a lineup more intelligently than that. Either a puddin' and a fake were batting second and third in the order, in front of the RBI man, or Casey, the Big Guy, was batting somewhere besides fourth. Either folly would be a plank-walking offense for the manager, who had painted himself into a coffin corner. This would be like batting Horace Clarke and Ray Barker, both dressed up as Yankees in this expansion-age masquerade, in front of Mickey Mantle. (And the fact that such a prospect isn't too shocking any more is a tipoff on what the Yankees have suddenly become.)

But the humpties, exceeding themselves in their zeal to give the Big Guy his cuts, took the manager off the hook.

Flynn let drive a single
  To the wonderment of all,
And the much-despised Blakey
  Tore the cover off the ball.

One sees Blake, the fake, lining a " 'tweener" up the alley in right center and Flynn cruising into third, where the coach has stationed himself a quarter of the way toward home plate, arms raised in the classic cease-and-desist sign, ready to tackle the puddin' if he had any bright ideas about trying to score: We're two runs down, and the Big Guy is coming up. But evidently that wasn't exactly what happened.

And when the dust had lifted
  And men saw what had occurred,
There was Blakey, safe at second,
  And Flynn a-huggin' third.

127

"When the dust had lifted" indeed. Beautiful. You score it a single and a throw. Flynn, that idiot, ran with his head down and it must have taken a Pepper Martin belly slide to make third, if he was a-huggin' it. Then Blake had a belated flash of brilliance and went for second on the play, and the throw almost got him, too. Couldn't anyone there play that game?

Nobody could manage very well, either. Presumably the manager of the New York nine was more sophisticated than the resident genius of Mudville (and what kind of league was that?). But, with the tying runs in scoring position and mighty Casey advancing to the plate, he didn't even go out to talk to his pitcher. Granted there was no television in those days, so managers weren't "on," but he had some things to say to his pitcher. He had to tell him he was out of his mind if he got anything over the plate to that big ape, with first base open. So he threw him two quick strikes, showing the kind of indiscreet valor that would have sprung Bill Rigney off the bench like a jack-in-the-box. And if there was nobody coming up behind Casey except another puddin', or fake, what was wrong with putting him on, anyway? You don't put the winning run on base, but sometimes you do. Bucky Harris did in the 1947 World Series, and that may have been the beginning of the end of him as Yankee manager. Right-hander Bill Bevens was pitching a no-hitter in Ebbets Field and winning it, 2–1, with two out in the ninth, but the Dodgers had a runner at second. Leo Durocher sent left-hand hitter Pete Reiser up to pinch-hit. He couldn't run, but anybody who had ever seen Pete Reiser play baseball found it hard to believe that he couldn't get out of bed on Christmas morning and hit, no matter how many outfield walls he had run into. Harris had Bevens give Reiser four wide ones and he limped to first.

BABE RUT

EARLE COMBS

BOB MEUSEL

JOE DUGAN

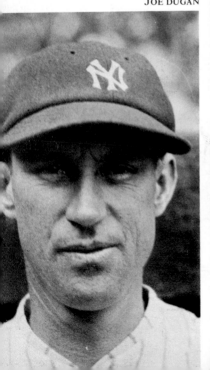

HERB PENNOCK

WAITE HOYT

MARK KOENIG

LOU GEHRIG

WALLY PIPP

TONY LAZZERI

RED ROLFE

RUFFING
CHANDLER

BILL DICKEY
LEFTY GOMEZ

JOE DI MAGGIO

TOMMY HENRICH

CHAI
KEL

FRANK CROSETTI

ALLIE REYNOLDS

WHITEY FORD

ED LOPAT

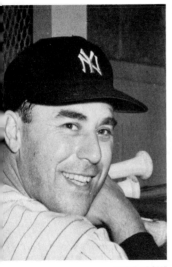

VIC RASCHI

YOGI BERRA

CASEY STENGEL

MICKEY MANTLE

NK BAUER

BOBBY RICHARDSON

STON HOWARD

BILL SKOWRON

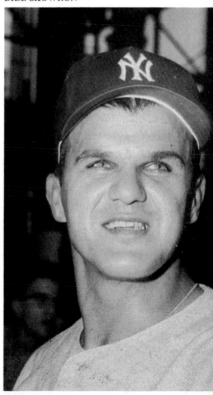

PHIL RIZZUTO

KUBEK

ROGER MARIS

(Trivia quizzers: Eddie Miksis ran for him.) So Harry Lavagetto hit the right-field wall for a double and the Yankees were beaten, 3–2.

The New York manager at Mudville lived dangerously, too. He assumed his man could execute, and he pitched to Casey, who disdainfully took two strikes and dug himself the deepest hole a hitter can find himself in. With an 0–2 count, there were a number of things the New York pitcher could have done with that pitch to Casey. Whitey Ford might have bounced a curve on the plate. Lew Burdette might have loaded one. Marv Grissom might have decked him. Anything, except another strike.* But the New York pitcher came in with it and Casey didn't cream that 0–2 pitch. He struck out, swinging, and the populace of Mudville was plunged into municipal depression. The Big Guy had failed them, and it was difficult to understand how he could have. It should have been so easy for him to hit one over the clock or the standpipe or whatever they had in centerfield in Mudville. You don't expect much

---

* But sometimes, as Dodger manager Walter Alston says, the unortho- dox is the percentage play. Sometimes you throw the strike because the hitter is "set up" to assume you won't. Willard Hershberger, a superflu- ous Yankee product who caught for the pennant-bound Cincinnati Reds in 1940 when Ernie Lombardi didn't, decided to try the unortho- dox one night in the Polo Grounds. Bucky Walters had an 0–2 count on Harry Danning with two outs in the ninth, a 4–3 lead and Mel Ott on first. Hershberger called for the fast ball, a strike at the knees, and Walters executed. So did Danning. He lined the ball over the score- board in left field. A short time later Hershberger, a moody little man, cut his throat and died in a Boston hotel room. A man would have to have a better reason for cutting his throat than the fact that he called for a fast ball over the plate and somebody creamed it. But some of those who knew Willard Hershberger have said that decision and re- sultant recriminations were a factor.

from the Cooneys and Blakes, but for Casey it should have been a piece of cake.

There was ease in Casey's manner
  As he stepped into his place.
There was pride in Casey's bearing,
  And a smile on Casey's face.

The Big Guy need not be an outfielder or a first baseman. He can be the infantry lieutenant who makes it sound reasonable, almost desirable, when he notifies his men that they are going on night patrol, because they know he is not afraid to go, and will know what to do when he gets there. He can be the editor who unscrambles the mess made by the puddin's and fakes and manages to get the paper out in some respectable form, inside the deadline. The Big Guy is a leader in a way, but not the hortative way. He doesn't tell you to win one for the Gipper; he *is* the Gipper, stronger and more capable than his fellows and willing to do more simply because he can do more. There are Big Guys in all areas of human enterprise because most people are little guys. The Big Guy is a superior being, in some way, maybe only physically; he didn't plan it that way, but he can't help it. There were Big Guys among the galley slaves, saving their wretched companions a few lashes by pulling a little harder on their oar, because they were able to.

People can tell right away who the Big Guy is, and they come to depend on him. His example can move them—shame them, perhaps—to greater effort and greater achievement, but it is his mere presence that is reassuring, comforting. If you never worked with a Big Guy, you don't know any better and you don't miss him when he's gone.

130

The trouble with the Yankees is that they always had a Big Guy, and now they have none.

From the middle of the summer of 1920, when Babe Ruth made it evident that he had only been warming up when he hit his record 29 home runs in Boston the year before, until the middle of the summer of 1965, when it became obvious that Mickey Mantle's tortured body was finally wearing out, the Yankees had been led by a super star. Not a mere first-magnitude star of Hall of Fame caliber like Bill Dickey, Phil Rizzuto or Yogi Berra, but men who performed feats that had never been performed in baseball before and probably never would be performed again. Lou Gehrig broke into the lineup in 1925, the year of Ruth's indisposition, and Gehrig was the American League's Most Valuable Player in 1936, the year DiMaggio arrived and attained instant stardom. In 1951, when DiMaggio was finished, Mantle showed up. In 1965, when Mantle was finished, nobody showed up. Not even a plain, ordinary first-magnitude star.

It was difficult to believe, early in the 1965 season, that the Yankees could be in as bad shape as they appeared to be. Elston Howard had put his arm out of commission by trying to play in one of those foolish, frost-bitten season openers in Minneapolis, with dirty snow piled up around the parking lot, and Mantle could hardly move. But the Yankees had always had injuries, and if things were that bad it was time to reach down into what was left of George Weiss's farm system and bring up a couple of replacements. The fact that they didn't, it was suggested to farm director Johnny Johnson, indicated that maybe the plum crop had finally dried up.

"The next Yankee star," Johnson said, "is Roger Repoz. There's no question about that." Then it was easy to believe that the Yankee Era was over. Consider Repoz' credentials.

The Decline and Fall of the New York Yankees

He was a big, strong left-handed outfielder who was almost 25 years old, and that was the first clue. Time was when a strong young man was considered precocious if he made the big league before his 25th birthday, but time was no more. The time had come, as Johnson had admitted, when they said the hell with it if they hadn't made it at 23. Repoz had hit 23 home runs—and .234—for Columbus, Georgia, in an allegedly Class A league in 1964, and the Yankees promoted him to Toledo, in the International League. As Johnson spoke, in early June, Repoz had spurted to the .300 mark. Joe Di-Maggio, in his last season in the Pacific Coast League, had a .398 average. Mickey Mantle, in his last full minor-league season at Joplin, Missouri, hit .383. Sent back to Kansas City for a quick Triple-A seasoning during his rookie year, Mantle hit .361. Other matriculating figures: Aaron .362 (and led the league in almost everything) at Jacksonville; Ted Williams, .366 and 43 home runs at Minneapolis; Mays .477, also at Minneapolis. Batting averages don't run that high any more in any league in this swing-from-your-tail age of the incomplete ballplayer, but almost no superstar had ever burst on the horizon without some kind of warning, and there was no glow in the sky over Toledo.

Repoz made the big league before his 25th birthday, in August. Not because he was ready, but because baseball men feel the obligation to "do something" for All Those Wonderful Fans when the club is going badly. It doesn't matter so much *what* you do, but it would look bad not to do anything. That is why so many nothing-for-nothing trades are made at the winter meetings.* Repoz hit 12 home runs in the 79 games

* Sometimes the blind pig finds an acorn. The do-something psychology won the Dodgers a pennant and general manager E. J. (Buzzie) Bavasi

he played for the Yankees in the remainder of the 1965 season. He also struck out frequently and wound up with a .220
average, and whatever latent stardom he had in him was
suppressed forever. Application of pressure can bring out the
best in some men, but only if it's there. Early in 1966 Repoz
was tossed into one of those do-something trades with Kansas
City. (The fact that Athletics owner Charles O. Finley, a
self-appointed Yankee nemesis, was willing to resume operation of the N.Y.–K.C. shuttle was another clue to the station
to which the Yankees had fallen. Finley was pledged not to
help the Yankees, as his predecessors in Kansas City ownership had so consistently, servilely done. But Finley, with less
baseball acumen than the late Branch Rickey, could see the
way it was with the Yankees. Along Mosholu Parkway in the
Bronx, up the road from Yankee Stadium, they would say
gornisch helfen.)

The 1966 winter meetings threatened to produce action,

---

the serendipity award at the 1965 meetings. Buzzie and Jimmy Campbell, general manager of the Tigers, were sitting around together as the
meetings droned into the final evening. Neither of them had done anything to speak of and they thought maybe they ought to. All he could
think of, Campbell said, was that he could use some kind of utility infielder. Bavasi said he had just the man: Dick Tracewski was quite
expendable. Fine, Jimmy said, but what would Buzzie take for him?
It was getting late. Oh, a pitcher, Buzzie supposed. Some kind of
pitcher. Just let me know. Campbell had just the man. He sent the
Dodgers Phil Regan, a very nice guy who had accumulated a 5.02
earned-run average. Considering that Tracewski had batted .215, the
deal seemed about even. Shuttling back and forth to Syracuse, however, Regan had learned some things. He had learned, among other
things, that a bit of moisture applied to the ball can have interesting
effects. As a relief pitcher with the Dodgers in 1966 his ERA shrank to
1.62. He won 15 games and "saved" 17 others and the Dodgers tiptoed
home free.

133

not only because the Dodgers, without Sandy Koufax, were in almost as deep trouble as the Yankees, but because the environs of Columbus and Pittsburgh are rather less distracting than previous sites where business was done, and not done, like Miami Beach and Fort Lauderdale. But the proceedings were perfunctory. The World Champion Orioles did something. They rewarded the loyalty of All Those Wonderful Fans by jacking up ticket prices. The Yankees did something too. Given second choice in the unrestricted draft of minor-leaguers, they reached deep into the Baltimore farm system and grabbed two teen-age prospects at $8,000 apiece. Then they made their big move.

They wheedled Bill Robinson, a 23-year-old outfielder, away from the Atlanta Braves and pronounced him the rightfielder, just like that. This appointment to stardom, perhaps the most premature lionization in American sport since the journalists elected Bill Bradley governor of Missouri while he was still working on his senior thesis at Princeton, accomplished three things. First, it let the over-the-hill Roger Maris know where he stood in case the Yankees couldn't unload him and, at salary time, he came in expecting to be supported in the manner to which he had become accustomed. Second, it told All Those Wonderful Fans, in effect, that indeed there was another Big Guy waiting in the wings. And third, theoretically, it gave the kid the kind of confidence he was going to need when he felt the load of responsibility they planned to shove on his inexperienced shoulders.

The second objective of the Yankee announcement was fraudulent in spirit. Playing at Richmond in the International League in 1966, Robinson batted .312, with 30 doubles and 20 home runs that established basic power. But he is a right-handed hitter, and nobody among the Yankees' accredited superstars, except the nonpareil DiMaggio, managed to be a Big Guy without batting left-handed at least part—much more than half—of the time. "Tell him to shoot for the foul lines," counseled Orioles manager Hank Bauer, a right-handed hitter with basic power who once, in 11 years as a Yankee, was able to hit as many as 26 home runs. "If he doesn't, he'll die in Death Valley." The reference was to the geography of left field in Yankee Stadium. Except for grotesque Fenway Park in Boston, Yankee Stadium is the only remaining playing area in the major leagues that is hermaphroditic, like a sailing ship with square- and schooner-rigging. Players talk about it like the blind men discussing the elephant: To left-handed hitters it is "the short porch," to right-handers "an airport." Partly because of the exigencies of New York City real estate, even in 1922, and partly, perhaps, out of embarrassment at making the right-field seats a chip shot, according to prescription, the architects of The House That Ruth Built made the left-field distances formidable and the center-field range impossible (for everybody but, one time, Mickey Mantle).

In the little handbook of statistics the Yankees issue to the press each spring, an item is the list of names of hitters who have hit home runs into the left-field bleachers, to the right of the bullpen. For all of the liveliness of the ball these 44 years, and the "whippiness" of the wispy bats that have come into vogue since World War II, it remains a very brief list. Joe DiMaggio, in a class by himself, is the only great right-handed pull hitter the Yankees ever had. Other than him, only Joe Gordon and his predecessor, Tony Lazzeri, could even be described as successful in shooting at the "airport" sector of the seats. The other successful right-handed hitters, like Howard and Skowron, made it because their power was distributed in all directions, principally right-center. Robinson, if he can hit that way, can become a first-magnitude star. That won't make him a superstar, and All Those Wonderful Fans will be disappointed.

The third stratagem, to give the new kid "confidence" by suggesting that he is something he isn't, is cynical. It is a two-edged sword and it usually cuts the other way. Informing a rookie that he has a chance to win a starting job is a fine, open-minded thing to do, something like Johnny Keane wanted to do with Bobby Murcer in 1966, before he was vetoed. But telling him he's first-string and leaving him to prove he isn't is something quite different.*

One very serious problem, when a rookie is pronounced a regular, almost sight-unseen, is that teammates who have been in the big league for a few years, trying to establish them-

* The St. Louis Cardinals last spring pronounced 26-year-old George Kernek their first baseman. He had good minor-league credentials and he had performed well in a big-league trial late in 1965. Besides, smiling Bob Howsam, the new-broom general manager, had traded away Ken Boyer, Dick Groat and Bill White, three quarters of the infield that won the 1964 pennant and World Series. They were getting old, it was explained. They were. They were also commanding the three highest salaries the Cardinals were paying, and one of the principal functions of a general manager is to keep a hold on the old overhead, even if the money he saves comes out of the nearly limitless coffers of beer baron Gussie Busch. Within a short time Kernek was dragging his .240 batting average back to the bushes. He may be back, and he may not. The Giants gave the big buildup in 1947 to Clint Hartung, and again to Andre Rodgers a decade later, both times obfuscating the fact that there was nothing else about the ball club really worth talking about. Hartung was the Ozark Ike phenomenon who couldn't be for real, and wasn't. Andy Rodgers, it seemed, might have become more than a journeyman ballplayer, but he wasn't nearly ready and the pressure ruined him.

selves, take notice, and they keep noticing. Their scrutiny is a greater pressure than anything the newcomer might hear from the stands. "Pheenom" is a dirty word. Except for giving a watch to the most promising rookie of the spring-training season, the Yankees have never put on any pheenom promotions. It was undignified, and they never had to. Now, presumably, they feel they have to—even if it is undignified.

To get Robinson, the Yankees sent Clete Boyer, their acrobatic-fielding, nonhitting third baseman, to Atlanta. The Braves tossed in Chi Chi Olivo, a charming, elderly, undistinguished relief pitcher, and the Yankees agreed to send a warm body to the Braves' Richmond farm when they had sorted out their nonentities. So it was Boyer for Robinson, even up. Boyer, except for 1962, when his average soared to .262 and he batted in 68 runs, was always a luxury to the Yankees. The spectacular plays he made at third were box-office, and as long as the rest of the men were executing they could afford having his bat in the lineup. Besides, there was comfort in the belief that Boyer could move over to shortstop any time the Yankees wanted him to, and do a superior job. (Stengel wanted him to in 1960, "but my owners say I got to play the other man.") By the time they wanted him to, in 1966, Boyer couldn't, or not well enough to justify his "out man" status at the plate. Boyer had to go, and who would have thought the Yankees would receive a pheenom in exchange?

New York reporters, as ill-conditioned as anyone for the prospect of starless Yankees, quoted baseball men's opinions that Robinson was destined for stardom. Paul Richards, doing his wheeling and dealing for Atlanta, spoke of Robinson's strong throwing arm. He also explained the Braves' reasoning in letting the young man go. "He couldn't crack our outfield for two or three years," Richards said. That meant Robinson couldn't replace Rico Carty, who is capable of hitting .330 but almost incapable of playing the outfield, or Mack Jones, a useful ballplayer but no one who has been rattling the doors of the Hall of Fame. The key commentary, however, came from Harry Dalton, general manager of the Orioles. He called Robinson "the kind you pay your way in to see."

Now that the erstwhile have-nots had broken up the Yankees, they were beginning to wonder whether it was a bright idea. The Yankees had long justified their eminence and arrogance with the argument that their august presence enriched the entire league. No matter how bad a team you have, you draw a crowd when you play the Yankees. Where would you be without us? The statistical evidence was irrefutable. In 1965, when the Yankees were a second-division team all year, the number of people who paid to see the Yankees in the other nine cities was 19.8 percent of the number of people who paid to see baseball at all in those other nine cities. There were more dramatic illustrations of the Yankees' drawing power on the road. In 1959, the Red Sox won a game in Yankee Stadium on a Thursday, then beat the Yankees in Fenway Park on Friday, Saturday and Sunday. A Red Sox team had swept a five-game series in Yankee Stadium in 1939, but nothing like that had happened since. And, by some vicissitude of the schedule, there was another game to be played in Boston Monday afternoon. If Turner's Law was correct and it was un-American to be enthusiastic over Yankee failure in the era of Yankee success, there must have been a startling number of subversives among the crowd that showed up. A few minutes after the scheduled game time a reporter, having dawdled over his free food in the press room, hustled out to his working place to see what he had missed. The field was vacant except for the two pitchers, who were just beginning to warm up. There was a buzz of crowd noise, but the customers seemed to be milling around in the stands. A look out the window over Jersey Street resolved the mystery. Fans were standing on line, trying to get in, and the management had postponed game time 15 minutes to accommodate them. Oh, yes: the Yankees lost.

But they did draw on the road. Oh, how they did! In 1965, when the Angels were playing their home games in comparative privacy in Dodger Stadium, victims of one of the outstanding recent examples of civic indifference, the Yankees were 11.1 percent of their schedule and 26.6 percent of their attendance. Now, suddenly, the Yankees didn't pack them in any more, and that was disturbing, if not downright frightening. Harry Dalton knew, as well as anybody, that the fans who drove down from Wilmington in 1965 to see the Yankees and, with their fellow Yankee-loathers, constituted 20.2 percent of Baltimore's attendance for the season did not come to see Bobby Richardson and Joe Pepitone, no matter how well they were executing. Most of them came to see what was left of Mickey Mantle, the superstar. When Dalton pronounced Bill Robinson "the kind you pay your way in to see," he wasn't rationalizing. He was rooting. If they don't pay, everybody's in trouble.

In 1919, the last year without Babe Ruth, the Yankees had a nice kind of team and they finished third, higher than they had finished since 1906, when the American League was still an expansion kind of thing. And they drew 619,164 customers, the most in their history. In 1920, with Ruth hitting his fantastic 54 home runs, they drew 1,289,422, a little

139

better than double. The attendance did not dip below the million mark again until 1925, the year Ruth was marked absent for half the season with his mysterious ailment. The Yankees drew 697,267, dropping almost all the way back to where their prosperity began. The correlation between attendance and the superstar was established forever, and it was underlined in 1935, when attendance fell to 657,508. That was the year of *Brother, Can You Spare a Dime?* But that doesn't explain it. The Yankees had drawn almost 200,-000 more the year before, when people were still singing *Happy Days Are Here Again* not in the torchy way Barbra Streisand does it but in a hysterically optimistic way that convinced even a nine-year-old they thought happy days would never be here again. But a man who is hooked on whiskey will contrive to get a drink, no matter what the Dow-Jones Average tells him. And a man hooked on baseball will find his way into the ball park, no matter what he has to fear besides fear itself. The vicarious participation in a game he can't play, and his childish, slavish identification with men who can, is the escapist fantasy that is the essence of what we call a fan. What was different about 1935 was that it was the first year Babe Ruth wasn't there any more, and a considerable number of his idolaters felt that some kind of sun had set and that there would never be another like it.

We are a people who prefer to pay more attention to the symbols of our times than to their symptoms. A color television set may be a symptom of intellectual decadence, but it is a symbol of affluence, so what the hell. The literature and the music of the 1920s, and the wildly embellished tales grandfather tells, suggest that anybody who tipped the fact that he gave a damn was in jeopardy of inquisition by that bright young fellow J. Edgar Hoover as to his patriotism. There had been that Great War, but it made the world safe for democracy, and who needed a League of Nations? The Volstead Act was a mild annoyance, but anybody in the know could get booze if he wanted it (and apparently everybody wanted it). The market kept going up and up. As President Coolidge said, "The business of America is business." Twenty-three-skidoo, and oh, you kid. Hello, suckers! Is everybody happy? Hell, yes. Nations need Big Guys in good times, too. Maybe, in a way, they need them more. The Big Guy of the 1920s couldn't be military, because there was no such thing as war, and he couldn't be political because the country was running itself, wasn't it? The symbol of a nation kidding itself could not be serious. And there was this Babe Ruth.

There was ease in Casey's manner
  As he stepped into his place.
There was pride in Casey's bearing
  And a smile on Casey's face.

The smile was the thing. George Herman Ruth was a loser who had become a winner, fitting Horatio Alger's stereotype of the really American values. First of all he was an orphan, and even Theodore Dreiser couldn't knock that for a beginning. Then (snicker), he wasn't any better than he ought to be. A big man with big appetites, he ate too much and drank too much. Training was for mere mortals, and Babe Ruth was something else. The symbol of the spirit of the 1920s had to be very important in a frivolous sort of way, and he had to be somebody who had fun. Babe Ruth was bigger than the game he played, important enough to revolutionize it. He didn't have to give a damn because he was naturally, splendidly talented and he enjoyed the hell out of it. Everybody he met was "Keed," unless he looked old enough to be "Doc." When finally he shook the Yankee management down for an unprecedented salary of $80,000, topping the President of the United States, a nation applauded. Babe Ruth was surely now the symbol not only of bigness and fun but of success.

We were an isolated, self-centered nation then, having learned precious little from the adventure of 1917–18, little influenced by other civilizations and interesting to them only as a kooky curiosity, a people who solemnly outlawed alcohol and then bathed frantically in expensive gin, who asked for your poor and your huddled masses and passed an immigration act to shut them out. We were a tight little continent, but we exported Babe Ruth, our national mascot. In the foxholes of Okinawa, a decade after the day he signed off with three home runs and laid down his bat, Japanese soldiers would be taunting Americans with what they had been taught from childhood was the supreme insult: "——Babe Ruth!"

Babe Ruth's figures seem almost as fabulous as the apocrypha that grew up around him, making him literally a legend in his own time.* His 714 home runs is a record far out of the reach of Willie Mays, the runner-up, even though Mays may end up playing 20 years without a crippling injury. Only eight men in history have hit more than 50 home runs in a season, with or without an asterisk, and Ruth did it four times. His lifetime

---

* Only a few skeptics doubt that Ruth pointed to the Wrigley Field bleachers before hitting that home run in the 1932 World Series. They point out that it was an acrimonious Series, played to the Yankee theme that the Cubs were cheap bastards for failing to give Mark Koenig, an ex-Yankee, his fair share of a previous Series pool. They theorize from this that Ruth was probably pointing to the pitcher's mound and saying, in effect, "—— Charlie Root."

batting average of .349 is the highest of all the Yankees, and it is topped only by Ty Cobb (.367) and Rogers Hornsby (.358). Despite his bandy-legged, top-heavy structure, Ruth was a good fielder and could run. Twice he led the Yankees in triples, and his 16 triples in 1921 were more than the fleet, graceful DiMaggio ever hit in a season. His achievements were as gargantuan as his appetites.

Babe Ruth was the biggest of the Big Guys, and nobody can ever get bigger, for the Yankees or anyone else, because history repeats itself only imprecisely. The exact circumstances that were made for him cannot exist again. The World Series records he owned—and at one time he owned most of the important ones—have gradually slipped away from Ruth, tied or broken by Yogi Berra or Mickey Mantle in the monotonous regularity of Yankee success. Maris, playing 161 games and swinging for a .269 average, knocked most of the magic out of the number 60, and 714 will probably go some day. Baseball will pump up the ball or bring in the fences or dilute the talent in the name of expansion until some big vegetable will amass a lifetime average of .203 and 819 home runs. The statistics will recede into the preterite, but the name may never fade out completely. Listen to eight-year-old kids playing ball in the street and it is unlikely you will hear the name of Ty Cobb or Joe DiMaggio or Rogers Hornsby. You will hear, occasionally, from the lips of a little boy who was born 10 years after Ruth died his agonized death, the name of the Babe. Men can become better baseball players than he was, and maybe a couple already have. But nobody can ever be as Big.

When horsemen sit around and swap lies, exaggerations and furtive recollections about the great steeds they have seen, somebody is sure to drop the name of Count Fleet, the Triple Crown winner of 1943. Nobody ever mentions the name of Blue Swords, who might have been a household word if he hadn't had the ill judgment to be foaled in the same year as Count Fleet. Walter Kelley, who trained Blue Swords, was once asked—he must have been asked more than once—when he first realized that Blue Swords, for all his excellence, would spend his career chasing Count Fleet. "The first time they ever hooked up," Kelley said.

It had to be that way with Babe Ruth and Lou Gehrig, the second of the Yankees' Big Guys, the supernumerary superstar. In 1925, the year Ruth was marked absent, the Yankees were trying to make do with ordinary, first-magnitude stars like Bob Meusel, Earle Combs and Wally Pipp. One day the veteran Pipp violated the corporate precept that it is dangerous to take a day off because it may show the management how unnecessary you are. He was replaced at first base by the rookie Gehrig, who took his job. That sort of thing will happen from time to time, but the veteran always assumes it will be all right because the kid will play himself off the team after a while. And Gehrig did. On May 9, 1939, in Detroit, when Pipp was 46 years old, Gehrig benched himself. He had played 2,130 consecutive games.*

Gehrig spent the first decade of his career in Ruth's shadow. Playing on the same team with the Babe was enough to obviate any possibility of being top banana, but hitting immediately behind him in the batting order was like following Judy Gar-

---

* The "Iron Man" label was tainted once, when Gehrig was indisposed and couldn't have played but they let him bat leadoff in the first inning, to keep the record intact, then put in the shortstop for whom Gehrig was, in effect, pinch-hitting.

land in a vaudeville show. All the magnificence of the stolid No. 4, displayed while the applause for the charismatic No. 3 was still echoing in the Stadium rafters, did about as much to distinguish Gehrig as Wendell Willkie's "me too" campaign against Roosevelt in 1940.*

A case can be made that Gehrig, and not Ruth, was the prototypical Yankee, clubbing the opposition into submission with an inexorable consistency and performing the task with dispassionate, if not completely humorless, efficiency. He, more than Ruth, set the distinguishing tone that would obtain through 15 years of Yankee teams to follow him. Attempts by Yankee publicists and broadcasters to sell the idea of traditional rivalries, or even feuds, with the Red Sox, Tigers or White Sox were doomed to failure because the men executed in their gray flannel rompers in the manner in which John L. Lewis once said F.D.R. had cussed out labor and management: "with equal fervor and fine impartiality." The fervor was usually as feverish as that of a hangman springing the trap. This very aloofness, manifested almost as indifference, was as maddening to Yankee victims as the frustration of defeat itself.

Being beaten by the Yankees could be as insulting as being spanked by a parent who wasn't angry ("All right, all right— if I should hit him, I'll hit him"). Gehrig in his indestructible, imperturbable way was the model Yankee for 14 years, making

* The Ruth-Gehrig gang do not hold the major-league record for back-to-back home runs. The record, 13 in a season, was set by the Maris-Mantle axis in 1960 and tied by them in 1961. This is also an annual item in the Yankee press book. The 1966 edition noted that the Yankees had hit tandem home runs three (3) times in 1965. The one-two men were Repoz-Lopez, Barker-Richardson and Repoz-Boyer. Murderers' *what?*

all the necessary plays at first base and very few spectacular ones, hitting 493 home runs and very few tape jobs that anybody remembers. His 184 runs batted in in 1931 still stands as the American League record, topped only by the 190 RBIs by Hack Wilson the year before, playing for the Cubs. Not Babe Ruth but Lou Gehrig was the most productive hitter in Yankee history, with 2,721 RBIs to Ruth's 2,518, and nobody else is close. Lou Gehrig was a great baseball player. But never in baseball history have so many been so unexcited about so much.

In 1927, Gehrig's first season of what should have been recognized as superstardom, he batted .373 and drove in 175 runs, which had never been done before. But you know what Ruth did that year. In 1932 Gehrig became the first man in modern (since 1900) history to hit four home runs in a game, but that wasn't the lead sports story in the newspapers the next day. John McGraw retired as manager of the Giants the same day. In 1936 Ruth was gone and Gehrig was the undisputed Big Guy of the Yankees, for a little while. He led the league with 49 home runs and 152 RBIs that year, and was the Most Valuable Player. But there was this rookie, an Italian kid from San Francisco, and he was a natural if you ever saw one. By the end of the season the name DiMaggio was first on the lips of the Yankee followers, and Lou Gehrig's magnificence was being taken for granted again.

Finally, on an afternoon in 1939, Gehrig was given the recognition he had always deserved, but he had to die for it. There was something wrong with him during the 1938 season. He played all the games, as usual, but his hitting fell off to a mediocre .294 and he seemed sluggish. It couldn't be his age, because he was the Iron Horse and, well, he'd always be there. But there came the day when the picture on the back page of the New York *Daily News* was of Gehrig, sitting on the steps of the third-base dugout in Detroit, watching Babe Dahlgren take infield practice. Gehrig had told manager Joe McCarthy that he realized he wasn't helping the team, and asked to be benched after 2,130 games. At the Mayo Clinic they told him it was lateral sclerosis, a pernicious degeneration of the spinal cord. Whether or not they told him he was going to die, Gehrig must have known it when he stood at home plate in Yankee Stadium that July day, responding to the cheers of a full house of Yankee followers, many of them seeing him as a human being for the first time as they saw him in the gray pinstripes for the last time. His farewell address was a study in dignity, Yankee or otherwise. "Though I may have been given a bad break," he said, "I consider myself the luckiest man on the face of the earth." They made a movie of Gehrig's life and it was about as bad as most baseball movies. But they called it *Pride of the Yankees,* and that wasn't too bad. No man ever gave the Yankees more to be proud of.

They gave Gehrig a job on the Parole Board and propped him up at his desk to listen to other losers tell of the bad breaks they got. But the iron body was a wasting shell, and soon even that became too much for him. Lou Gehrig died in 1941, the year DiMaggio put on his 56-game hitting streak, led the Yankees in just about everything and was pronounced more valuable than a .406 hitter. The Big Guy was dead; long live the Big Guy.

If there was a murderous *joie de vivre* to Babe Ruth and an industrious serenity to Lou Gehrig, DiMaggio's indelible impression was a functional *sang-froid*. There is certainly no such thing as a perfect baseball player, but nobody ever played the game as nearly flawlessly as DiMaggio. He finished far behind Ruth and Gehrig in almost all the offensive departments (though the three years he lost in World War II would have closed some of the gaps), and most of his final figures do not exceed the brittle Mantle's by much. Other than the hitting streak he holds no important records, and other men have hit .325 lifetime without making the Hall of Fame.* But the sign of greatness horsemen look for in their steed is not how fast he went but that "he done it easy." DiMaggio done it easy, sometimes almost ridiculously easy. Other men have run faster and hit for more power and higher average than DiMaggio, and the young Willie Mays made some plays in the field that DiMaggio wouldn't have. But nobody ever ran as fast without seeming to hurry, hit with crunching power and fine consistency without seeming to swing hard, and made truly great catches and throws so effortlessly. Perhaps the definitive memory of DiMaggio is his picking off a long drive with a going-away catch for the final out of a World Series game against the Giants and continuing up the steps to the visitors' clubhouse of the Polo Grounds without breaking that long, loping stride. He had done what was needed to be done, and there remained nothing to do. Another man might have

---

* Voting for baseball's Valhalla is as capricious, and the reasoning behind it as specious, as other selective methods employed by the National Pastime. Joe Medwick batted one point lower than DiMaggio and made 257 more hits, but he sits in Musial & Biggie's restaurant in St. Louis and laments that he does not make the Hall of Fame because a lot of people down here do not like him, and he is right. The flamboyant Dizzy Dean makes it immediately with 150 victories, but the workhorse Charley Ruffing, with 273, all but 42 of them with the Yankees, has to wait two decades for his due.

exultantly heaved the ball into the bleachers, or waited to greet the winning pitcher, but Joe DiMaggio was not another man. There were no frills about the way he played his game, and there was no wasted effort.

The closest thing to flamboyance DiMaggio ever showed the Yankee followers was a barely perceptible touch to the bill of his cap as he crossed the plate after a home run, or trotted in from center field after an especially superior play, like the "impossible" catch he made of Hank Greenberg's 440-foot drive to straightaway center field in 1940. But there were days when DiMaggio felt that cap-tipping was an unnecessary frill (which from any adult point of view it is, of course), and there were days when Joe Dimaggio was roundly booed by his followers. In his first years as a Yankee, his basic coolness was interpreted by the followers as arrogance, and their resentment was fanned by New York columnists who made a public issue of his failure to give mawkish recognition to the mawkish recognition he received, and deserved.

But there was another area of discontent among the natives. DiMaggio posted averages of .323, .346 and .324 in his first three seasons, and in his sophomore year he led the league with 46 home runs. Then in 1939, with Gehrig retired, he put on the Big Guy mantle and it fit. DiMaggio batted .381, an average that was thereafter topped only by Ted Williams in the American League and by nobody in the National, and he won his first MVP award. Big Guys had been paid big money before, and DiMaggio, a married man by then, figured it was about time for him to have some of it. Toward this end he retained one Joe Gould, an agent type, as his business manager. Well, sir, there was a fuss the like of which would not be heard again until 1966, when Sandy Koufax and Don Drysdale decided that agent-attorney Bill Hayes might wheedle more money out of Dodgers owner Walter O'Malley than two pitchers, acting by themselves, might expect. New York columnists went on another crusade, this time to protect the Yankee treasury from the greed of the best baseball player alive.

DiMaggio got his money, or enough of it, and the followers got over their resentment. So did the columnists. DiMaggio did not charm them by any noticeable change in his detached attitude, but he overwhelmed them with his sheer excellence. The followers would not come to believe until after the 1951 season that money was not everything to DiMaggio. Age and injuries had reduced him to part-time play, with a .263 average and only 12 home runs. He was in the six-digit pay grade by then, and had been for several years. But in his 13 seasons the Yankees had won 10 pennants and nine World Series, and Messrs. Topping and Webb felt they owed him a debt of gratitude. They also felt that some of the followers would pay their way in to see DiMaggio, even as a pinch-hitter. The new kid from Oklahoma had shown promise in his rookie season, and Yogi Berra was the MVP. But the horizon seemed void of superstars at the moment. So they asked DiMaggio if he'd stick around for another year, at the same rates. Joe said thanks, but no thanks, and went out of the game as he had played it, with dignity and grace.*

* DiMaggio could spill soup with dignity and grace. He never looked better looking bad than on a June day in 1944 in Honolulu Stadium. S/Sgt. Joe DiMaggio of the Seventh Air Force had homered off Lenny Kasparovich, and now he had doubled to right center. Jimmy Wasa, the little Nisei second baseman, stood beside the six-foot-two DiMaggio as he took the relay throw, and the scene was reminiscent of T. A. Daly's line in his poem *Baseball in de Park:* "The captain of the Never-

The graybeards of the dugout and the press box, and the old scouts, sometimes say of a certain player that they saw him coming. All you had to do, they say, was see him run across the field, or swing a bat a couple of times, and you knew there was greatness there. Some have said it of Pete Reiser or Willie Mays or Henry Aaron (though usually they don't get around to saying it until the subject person is a 10-year man with a couple of MVPs tucked away). Some have said it of DiMaggio, and his is one case where they might even be right. Somebody may have played the game better than he, but nobody ever looked better playing it.

Mickey Mantle might have played it better. The assumption is inescapable that Mantle might very well have been the best there ever was if he had ever, even for a short time, had the

---

sweats was all of three-foot-three." Wasa was a member of the Hawaii Braves, a homebred team that was a sparring partner in the league with the Seventh Air Force, Ewa Air Station, Schofield Barracks and other service teams, all loaded with big-league talent, and the big, bushy-browed Kasparovich was taking his lumps from the Air Force team, which included Joe Gordon, Ferris Fain, Mike McCormick, Walter Judnich and other notables besides DiMaggio. "Now watch," a sophisticated 18-year-old Marine counseled his buddy from Council Bluffs, Iowa, whose closest previous brush with the big league had been striking out against Rex Barney in high school. "You hear about how DiMaggio hits and fields, but they never mention what a great base runner he is. Just watch." Kasparovich, his gray uniform dark with sweat, came to a stop position, whirled clumsily and threw to second. Jimmy Wasa took the throw and Joe DiMaggio, sliding gracefully back to second, was out by six feet. "I see what you mean," the Council Bluffs wise guy said, and the air was filled with the hoots of soldiers, sailors, Marines and Hawaiian chauvinists. DiMaggio arose, took one swipe at the dust on his pants and trotted to the dugout, deadpan, as flustered and embarrassed as if he'd just hit a grand slam off Mel Harder. Egg wouldn't stick to his face.

151

full use of his splendid body. Given the divine power to create a baseball player, the perfect baseball player, what attributes would you give him? The brute strength, of course, and the reflexes to hit the long ball as far as man has ever hit it, and the scatback speed to reach first base in 3.1 seconds, to beat out all the short balls that aren't perfectly handled and some that are. You would make him six feet tall, or a shade under, because excessive height would lengthen his batting stride and the arc of his swing, increasing the margin for error that plagues the Frank Howards and other giants, and because a man of that size can have what the scouts call "infielder's agility"—more or less the measure of lateral maneuverability by which most welterweights exceed most heavyweights. You would like him about 195 solid pounds, with no tendency to fat that would impede him when he reached the early thirties, his most productive years; the records demonstrate that weight above the 200 class does not increase hitting power and is disadvantageous in every other respect. You would naturally give him the hands of Willie Mays, who would have made them forget about a lot of shortstops, and an arm of the strength of Rocky Colavito's and the pinpoint accuracy of Carl Furillo's. And you would play him in center field, where a man who can do everything is of maximum value to his team. (There is an argument that he could be more valuable at shortstop, but he wouldn't last as long, and time is the fourth dimension of a great athlete.)

Grant that you can't have everything. But except for hands —baseball's generic term for the ability to catch the ball— that were better than adequate but not much better, and a throwing arm that was strong but a bit scattery, Mickey Mantle had it all. But the Yankees never really had all of

Mickey Mantle. He came out of Commerce, Oklahoma, at the age of 17 with a history of osteomyelitis, a bone deterioration, and there was serious question how long he would walk, much less play baseball. In his second World Series game as a Yankee he stepped on a drainage cover in the outfield and injured an ankle that would never be quite right again. That was only the beginning. The left knee, the right ankle, the right shoulder, a pulled hamstring muscle that sent him screaming to the ground as he crossed first base in an all-out effort to beat the throw for the last out of a Yankee defeat. The broken foot. Surgery on both knees, and then the shoulder. The definitive memory will be of Mantle, batting left-handed, striding and taking a pitch and almost falling down as that weak, painful right ankle buckled under his weight for the thousandth time.

With that treacherous right ankle and a right shoulder—the pivotal source of power for a man batting left-handed—that had ached since the 1958 World Series, here is what Mickey Mantle did on August 12, 1964. Off White Sox right-hander Ray Herbert, he hit a ball into the center-field bleachers, over the green 22-foot batting screen behind the monuments to the Yankees' earlier Big Guys—502 feet from home plate. In 1963, restricted by multiple injuries to playing in only 65 games, and part-time in many of them, he came within a couple of feet of erasing the fact that no fair ball has ever been hit out of Yankee Stadium. He hit the façade over the third deck, 106 feet above ground level and perhaps 390 feet from home plate, and those who were there testify that the ball was still going up. In the World Series that year Mantle, who would have been scratched by the track veterinarian if it had been a horse race, played in all four games.

The Decline and Fall of the New York Yankees

He made only two hits, but the second one, off Sandy Koufax, was that tee shot into the bleachers that kept the Yankees alive until the last out of the final 2–1 defeat.

The Yankees never had all of Mantle, but they always had all the Mantle there was and sometimes, it seemed, more than there really was. Ruth, Gehrig and DiMaggio led the Yankees across the great plateaus by the example of their excellence, but only Mantle led by inspiration. His teammates would see him limp as he tried to run, and grimace when he tried to swing. They would see him starting, long before game time, to begin wrapping his aching legs in yards and yards of bandage. They had been aching and wrapped so long that he no longer needed help from the trainer. Mantle applied the bandage as routinely as another man would tie his tie. They knew how he felt, even though he never complained. He would kid his miseries, with the earthy, witty sense of humor that emerged as he grew older and more miserable. One night he, Tom Tresh and Roger Maris all had injuries that should have kept them out of uniform, but they all played. As the three limped in from the outfield after an inning and met near the dugout, Mantle said: "All we need is a flag and a drum."

But they all played. "The guys know how much he hurts," it was once explained by Mantle's very professional buddy, Whitey Ford, "and they figure that if he can play, they can, too. And they feel like putting out a little more because of what he's going through for the club." The guys never felt it more than during the 1961 World Series against Cincinnati. Mantle had put in a good season, a fairly healthy one for him, but in late September he developed an ugly, painful boil on his rump. Just before the Series began it was decided that it would be impossible for Mantle or anybody to play with such an affliction, and Dr. Sidney Gaynor cut it out. The operation left a cavity in his buttock that would have concealed a golf ball, but it was packed with gauze and Mantle played, or tried to play, in two games. Midway through his second effort he had to quit. When he trotted from the outfield to the dugout to leave the field, his pants leg was full of blood. The spectators didn't notice, but Tony Kubek did. "After the game," Kubek said, "he was lying on the rubbing table and you could see it. Most of the guys took one look and left. They couldn't take it. I don't know why, but I stayed and watched while they treated it. It was awful. You could see the bone. I knew then what kind of guy Mickey was."

Mickey was the kind of guy who knew quite well that any injury to his battered legs could finish a career that had moved him into the six-digit-salary neighborhood, but he was the kind of guy who stole bases. "How can I stop him?" asked Casey Stengel in 1959, when Mantle tried two dozen times to steal a base for a team that was going nowhere. And he made it 21 times. Even in 1965, when running at all was an agonizing chore, Mantle took off five times and got there four times. His get-there average for his first 15 seasons was .806, which compares favorably with almost anybody's. One of his strangest but most impressive feats was his belly-squirm back to first base in the ninth inning of the last game of that bizarre 1960 World Series, when the Pirates' first baseman, Rocky Nelson, stood ready to tag him. It looked silly, but it was a feat of agility that would have been remarkable if it had been accomplished by a man with a sound body.

So is his record. Mickey was the kind of guy who not only used no excuses, but needed none. His 23 home runs in the 1966 season gave him a total of 496, sixth on the all-time list.

The Decline and Fall of the New York Yankees

He hit .353 and .365 in consecutive seasons at the beginning of the decade in which hitting for average went out of style. In 1966, when Triple-Crown winner Frank Robinson—the first since Mantle, 10 years earlier—led the league with a .317 average and there was only one other man over .300, what was left of Mantle hit .285 in the 108 games he was able to make. His 18 World Series homers, breaking Ruth's record of 15, will stand up for some years, and maybe forever, now that dynasties have been legislated out of style.

Mickey was the kind of guy who grew up to the stature that his talents imposed upon him. He was almost incredibly naïve when he became a Yankee in 1951. As an 18-year-old shortstop at Joplin, Missouri, the year before, he had torn up the Western Association with a .383 average, but New York was something awesomely else. Even at the end of the 1952 season, which established him certainly as a big-leaguer and probably as a rather special one, his eyes could be easily opened. As the Yankees worked out in Ebbets Field before the World Series opened, Casey Stengel took Mantle to the outfield to explain to him some of the vagaries of the caroms that might come off the right-field wall. "I told him I played it once," Stengel said, "and he looked amazed. I guess he thought I was born a manager, at age sixty." As late as 1958–60, when he struck out 120 or more times for three straight seasons, leading the league, Mantle very nearly wore out the water cooler in the Stadium dugout by taking out his post-strikeout chagrin with vigorous kicks. Then, possibly because of the ageing experience of two "bad" seasons, the kind most players would love to have just once, or possibly because of the boos that went with them, Mantle seemed to mature. He would never be a public speaker, but the painful shyness, sometimes manifested in surliness, became at least less painful. Mickey would never learn to accept failure with equanimity, but there was a kind of calm about him. Whitey Ford, as long as he remained a Yankee, would be the chairman of the board, but Mantle became a young elder statesman. Young players, or for that matter old players, would stop at his locker and talk on their way to the shower room.

And there were no more boos. As DiMaggio had worn out his critics with his sheer excellence, Mantle had quieted his with his raw courage. Nobody will ever know whether Mantle had the most talent of all the Yankee Big Guys, but nobody should ever doubt that he had the most guts.

Big Guys don't have to be big. One Yankee who was as instrumental as any in maintaining the 45-year dynasty was by baseball standards diminutive (a word all sports writers must learn in their rookie season). Edward Charles Ford, of the Astoria, Long Island, Fords, stands five feet, ten inches tall, at the most, and he was a winning pitcher. All general statements made by Leo Durocher are suspect of intemperance, but one of his pronouncements applies to Whitey Ford's pitching career: "Don't tell me how many he won. Tell me how many he lost." By the Durocher formula, a pitcher who has a record of 21–11, as Warren Spahn did with the pennant-winning Braves of 1957, is a 10-game winner. This is based on the theory that a man can pitch ostensibly well but still make enough mistakes to lose a game he should have won. Whitey Ford very seldom lost a game he should have won.

Another rule of thumb for reckoning a pitcher's validity, and one more reliable than Durocher's presumption of guilt in defeat, is a comparison of the pitcher's winning percentage with that of the team for which he was pitching. Of all the pitchers who won an overall total of 20 or more games for the Yankees in the 1920–66 period (there were 57 of them), only two had winning percentages under .500, and they were both one game under. So you are supposed to be a winner with the Yankees. But consider that the Yankees' winning percentage in the years Ford has worked for them is .580, and his percentage is .696. This suggests the converse of the Durocher theory: that Ford, here and there, must have been winning a game he should have lost.

And so it seemed. In 1964 Whitey had arm trouble (serious enough to call for complex surgery at the end of the season) and won only 17 games, but eight of them were shutouts, arm trouble and all. With a reputation for frailty, and for being a "cold-weather" pitcher, Ford has been in more games than anybody who ever pitched for the Yankees, pitched more innings than anybody but Ruffing (and 42 more innings would take care of that detail), struck out more batters and won more games, and his career earned-run average is 2.76.

The frailty rap stems not merely from Ford's stature, but from the fact that he would frequently signal the bench to warm up a relief pitcher when he anticipated that he was tiring or losing his stuff, rather than waiting for his mentors on the bench to figure it out for themselves when the game was out of control. In this way he made a big man out of reliever Luis Arroyo in 1961. Ford finished only 11 of 39 starts, but he won 25 games and the Yankees won the pennant.

You can be a Big Guy with your head, too. Ford's intellectual background, consisting largely of Manhattan Aviation High School, does not qualify him for consideration as dean of the Harvard Law School, but he is not Ned in the Third

Reader. There is a basic shrewdness about him that would have made him valuable in any endeavor. His highest strikeout total for a season—209 in 1961—pales away to insignificance when compared to Sandy Koufax' figures. But if Koufax' fast ball and Ford's had ever met head-on, Ford's would have bounced back. Ford had to do it all with stuff, control and con. He had to think of details that went unconsidered by other pitchers. His pitching pattern for the first few innings of a night game in Cleveland, for example, was different. The town is in the eastern time zone, you see, but it is 405 miles west of New York, as the airlines fly. So the treacherous half-light lasts 20 or 25 minutes longer. Whitey Ford thought of things like that.

Con artist. New York wise guy. Honest man. Ford would eschew the I-just-do-my-best-all-the-time pablum and admit that it was more difficult to concentrate on pitching against the Athletics on a hot day in Kansas City than to get "up" for a night game in Yankee Stadium against the contending Orioles. Anybody who had seen him pitch the money games would have assumed that, but Whitey Ford would admit it. Nor would he flee to the sanctuary of the trainer's room when the reporters were coming to ask why he was belted out in the third inning. Ford would be waiting, and he would be in an area of the room where there would be space for his inter-rogators. "Can I get yez a beer?" he might ask before the interview began.

Ford's singular achievement as a money pitcher was his string, through the 1960 and 1961 World Series, of 33⅔ scoreless innings, breaking the record Babe Ruth set with the Red Sox before they hyped up the ball for him to hit. (How you can add ⅔, a part or parts of a scored-upon inning, to a succession of scoreless innings is a little mysterious, but that's the way they do things in baseball, because they always have.)

His second shutout of the Pirates came in the sixth game of the '60 Series, so there was no chance he would be called on in the seventh game. Whitey always took meticulous care of himself, but Whitey also liked a dram of Scotch, and how long did it take to get ready to pitch? About 48 teetotal hours, so yez couldn't get Whitey a beer the night before he was pitching, or the night before that. But now school was out, and so was Whitey. He didn't have the kind of arm that "comes back," and using him in relief would be the last thing in Stengel's mind, so Whitey might as well begin to celebrate the victory the Yankees would win tomorrow. By early evening his celebration was well under way in a place called Danny's. Two mature ladies seated themselves at a table nearby and popped off about how the Bucs would surely win the next day.

"Oh, they will not," Ford said. "They don't have a chance."

The ladies, without a clue to who he was, pursued the argument. Ford met the challenge, carefully keeping the debate on the uninformed plane of the most asinine baseball discussions he had heard in the Ivy Room, the place in Astoria where his father tended bar.

At length two little girls approached him and said, "Mr. Ford, would you please sign this?"

Whitey signed the autographs and looked at his two lady adversaries. "Now," he said, "don't ya feel silly?"

If the ladies were at the game the next day, when Ralph Terry came in to pitch to Bill Mazeroski, leading off the bottom of the ninth, they may have had the last laugh. There was no chance he would be called on for service in the seventh game, so Ford had taken a few more Scotches before retiring.

Well, there was *almost* no chance Stengel would need him, but the weird game was 9–9 and a lot of pitchers had been used up. So, as Terry took his warmup pitches, a southpaw wearing No. 16 was up and throwing in the Yankee bullpen. A moment later Yogi Berra, the left fielder, stopped running and watched Mazeroski's home run land in the trees.

No. 16 didn't have to pitch. Probably he was just a decoy anyway, to make Pittsburgh manager Danny Murtaugh wonder. Stengel wouldn't really bring him in, with no rest—would he? "I couldn't have pitched," Ford said. "No, it wasn't the hangover. My arm was dead. Just tired." Whitey Ford couldn't have come in and got one man out. Not unless he thought of something on the way.

Ford really couldn't throw in the last game of the 1964 Series, and after it was over he had an operation that did something to a nerve that made it impossible for him to sweat on the left side of his body. Standing on the mound after a few innings, looking as if half of him were home and the other half on the road, he looked weird, but he could pitch again. In the 1965 season he was 16–13, which was creditable considering the kind of treadmill team the Yankees were. But in 1966 it was wrong again and Whitey was almost non-existent, with a 2–5 record. After that season they cut him again, transplanting a vein from his right thigh to his left shoulder. The operation was supposed to restore normal circulation, and at least Whitey could sweat again. At age 38, he had been repaired like a hand-me-down rag doll, and he said he hoped it would work this time, but he didn't seem optimistic.

The Yankee management talked about turning Mickey Mantle, at 35, into a first baseman, to drain the last drops out of him, too. The Yankees, for the first time since Babe Ruth hit that home run in the Polo Grounds, were without a Big Guy—even a little Big Guy.

It was a lonely feeling, but there was no panic. It was much too late for panic.

7

Crop Failure

HOW DO YOU find a Mickey Mantle? Well, these days the first step is to finish last, so at least the Yankees are on the right track. Among the 20 major-league teams, they have first choice in the free-agent draft of June 1967. If the college boy or high school graduate (or dropout) they choose happens to be *the* free agent of the year, he could be the new superstar. The price is strong, however, against his even being of big-league caliber. After making that eggs-in-one-basket stab, farm director Johnny Johnson will have to sit back and flinch as the other 19 teams pick over the other bright prospects for whom the Yankees would spend important sums, and all of them will be prospects the Yankees know about, because their reconnaisance of the boondocks is still just about the best in baseball. But it doesn't work any more: Look but don't touch, is the motto.

The system worked beautifully for 30 years. If you panned enough gold, you found a nugget. In 1932 general manager Ed Barrow was fairly sure that owner Jake Ruppert's money could outlast the Depression and that talent could still be bought. The have-nots—the owners who were engaged in no business but baseball—were hurting at the gate and had to deal their stars to the beer barons and timber magnates. Connie Mack's Athletics, one of the finest teams ever assembled and the champions of 1929–30–31, became the White Elephants as people began staying away from Shibe Park. He yielded Mickey Cochrane to Detroit and Jimmy Foxx and Lefty Grove to Boston. Multimillionaire Tom Yawkey, who had taken over the Red Sox and rebuilt Fenway Park in 1933—a year when many other owners were trying to figure how to pay the groundskeepers—took a fancy to Joe Cronin, the shortstop who had managed the Washington Senators to the '33 pennant. He offered Lyn Lary, a journeyman short-stop, and $250,000. Clark Griffith, the Old Fox whose penurious policy inflicted a one-man Depression on the nation's capital for a generation, never could see keeping expensive players around when cheap ones would fill the uniforms. He wasn't about to turn down that kind of money, even for his son-in-law.

There was talent to be had, but Barrow saw a cheaper way to get it. You could buy a good horse, too, but the most successful stables bred their own. Why couldn't a team develop its own players? Ruppert's money had brought Tony Lazzeri, Frank Crosetti, Lefty Gomez, Bill Dickey and others from various minor-league teams, and there was the nucleus for the next plateau of the Yankee Era. But if you owned the minor-league teams, you wouldn't have to pay for the players. Branch Rickey, with the St. Louis Cardinals, had developed what came to be known as a "farm system," buying control of clubs on graduated levels of the minors and stocking them with young prospects (and used-up professionals, who would work cheap, either because they were "baseball bums" who didn't know how to do anything else for a living, or simply because there wasn't much to do for a living during the Depression). The shrewd Barrow could see that Rickey's farms were bearing fruit, producing a team that would soon be a champion. He envisioned a Yankee farm system that could produce talent in such a steady, self-perpetuating flow that the Yankee dynasty might go on forever.

To run such a system he hired George Weiss, who in the early 1920s had turned a sick New Haven franchise into a going concern, then moved on to Baltimore, where he not only turned out consistent winners but turned a nice dollar peddling players to the big leagues. If Weiss didn't know baseball's bushes like a native guide, he knew men who did. Such a system called for talent scouts, and Weiss selected his scouts as meticulously as he expected them to select players.

Scouting was easier in those days because of the Depression. An 18-year-old kid who couldn't find a job could join the Army for $21 a month, but that was frowned upon as a bum's way out because armies were for wars and there weren't going to be any more wars. It was considered more honorable and edifying to enlist in the Civilian Conservation Corps and chop down trees in exchange for food, a bunk in a barracks and pocket money. By the middle 1930s, Rickey's farm system was being called a chain gang, but by CCC standards baseball salaries weren't so bad, and the hours certainly were better. Besides, there was the pot of gold at the end of the rainbow. A boy who could make himself believe he had ability could see himself, someday, making as much as $20,000, like Hubbell.

It is unreasonable to assume that Carl Yastrzemski Sr. could have been anything like the kind of hitter his son is, but if "great sandlotter" isn't a contradiction in terms, he was the greatest, including his son, who ever played on Long Island. He might have made a marginal big-leaguer and he was certainly equal to the high minors—which in the 1930s played better baseball than some that is shown on network television in the 1960s. The Dodgers offered him a contract in 1939, calling for $75 a month. He might have gone, but there was Carl Jr., the baby, to think of. Carl Sr. went back to the potato farm in Bridgehampton. The rest of the country was emerging from the Depression, but baseball wasn't about to. These boys had to understand that their apprenticeship for a pittance was an investment, a shining opportunity to share the glories and rewards at the top.

Under such circumstances, scouting was like shooting fish in a barrel for the Yankees' bird dogs, not only because they had the most attractive product to sell but because they knew what they were looking for. You find a Mickey Mantle because you have a Tom Greenwade out hunting for him, and if you don't know who Tom Greenwade is, you get the point. He's a skinny guy out of Willard, Missouri, and scouting is his profession. He never pivoted a double play, and neither did Paul Krichell, Joe Devine or Bob Connery, the men Weiss picked to do his picking. But he knew how the pivot should be made, and so did they.

In too many baseball organizations in the past (and some in the present), the scouting staff is the counterpart of the Retirement Row that clutters up the roster of most newspapers and, presumably, other enterprises. A man who has outlived his usefulness or simply established his incompetence is pigeonholed in a "job" where he can't do very much harm.

166

The harm, of course, is in leaving no room for a man who could do a job well. So it has been with many scouting staffs, most notably the Red Sox, for almost 30 years of Yawkey's ownership. Because he has a great accumulation of money and because he has always kept to himself, spending the summers in his remote rooftop box at Fenway Park and his winters on his South Carolina estate, the presumption has been made that Yawkey is some kind of Scrooge. In fact he is an old softy, and his sentimentality hurt his team in two ways. He has always overpaid his players, rewarding mediocrity consistently and nonfeasance frequently. And he has developed overweening affection for certain players, keeping them around for two years or more after their inefficacy was well established and their trading value nil. Then, instead of letting Good Old Joe go back to the farm when he'd had it, Yawkey would "give him a territory"—make him a scout.

Just as jockeys are the world's worst handicappers—and for similar reasons—emeritus ball players often, if not usually, make the worst scouts. A pitcher is usually competent to judge a pitcher, and a hitter sometimes can evaluate a hitter. But only if he can clear his mind of the idea that his way was the only way. Objectivity in these areas runs almost in inverse proportion to the success the scout enjoyed during his own career, by his own techniques.

Wally Moses is a notable exception. With his smooth, classic swing he made 2,138 hits in his career and once batted as high as .345. Yet in proctoring a pre-game drill to get Joe Pepitone out of a slump, Moses counsels him not toward perfection of his style but back into the same unorthodox "mistakes" that make him a dangerous hitter. Moses is the most effective batting coach in the business, and Elston

Howard once explained why: "Wally don't make you hit his way; he makes you hit your way."

An ex-player's preoccupation with the position he played tends to circumscribe his view of other phases of the game. There haven't been many better players than Duke Snider, who hit 407 home runs and might have been recognized as a truly great center fielder if the structure of Ebbets Field had given him room to roam. But when he reluctantly acquiesced to manage the Dodgers' Spokane farm team in 1965 after Pete Reiser was stricken with a heart attack, the Duke feared the worst and it happened. His limited knowledge of pitching and the snap judgments he made in his doubt and confusion probably set back several young prospects a year or so.

It is an oversimplification to state that mediocre players make the best managers, but there is evidence in the record. Joe McCarthy never made the big leagues, and Ralph Houk barely did. Just about everybody who came up through the Braves' farm system during the 1950s says the late Ben Geraghty was the best he ever played for. ("I could tell right away that I wasn't good enough to play," Geraghty once said of his brief term as a Dodger infielder, "so I knew I'd have to pay attention, and learn everything I could, if I wanted to stay in the game.") Leo Durocher was once popularly known as The All-American Out, and Gene Mauch, the gutsiest and most inventive of the young crop of managers, accumulated a .239 average while shuttling around to six big-league clubs. The senior managers of the moment are Bill Rigney, a career sub with the Giants, and Walter Alston, who struck out in his one at-bat with the Cardinals.

Maybe nonplayers don't make the best scouts, but it seems to work out that way. Maybe, like good reporters, they pay attention because they go uncluttered by the assumption that they know everything. The only star on the roster of Yankee scouts is Dolph Camilli. There are other recognizable athletes, like Atley Donald, Buster Mills and Jimmy Gleeson, themselves Yankee farm products.* Most of them, however, are as anonymous as Yankee scouts have always been. Much more so, in fact, because it's a different game, in a different economy, in a different country, in a different world. The Barrow-Weiss system, which worked with such overwhelming efficiency in the 1930s, went out of style in the 1950s.

"There was a time," veteran Yankee-chaser Al Lopez said in 1965, when he was managing the White Sox and the Yankees' problem began to look serious, "when they had not only the best team in this league but the best two in the minors." There surely was. The Newark Bears of 1937–38 would have raised hell in either major league, and the Kansas City Blues wouldn't have finished last. They were the crowning gems of empire, the culmination of all the glorious, burgeoning fruition farmer Weiss could have envisioned when he went out to plant the seeds. In only five seasons, his crop had grown to where it towered over all others and flourished, from its Class-D roots to its Triple-A plums. Of course the Bears and the Blues met in the Little World Series of 1938, and of course it went seven games because Weiss's best of all possible farm systems had the delicate balance of a watch movement.

The handwriting on the wall was perfectly clear by mid-1965, but American League managers, conditioned to Yankee

* Gleeson was added to the list because he became a Yankee coach on an old-buddy basis when Yogi Berra became manager and went down in flames with Yogi at the end of the season.

169

resilience, were reluctant, or at least cautious, about believing it. "Everybody's brave," said Los Angeles Angels manager Bill Rigney, "when those guys are in the hospital. I want to hear what kind of talk there is when they get out." Mantle, Maris and Howard were injured. "There is no way," Oriole manager Hank Bauer said, "to replace guys like them." There wasn't any more, but there used to be. Had the 1938 Yankees needed to replace, or at least temporarily substitute for, DiMaggio, Tommy Henrich and Bill Dickey, they could have had Gleeson (.310), Charley Keller (.365) and Buddy Rosar (.387) from Newark within the hour. Had anything gone wrong with veteran shortstop Frank Crosetti or rookie second baseman Joe Gordon, a phone call to Kansas City would have brought in Eddie Miller. Merrill May could have done the job at third if Red Rolfe had been hurt. Pitching trouble? Ernie Bonham and Atley Donald weren't quite ready, but Joe Beggs and Marius Russo were just about ripe. Enemy managers in those days read the *Sporting News* and felt like the visiting coach watching a 67-man Notre Dame squad pour into the stadium at South Bend.

The beautiful thing about Weiss's system was that it was self-sustaining. It had been necessary to bring Gordon up for the 1938 season, and Keller was ready for 1939. In a year or so they'd need Phil Rizzuto, Billy Johnson, Johnny Lindell, Bonham, Donald, Russo, Borowy. Gerry Priddy would get a fast look and a train ticket, and Rosar was to last through the war. But Miller, Joost, Gleeson and Beggs were for export. So were Joe Gallagher, Walter Judnich and Mike Chartak (and there have been far inferior outfields in the big leagues to what they would have been as a unit). Mickey Witek could play a little for somebody—and the Giants were in trouble. George

McQuinn was drafted away but couldn't hurt them much, playing for the St. Louis Browns, and you could always get him back if you needed him.* They were sent away, mostly for money (who needed to trade?) to restock the farms with brighter prospects.

So well did the system work that the Yankees' march was barely slowed by World War II. In 1943, without DiMaggio, they won the pennant and whipped the Cardinals, who had rudely upset the Yanks in 1942 and threatened a rival dynasty. Most of the varsity was gone in 1944, but George Stirnweiss, a Newark alumnus who normally would have been peddled away, replaced Gordon and hit .319. He, along with Lindell and Nick Etten, gave Bonham, Borowy and the others enough runs so that the Yankees still had a shot at the pennant as the final four-game series opened. They were swept by the Browns. In 1945 Stirnweiss led the league with a .309 average, but manpower became so short that Herschel Martin, a short-ball hitter with the pitiful Phillies of the late '30s, wound up batting fourth. The big fellows were back in 1946, but Weiss saw mixed blessings in the reconstruction as the Yanks finished third. DiMaggio had an indifferent (.290) season and led the team in hitting. Gordon fizzled completely, to .210. Chandler had his last great season, but he was getting along in years and Borowy had gone to the Cubs for money in a weird "waiver" deal in the middle of the '45 season. There were some good-looking kids coming up: Frank Shea, Bevens and Vic Raschi, a 27-year-old who had long been kept in the

* They did need McQuinn, as a matter of fact, in 1947, when after his unconditional release by the Athletics the winter before, he hooked on with the Yankees in spring training and went on to hit .304 as the first-string first baseman on a pennant-winning team.

vineyards for lack of a breaking pitch, but kept impressing everybody with his control and his angry-man guts. Weiss knew the farm system would produce, as it always had, but there were complications.

Ruppert had died in 1939, and in 1945 his heirs had sold the franchise for $2,800,000 to a three-man syndicate (the remaining two of whom would sell 80 percent of it to the Columbia Broadcasting System in 1964 for $11,200,000). The new owners were Dan Topping, a swinger who had inherited millions of dollars worth of tin and banks; Del E. Webb, a carpenter who had thought big and made his fortune as a contractor; and Larry MacPhail. Topping, who had put considerable money in sports ventures that were not at all dynastic, and Webb, who was very busy putting up buildings and laying down sidewalks (with his imprimatur in them) from coast to coast, might have been content with a state-of-the-union address from Weiss on the farm products that were ready, or nearly ready, for harvest. If Aaron Robinson wasn't the catcher to replace Bill Dickey, there was this Berra at Newark. He didn't *look* like a ballplayer, and his catching was still a little sketchy, but what a hitter—a natural. And Bobby Brown, a good-looking left-handed hitter.

MacPhail, however, didn't have that kind of patience. He had been a man who needed a happening to make his day complete, ever since World War I, when he essayed to kidnap the Kaiser. He had caused night baseball to happen in Cincinnati, in 1935. He had taken over a sad seventh-place team in Brooklyn, made Leo Durocher the manager and turned it into a pennant winner—and a money-maker—in three years by a series of shrewd deals. He had told the Dodgers of 1942—a too-proud band by then that included Dixie Walker, Joe Medwick, Curt Davis, Pete Reiser, Billy Herman, PeeWee Reese and Kirby Higbe—that they were going to blow a seven-game lead. They had laughed at him, and blown the pennant. Mac-Phail ran a ball club the way LaGuardia ran City Hall, and this return-to-normalcy jazz was not for him. Neither, especially, was Bucky Harris, the mellow, much-traveled manager Weiss had chosen after Joe McCarthy chucked the bit early in 1946 and Dickey discovered, as he had suspected, that managing wasn't his kind of work.

So the Yankees made a deal. They sent Gordon to Cleveland for Allie Reynolds, a hard-throwing, wild sort of right-hander who had a way of getting himself beat. It was the kind of trade that could have boomeranged, for Gordon, despite his troubles in 1946, had four of his best seasons left in him, and in 1948 his 32 home runs and 124 RBIs helped beat the Yankees out of the pennant. But if the Doctrine of Transvestitism —put the Yankee uniform on him and he becomes a better player—ever applied to anybody, it applied to Reynolds. As a Yankee he suddenly developed that "winning habit" Whitey Ford talks about. In 1947 he won 19 games and the Yankees won the pennant by 12. In the next several years he won 131 games and lost only 50. He didn't always pitch complete games (the gag of '47 was of the two-headed pitcher, Reynolds-Page), but he pitched many, many innings and he finished games for other people. And there was a time, around mid-century, when Allie Reynolds, pitching to one batter with the tying run in scoring position, was as difficult to hit as any man who ever threw a ball in anger.

By then Larry MacPhail couldn't have cared less. The whole conservative Yankee setup wasn't for him, as his partners found out at the victory party after the 1947 Series. There was an argument that just about became a brawl. MacPhail picked up his marbles, or picked up a substantial check for them, and went back to his farm in Maryland. Things returned to normal and the talent flowed on, in waves. The Bauers and Berras were followed by the Mantles and Fords, who were followed by the McDougalds and Skowrons and Andy Careys, and then came the Kubeks and Richardsons. When Harris was sacked as manager after the 1948 season, Stengel took over and the Yankees scaled the plateau that would go on, almost without interruption, to the horizon. The ultimate refinement of the farm system had been attained. As Lincoln Steffens said of the Soviet Union after a visit there, George Weiss had seen the future, and it worked.

It would always work. When Topping pronounced Weiss too old, along with Stengel, after the 1960 season, he could walk the plank sustained and soothed by the unfaltering trust that he had left his monument behind. In 1962, when Weiss was trying to bring order to the straggling New York Mets, the Yankees' farm system brought forth Jim Bouton, Tom Tresh and Phil Linz. The 1963 crop yielded Al Downing, Joe Pepitone and Hal Reniff, and another pennant. The Yankees struggled home free again in 1964 as the farm produced Mel Stottlemyre in mid-season, just in time. For 1965 there was . . . ? There was Jake Gibbs, a bonus boy. The rookie of 1966, the little guy who had to wear Mickey Mantle's shoes for a while, was Roy White. Thus, the last two plums out of the cornucopia were a bonus boy and a Negro, and thereby hangs most of the tale.

George Weiss always seemed like a guy who never had any fun, but that wasn't so. They say he swung pretty good in his younger days, and there were signs in his latter days with the

Yankees that this was so. He liked to bet a horse, but he could bet and then watch the race as excitedly as if he were watching the grass grow. He liked a drink, but he was a washout at a cocktail party because small talk was impossible for him and any kind of talk was improbable. There were times, though, when a couple of beakers of grog would loosen him up in an among-us-boys situation.

It happened one night in Washington, at the winter meetings of 1958. After a couple of belts George began to talk. He ran on for almost an hour and a half, and he was pretty funny. But did he talk about Gehrig or DiMaggio or Stengel or Larry MacPhail? No, he talked about Newark. He was still talking about Newark on that day in Shea Stadium, after the 1966 season, when he announced his retirement as president of the Mets. The formal statement was brief, of course. He said he was culminating a life of "the happiest kind of work I could indulge in." He couldn't resist a mild crack at the Yankee management: "This time I go out with the right kind of taste in my mouth." He said the thing of which he was most proud was hiring Casey Stengel as a manager twice. But when the press conference disintegrated into a bull session, George Weiss talked about Newark. "Those were the good old days," he said. "The 1937 Newark Bears. There was a team."

There was a way of life. Weiss was retiring to his home in Greenwich, Connecticut, where he hung around in 1961, during his hiatus between the Yankees and the Mets. George wasn't good at hanging around. "I married George for better or for worse," his wife, Hazel, is reported to have said during that long season, "but not for lunch." If Hazel calls George for lunch someday and he turns up missing, she might call the Newark police department and ask them to take a look around the haunted house that is now Ruppert Stadium. They might find George sitting there, reminiscing about the time in 1939 when Bob Seeds hit all those home runs and Weiss was able to peddle him to the Giants for cash. "Look on my works, ye mighty, and despair."

They call them the bushes, and that's a dirty word in baseball, but a man can carry a torch for the minor leagues, just as he can for a girl he knew somewhere, a long time ago. Buzzie Bavasi of the Dodgers, an architect of championship teams and probably the sharpest, most pragmatic baseball executive alive, still says, "I'm a minor-leaguer," and he says it proudly. When he says it he is thinking of his days as a youthful "executive" at whistle stops like Nashua, New Hampshire, and Americus, Georgia, riding the buses and soothing the homesick and filling in at second base, with rather disastrous results, when the team became more short-handed than usual. He is thinking about the frustration and the challenge of the impossible alchemy of trying to make chicken salad out of chicken soup—and in an occasional, marginal way succeeding. No man creates another or gives him talent, but there can be great joy in giving a man the counsel, the encouragement or merely the opportunity to achieve, and there is a necessarily quiet exultation when he does achieve.

Bavasi is a sentimental man, and Weiss, as much as anybody (with the possible exception of Hazel) is able to tell, is not. But he was in love with an idea, and he married it. Newark was the prep school for champions, Groton to Harvard. It was George Weiss's wonderful one-hoss shay, the working model of a painstakingly developed concept of perfection. There is beauty in the realization of an idea, and a man can fall in love with it. He also can get stuck on it, like a needle on a broken

176

record. Weiss's idea was perfect for its time. The only trouble was that they changed the time on him.

While DiMaggio was hitting home runs for the glory of the Seventh Air Force, the Congress of the United States was passing the G.I. Bill of Rights. While Weiss was trying to live with Larry MacPhail, Branch Rickey had a happening of his own over in Brooklyn, introducing the first Negro to the National Pastime of the land of the free. While Weiss was busy getting Stengel the men who could execute, people stopped going over to the Lowerys' to watch television because they now had one of their own. While the Yankee scouts were tempting American youth with a pinstripe uniform and all the tradition they could eat, other procurers were offering them money—big money. And then, as the Yankees' nonpareil scouts kept beating the bushes for the diminished number of talented kids who would rather be Yankees than rich, the other owners were passing rules that would allow them to harvest the crops George Weiss had planted.

Newark was the graduation platform for the best of all possible farm systems, but farm systems were out of style. The last important Yankee out of Newark was Yogi Berra, and the last significant product of Kansas City, before it was declared big-league, was Moose Skowron, in 1953. Long before that, the Yankees had gradually, imperceptibly, fallen back on the Jake Ruppert–Ed Barrow method of acquiring victory: buying and trading. The Raschis and Martins and Kubeks and Boutons kept coming from the farms, or what was left of them, but what kind of plateau would the Yankees have been on from 1947 through 1964 without Allie Reynolds, Ed Lopat, Gene Woodling, Johnny Mize, Irv Noren, Johnny Sain, Enos Slaughter, Bobby Shantz, Bob Turley, Don Larsen, Art Ditmar, Hector Lopez, Roger Maris and Pete Ramos? Those are a few of the key people for whom the Yankees sent money, or warm bodies, while they were winning 14 pennants in those 18 years. Without them—without half of them—the Year the Yankees Didn't Win the Pennant would have been a commonplace, and the world might never have known about Gwen Verdon. Nothing happened to the Yankees in 1965. It had been happening for years. The farm system couldn't do it any more.

There was a simple problem of numbers, which the Yankee management took a while to recognize, with a built-in solution, which the Yankee management took a long time to take advantage of. College during the Depression, and before the Depression, had been for rich kids, or for kids who had the motivation to wash dishes while the rich kids were going to parties. Whether this was literally so or not, it was an American attitude, and American attitudes are hard to shake. The G.I. Bill changed that. Many kids, children of middle-class families who never thought of college before Pearl Harbor, were taking it for granted by V-J Day. What the hell, it was free, and you got $65 a month. Many parents of middle-class children who had thought of college as a luxury before Pearl Harbor now insisted on it. The G.I. Bill did not create any valid intellectual climate, but the new technology and the new technocracy demanded college as a prerequisite for success. "The only jobs that's open is for guys with a knack," said part of the lyric of a popular Louie Jordan record of the immediate postwar period. Potential second basemen were becoming certified public accountants. Maybe it was as un-American as knocking apple pie, but not so many kids had the desire to be ballplayers any more. Oh, they wanted to play, all right, but

Kearney, Nebraska, for $160 a month? Are you kidding?

The Yankees had recognized the situation before they tumbled off the last plateau. "Before the war," Johnny Johnson said as Johnny Keane was trying to make do with Roger Repoz and Ray Barker in 1965, "not many people went to college. Now almost everybody does. Baseball isn't much in college, so very few get to play and the others lose interest." That wasn't exactly so either. By 1966 the colleges, the 533 of them with varsity teams, had become the richest source of talent. Organized baseball acknowledged this last winter when it resolved to stop raiding at the sophomore level—where Rick Monday was at Arizona State when the Athletics gave him the money after the first free-agent draft in 1965. Henceforth, they said, they would not "touch" a player (although they might whisper in his ear a little) until his class had graduated. This was a courtesy extended to the colleges by professional football and basketball for years, principally because they could not exist without using the colleges as their "farm system," and because a college coach here and there would get in on the act, advising a prize boy as to which team he should choose and consenting only to the team that was nice to the boy and to the coach. Baseball didn't worry about such niceties, and pro football doesn't have to, either, since the merger. But there's always Representative Celler (D.-N.Y.) to think about, and the free-agent draft really might be unconstitutional. The somebody who's sooner or later going to blow the whistle could be a college coach.

"We don't have the quality of player we used to have," Johnny Johnson said, "but neither does anyone else, because it just isn't there any more." That was 1965, and Johnson was right. But there had been a decade or so when the Yankees weren't getting that top-quality player and some other teams—most other teams—were. "I ain't underrating Elston Howard," Billy Martin said, attempting to explain the strange collapse of his old buddies, "but there were years when they wouldn't have won the pennant with five Howards if they didn't have Mickey." There were also years when the Yankees could have had five Elston Howards, cheap. Had they actively, sincerely scouted Negro players in the late 1940s, or even in the early '50s, they probably could have signed a half-dozen in the Doby-Irvin-Campanella class. That would have been only temporary sustenance, but a dozen more of the Aaron-Banks-Bruton wave might have followed, because they would have been convinced that the Yankees wanted, or at least didn't object to, Negro players. But the Yankees were as slow as the Tigers, and almost as slow as the Red Sox, to make the Pastime National.

"You know why the National League is better," said Alvin Dark in 1961. "Because of the colored players." Indubitably, as a cursory glance at the leading batters on a given day showed then, and shows now. But that was only because the National League, or most of it, had stolen a march in signing Negroes while the American, or most of it, moved with deliberate speed. It didn't mean Negroes were better athletes, Alvin Dark to the contrary notwithstanding. "Sure they're better," said Dark. "They have different muscles." And, of course, that great sense of rhythm and those irrepressible high spirits. While Dark's theory may never be included in a physiology text, even for use at Louisiana State, it is sociologically valid as an expression of baseball's majority attitude toward Negro players. "It don't matter what you think about 'em," Casey Stengel's voice was once heard rasping over a hotel transom in Cleveland, "you could give me an all-star team of 'em and I'd beat everybody."

An all-Negro team is quite plausible, and something close to it would have happened by now if all the scouting and trading were done on a merit basis, irrespective of pigmentation. But it won't happen in the foreseeable future because baseball still applies a *sotto voce* quota system to the employment of Negroes. Ironically, Branch Rickey, who made a place for Jackie Robinson, invented the quota system. "None of us is color-blind, boys," Rickey said at the Duquesne Club in Pittsburgh in June 1962. "Some of us just squint a little better than others." That, he admitted, was something like what he told the Dodgers' owners when he announced that he was selling Sam Jethroe to Boston, notwithstanding his conviction that Jethroe could have made the Dodger team the next season. He'd have been the fifth Negro on the squad, and Rickey figured four was just about right.

"And the great thing," said one of the many big-league scouts hanging around Rick Monday at Tempe, Arizona, before the first free-agent draft, "is that he's white." The fear of Negroes' "taking over" the game is endemic. William Faulkner once suggested to his fellow Mississippians that their fear that the Negro, given the opportunity, would take all the good jobs and marry all the pretty sisters and their assertion of his inferiority were contradictory, if not mutually exclusive. The consensus of baseball people is that Negro players are, in some mysterious way, superior, and they gloomily point to the record. Since 1949, when Jackie Robinson was the Most Valuable Player, 13 of 18 MVPs in the National League have been Negroes. So have 10 of the 18 batting champions. (There will now be some ethnic static about whether Roberto Clemente and Matty Alou, being Latins, are Negroes. No distinction is made for the purposes of this argument because no distinction is made by baseball executives in applying the quota system.)

If Negroes and Latins are "taking over" baseball (and the concept of Pumpsie Green and Earl Wilson controlling the Red Sox is almost as funny as that of Chiang Kai-shek's containing the Chinese mainland), it is by the same process and for the same shriekingly obvious reasons that they "took over" boxing. Taking a punch for $175 on Friday night is, from a point of view, preferable to riding a garbage truck all week for $75. There are more avenues of endeavor open to Kenny Washington Jr., a Dodger farmhand, than there were to his father when he went to UCLA—on an athletic scholarship—30 years ago. There are Negro lawyers and accountants, and most newspapers these days even have a real, live Negro reporter. Banks and utility companies have gradually opened quotas, most of them as liberal as the McCarran-Walter Immigration Act. But there was not, at last count, a single Negro in the plumber's union in the city of Cincinnati. That "better money in industry" cited by Johnny Johnson as one of the reasons Yankee scouts are having trouble finding the Yankee-type prospect is less available to Negroes than to whites. And a Negro boy, partly for economic reasons, is less likely to go to college. It could be that separate-but-equal school systems—whether segregated in the south or ghettoized in the north—do not prepare him. It could be that the intellectual climate of a poor home, where survival is the name of the game, does not inspire him. And it could be that many colleges, as well as baseball and telephone companies, have unwritten quota systems.

Negroes are available to sports in numbers disproportionate

to their percentage of the population because sports are available to them. Before Jackie Robinson, and since, they gravitated to the entertainment fields for the same reason—to turn their "natural sense of rhythm" to something more profitable, and more enjoyable, than swinging a sledge hammer or operating a shirt-ironing machine. But to equate all Negro players with Frank Robinson is to say that all Negro entertainers are Sammy Davis, Jr. It seems at times that there are no bad Negro ballplayers, but that is an illusion. Some of them have been awesomely inept, but they didn't stay around long enough to be noticed. (Some of them were awesomely inept by design, so they could be tried and found wanting. "There, you see? We tried one and he didn't make it. What do you want from us?") Does it not follow that if so many Negro players are available, and if the quotas vary from none (within the last decade) to eight (very recently), those who survive the screening ought to be superior? Wouldn't it follow that if the terms were reversed, and if the quota of white non-Latins on each team were set at 10, the process of elimination would leave 10 men of exceptional skills? Would the cry then be that the game was being "taken over" by Aryan *Ubermenschen?*

Baseball takes only the best of the Negroes and Latins. Or those teams that can get them do, and the Yankees are not one of them. Certainly, ignoring a talent pool that represented more than 10 percent of the population and letting most of their rivals steal a march of five to ten years was short-sighted. If you're scouting ditch-diggers, you figure to find a better pick-axe man among 200,000 people than among 180,000. And you figure, as Jim Turner would put it, to create a better product. The Yankees weren't worried because their product was good enough as it was, but the lasting effects of the self-defeating policy wouldn't be felt until much later—like now.

Not George Weiss nor anybody in the organization would admit the Yankee policy was lily-white. They sent Vic Power away, they said, because they didn't need him. Anyway, they had Elston Howard, the lone Jew at the country club. They were scouting Negro players, they said when the people picketed Yankee Stadium, and as soon as they found one who measured up they'd sign him. They didn't want to hire a player just because he was a Negro. That would be as bad as not hiring a man because he was a Negro, which was the idea some people were getting about the Red Sox. They had Jackie Robinson for a tryout, and their scouts knew about Willie Mays. But they were going to wait for a Negro player they could be pretty sure about.

Ultimately the Red Sox came up with Earl Wilson, and then Pumpsie Green, who didn't have a prayer of being a big-leaguer. Then the flow of Negro talent stopped. It wasn't policy, owner Tom Yawkey said in 1965. Hell, he'd always employed Negroes on his place in South Carolina. The trouble was that the word seemed to have gotten around that the Red Sox didn't want Negroes, and the scouts were having trouble signing them.

That word got around about the Yankees, too. Their 1966 roster included five Negroes and two Latins, but only three of them were farm products.

The attitude of Negro/Latin players toward the Yankees now is academic, because the free-agent draft places them in the same either-or situation as everybody else. They can play for the Yankees or not at all. But that rule will be rescinded shortly, not necessarily because it is arrantly unconstitutional but because none of the several anti-bonus rules has ever lasted more than a few years. Then the Yankees may have a problem. The prestige and the money of being a Yankee used to be reasons enough to override almost any objection, but that time is no more.

While Yogi Berra was playing at Newark in 1946, somebody at RCA was perfecting the Orthicon pickup tube, which would be a television screen on which you could really see the picture. And there went George Weiss's wonderful one-hoss shay. Drooling at the revenues the new medium promised, baseball prepared to eat its young. The Newark franchise survived for a couple of years, but it was dying, and so, within the next decade, would all the minor leagues except those few the parent teams would subsidize to keep them as proving grounds. In 1950 there were 7,500,000 television receivers manufactured in the United States, and by 1955 not having one was like not having a bathtub (and some people without bathtubs had television). It was, as promised, a most lucrative market, and baseball flooded it. It was unreasonable to expect a fan to pay money to see the Newark Bears, no matter how good their old days may have been, when he could sit in his living room with a supply of cold beer and watch Joe DiMaggio for nothing. It was less reasonable to expect fans in Terre Haute to pay tribute to the local club when the Cubs or White Sox were on television, and they didn't. By the middle '50s the minors were pretty much reduced to staging areas. For some years a healthy minor-league club could draw a decent crowd on a weekend, but by the early '60s network shows like the Game of the Week put an end to that. The farm system was not only obsolete but nonexistent as an agency to develop talent.

If the gold couldn't be panned any more, there had to be a

way to get instant nuggets. There was, a way Jake Ruppert would have suggested immediately. Money. The times had changed baseball, but the wheel had come full circle. If there couldn't be quantity any more, there could be quality. If the Yankees had the best scouting system—and with the possible exception of the Dodgers, they still did—they could find the best young players. Easy. Then they could offer them the most money, or enough money, combined with the privilege of being a Yankee, to stay far ahead of the field. This new era was going to be a little rough on the have-nots, because only money would talk, but the Yankees had money.

The bonus foolishness began, modestly enough, in the late 1940s. The Phillies gave $25,000 to pluck Robin Roberts off the Michigan State campus in 1948, and the same year the Boston Braves gave Johnny Antonelli $65,000. Antonelli had to sit on the bench for two years because the have-nots had begun passing rules to equalize things. By the early '50s the thing began to run wild. The Pirates gave an alleged pitcher named Paul Pettit $100,000, spread over 10 years in which they wished they hadn't. The Red Sox gave southpaw Frank Baumann a hundred grand and he promptly embarked upon a career of arm trouble. The Orioles, moved from St. Louis in 1954 after the lords of baseball punished owner Bill Veeck for original thinking, came under new, ambitious management in Baltimore, and big money was handed out to a number of young men. In 1956 the Braves, flushed by the startling success of their Milwaukee honeymoon, got wholeheartedly in the act. Even the Giants, withering in New York, gave away a $60,000 bonus to Mike McCormick, a 17-year-old pitcher.*

* McCormick may be the classic example of the world-owes-me-a-living attitude of some of the young men who become opulent because

The Dodgers had been conservative through the early years of the bonus race, handing out only modest sums like Sandy Koufax' $14,000 in 1955. But when they got to Los Angeles in 1958 and Walter O'Malley saw what kind of money he was going to make, he began to justify his principal argument for leaving Brooklyn: that only with big money could the Dodgers compete with the Milwaukee Braves in the bonus field. (And, of course, bonus money can be written off as operating expenses rather than paid in corporate taxes.) Large checks went to Ron Fairly, Frank Howard and Earl Robinson. The lid was off. In the next few years the Giants gave $60,000 to Gaylord Perry and $150,000 to Bob Garibaldi. The Pirates gave an alleged $175,000 to third baseman Bob Bailey, and the Cubs, it was said, gave even more to one Danny Murphy.

The Yankees came up with Jake Gibbs, for $100,000, so nobody could say they weren't spending any money on bonuses. That was a record for them, and the next year they almost topped it, offering $125,000 in the auction for Garibaldi. He didn't go for it. The Giants were near his home, in Stockton, he explained, and maybe that was it. But lesser

---

of their physical gifts and good fortune. He was big and handsome and he had a bonus, and he married his high-school sweetheart as soon as he cashed the check. The two-year rule was still in effect, but McCormick didn't have to sit on the bench. The Giants were so far back in the standings and their pitching so woeful that Mike was able to pitch 75 innings in 1957. The next year, at 19, he was a regular, and by 1959 he was an accomplished pitcher, with a fitting salary. One day that year he pitched well and was beaten by a broken-bat single or an error or some other cruel stroke of fate. Bob Stevens, the chronicler from the San Francisco *Chronicle,* approached McCormick in the Seals Stadium clubhouse after the game and commiserated. Damned shame, he said, to pitch that well and lose. "Well," Mike said with a deep sigh, "that's the story of my life."

players the Yankees had scouted were taking much lesser bonuses and signing with other teams. That old pinstriped magic couldn't be fading, because the Yankees were still winners. The trouble was that money was talking, and George Weiss was mum.

"In running a ball club," said Cleveland Indian president Gabe Paul in 1965, as people began asking other people what was happening to the Yankees, "we all make mistakes. And sometimes it takes a long time to catch up. An awful long time." There were times—long, long times—when the idea of error in the computer-efficient Yankees' Corporate Concept would have been ludicrous. They didn't make mistakes. But times had changed, and the Yankees hadn't.

"They didn't feel it was necessary for them to compete in the bonus field," Paul said. "During that period they didn't produce the reservoir of talent they might have. Then, when they got to where they felt they might go into the bonus market, it was too late."

It was too late because the Yankees, as they sank to their knees, were struck three heavy blows. The first-year rule, yet another manifestation of the owners' mistrust for each other in bonus competition, was the first. They could sign a bonus player, but he would have to be kept on the "big" roster for a year before he could be optioned out to learn his trade. The Yankees had carried Tom Carroll and Frank Leja, but they could no longer afford that sort of thing. By 1966 they needed all the Lou Clintons and Ray Barkers they could find. Then came the free-agent draft, tying the hands of the Yankee scouts. The bird dogs could still point, but they couldn't retrieve. And then the unrestricted draft of minor-leaguers. Billy Murphy is a highly unlikely nugget. He seems to be a good-field, no-hit outfielder, the kind that can be shaken out of any tree. But whatever chance Murphy had the Yankees lost in the first unrestricted draft in December 1965. They couldn't fit him on their winter roster of 40 names, so the Mets grabbed him for $25,000. It probably was no great loss, but these days a warm body is worth $25,000, and they let you keep only 40 warm bodies. On June 7, 1965, the Yankees had 154 players under contract. If the Yankees' scouting was still as astute as Johnny Johnson preferred to believe, their farms were sharecroppers in the service of 19 other teams.

"Once," said Tommy Henrich, an ex-Yankee who played 1,284 games and hit 183 home runs on two of the plateaus, "they could go to Newark for players. Now they look to Columbus, Georgia, so-called Double-A." Newark is one with Nineveh and Tyre.

How do you find a Mickey Mantle?

Hell, how do you find a Myril Hoag?

8

Tearing Up the Pea Patch

TURNER'S LAW—that paid attendance should be in direct proportion to excellence—took a beating in 1959; when the Yankees attracted more customers (1,552,030) in finishing third than they had in any of the previous six years, in which they won the pennant five times and scored Stengel's moral victory of 1954, finishing second with 103 victories. The better-mousetrap theory rallied in 1960 as the Yankees drew 1,627,349. Attendance soared to 1,747,736 in 1961, the highest figure in a decade. It wasn't hurt by the fact that Yankee excellence was muted enough to allow the Tigers to stay close into September, or by Roger Maris' run at Babe Ruth's home-run record—a race in which, significantly, Mickey Mantle was alive until the last two weeks and was the overwhelmingly popular favorite of the Stadium crowds.

But by the end of the 1963 season there were evidences that somebody had been tinkering with the verities of Turner's Law. The Yankees, most of them outspokenly happy with the new life under Ralph Houk's baseball-can-be-fun regime (the remarkable implication being that winning ten pennants and

collecting eight winner's shares under Stengel had been drudg-
ery), had won two pennants, making it four in a row again.
They had been obliged to part with such as Duke Maas and
Bobby Shantz to help stock the two expansion teams, but the
empty lockers had been filled quickly by the arrival of Bouton
and Tresh, Downing and Pepitone. Maris had tapered off
sharply after his assault on Olympus, but Mantle had punished
his aching bones to win another MVP in 1962. Everything
was just about as all right as it could get. Yet attendance
slipped by a quarter-million in 1962 and by almost 200,000
more in 1963. The gate for the latter year was 1,308,920, the
lowest since 1945, when Herschel Martin and Tuck Stainback
were masquerading as Yankees and Snuffy Stirnweiss was the
ersatz Big Guy. What was going on here?

Well, something was going on across the river. The National League had expanded, too, and there was another
wheel in town. In the Polo Grounds, that dreary relic on the
other side of the Harlem River, they were trying to play big-
league baseball with a collection of has-beens, like Gus Bell
and Charlie Neal, and never-wases, like Elio Chacon and Ken
MacKenzie. That was funny enough, but they had also filled
the empty uniforms with Rod Kanehl, who never had a chance
to be a Yankee, and Marv Throneberry, who flunked every
chance he got.

People were actually paying money to see such merry-
andrews, and the worse the Mets played the more the fans
seemed to love it. They weren't fans, really, but a bunch of
nuts, mostly kids, who came in with banners made from bed-
sheets—the kind of thing Yankee Stadium ushers would have
suppressed with cool efficiency, if they ever got through the
gate in the first place. "Marvelous Marv," indeed! It was like

a conspiracy. The Dick Youngs, Jack Langs and Harold Rosenthals, who had covered the Dodgers of Brooklyn and carried a torch for them ever since O'Malley spirited them away (and the author cops a plea), were giving the upstart Mets a press that was not only more benevolent than any that "my writers" had ever given Stengel's Yankees on their loftiest plateau, but downright affectionate. The ragtag Mets drew only 1,080,108 in 1963, as they finished emphatically last, but that was only 228,812 less than the Yankees' attendance. That was also in the Polo Grounds, the ramshackle monstrosity of archaic architecture in a "bad" neighborhood, where "nice" people were supposed to fear to tread. (It is a remarkably consistent coincidence in baseball that every time attendance sags, the management notices the deterioration of the neighborhood.) The following year the Mets would move into a modern stadium—built with public funds, yet—in Flushing Meadow, adjoining the World's Fair. Surrounded on all sides by major arteries of traffic, it would have no neighborhood except its own vast acreage of parking lots.

Worse yet, Charles Dillon Stengel, dismissed by the Yankee brain trust as too old after the 1960 season, refused to fade away. He hung around like the ghost of Banquo—or, more aptly, the Spirit of Christmas Past—and made the wistful venture across the Harlem seem a little less preposterous by his presence. On a day when Kanehl or Throneberry or Richie Ashburn didn't say something quotable (and there weren't many such days), Stengel did. The Mets in tenth place got more ink than the Yanks in first as one of Stengel's favorite descriptives, "amazin'," because not merely an adjective but a substantive for the Mets. They were lousy, but they were cute, and Stengel was their prophet.

It is difficult to combat cuteness with intrinsic qualities, like ability, and the Yankees were at a juncture for decision. They had been over that road before, and recently. Defeat by the Pirates in the crazy World Series of 1960 had nothing to do with the dismissal of Stengel and Weiss.* The principle problem was that coach Ralph Houk, a man's man whose baseball acumen and qualities of leadership had been clearly established in three seasons as manager of the Denver farm, was feeling pangs of ambition. He had been a coach for the Yankees for three seasons, and he had heard offers to manage other big-league teams. It would have been unreasonable to expect Houk to wait around for George Weiss to cut the uniform off the perennial Stengel, because that probably never would have happened. On the other hand, Topping didn't want to risk losing Houk. It is preferable to have an organization man as manager, and it is ideal to have one who had won the confidence so many of the players had openly expressed in Houk. So Stengel had to go. The decision was objectionable to Weiss. And if you're cleaning house there's no point in fooling around. So Weiss at 66 called Hazel and said he'd be home for lunch.

The wonderful one-hoss shay was rolling smoothly anyway, and what could louse it up? The nonwinning hiatus of 1959 had been one of those things, and some people had whispered that Stengel's advancing age was a contributory factor. He was beginning to forget things, they said. The talent was still

---

* To stress that fact, shortly after the double deposition, a press conference was held at which it was announced that there would be no salary cuts, despite the bitter disappointment. The New York press may never have been affectionate toward the Yankees, but it was usually benign. Nobody at the press conference picked up on the fact that the players most likely to be cut had just been dumped into the expansion pool.

coming in from the farms, and Houk would (and did) supply the vital, dynamic leadership on the field. Weiss's system, which had functioned with unparalleled efficiency for almost 30 years, could surely recapitulate itself under a caretaker management. Roy Hamey, a gentle, personable man who had attained no heady plateaus of success in his stewardships at places like Philadelphia and Pittsburgh, was made general manager. The realignment violated Miller Huggins' hallowed rule against breaking up a winning combination, but the Yankees were exceptions to almost all rules, including their own. They could do anything they wanted to. "It was a concept," wrote Leonard Koppett of the New York *Times*, "based on the arrogance that came with decades of supremacy." And it worked, or seemed to, for four more years.

The canon of The Corporate Concept that executives do not execute as well after age 60 as they did before has been dramatized in such forms as Rod Serling's television drama *Patterns,* and perhaps suspicion of dotage was the reason Stengel and Weiss had to go. Could there, on the other hand, be a situation in which an organization functioned *too* smoothly? Wherein a chief who hadn't done much lately would feel the need to justify his existence by a command decision, like firing an Indian? Michael Burke, the new Yankee president, who knows something about corporate tyranny (he worked at CBS under James Aubrey), says it is possible that executives sometimes execute just for the hell of it. The postulate could be that if money can burn a hole in a man's pocket, authority can burn a hole in his head. But the Yankees made the decision sound logical, as usual, and success continued to succeed—except that a lot of people stopped paying money to see them win.

One reason another change had to be made at the end of the 1963 season was that Hamey was in poor health and wanted to retire. Good general managers are hard to find, which is why there are so many bad ones. Ideally the chief executive should not only combine the pragmatism of the market place with a conversant knowledge of the game, but should be an organization man, familiar with the personnel and policies of the store he is going to mind. The Yankees had Jack White, who fit the prescription; he had been ticket manager in New York and general manager of the Richmond farm. There was another notion, however, that captured the imagination. Ralph Houk had advanced steadily from third-string catcher (he had 158 at-bats in five and a fraction seasons as a Yankee and never hit a home run) to minor-league manager to big-league coach to big-league manager. Now if he became general manager, he would have achieved the sort of neat completeness Americans like to their success stories, wouldn't he? And why couldn't he be general manager? He had no experience, but he was bright enough, and certainly tough enough, and the laissez-faire atmosphere of Hamey's interregnum had established that the store could just about mind itself anyway. Considered in its entirety, there was a niceness about the idea.

Putting a tie on Houk and making him stop chewing tobacco would not in itself make the Yankees cute enough to combat the menace rising in the east, but there was another way. All right, so Yogi Berra wasn't really a character. So he wasn't even especially interesting. Who knew? If there had not been a Yogi Berra, it would have been necessary for those attempting to write cute copy about the Yankees to invent him, and they did.

195

He *looked* funny in the first place, atypical among the tall, clean-limbed Yankee specimens, and occasionally he even said something funny. Bill Dickey, he said, "taught me experience." That was pretty good, but maybe the best was his advice to the guys about a restaurant in Minneapolis. It was a good place to eat, he said, "but nobody goes there anymore because it's too crowded." Yogi was, as Casey Stengel once described him, "a rather strange fellow of very remarkable abilities," and that should have been good enough. But it wasn't. "The great mass of the public," wrote Matthew Arnold at about the time Candy Cummings was inventing the curve ball, "will never have any ardent zeal for seeing things as they really are." So it was with Yogi. The malapropisms and the solecisms were there in great supply, the stuff to build a quote from. All a man had to do was move a word here and there and what had been fairly amusing became funny. Quite a guy, after a few years, was Lawrence Peter Berra.

The Yankee management, however, was not merely casting *Hellzapoppin*. Yogi was loveable and everybody thought he was funny, so the turnstiles would have to be oiled up to handle the action. But between curtain calls Berra would have to manage a little, and what recommended him for the job? Nothing much, but who knew? In the first place it is an American folk belief that Good Old Joe can be a baseball manager just because he's Good Old. Yogi was old, by baseball standards—he had become 38 and supernumerary in 1963, when Elston Howard became Most Valuable Player—and he was almost incomparably good. Lifetime .285, with 358 home runs and 1,430 RBIs, 30 more than Mickey Mantle had at the close of the 1966 season, he was three times MVP.

His remarkable abilities were terribly tangible, but there was a quality about his performance that passed all understanding. He had only a nodding acquaintance with the strike zone and he sent pitchers away mumbling to themselves about base-clearing doubles he hit off deliveries that other hitters would have interpreted as pitchouts. Worst of all, he had the uncanny capacity for hitting the bleeder—the ground ball with eyes or the pop fly to nobody—at the very time when the enemy pitcher seemed to have the Yankees beaten and was thinking about asking for a new contract. Besides, Yogi was a catcher, a very good catcher, and as everybody knows, catchers make the best managers. Catchers are all very shrewd because they are always In the Game.

Yogi knew the game. He was not dumb, as stereotyped. But a hundred thousand shipping clerks and truck drivers who never got closer to the big leagues than the television screen in their friendly neighborhood tavern can tell whether it is time to bunt or hit away, or when a pitcher is running out of gas. There is more to managing than that. Twenty-five men, baseball players or insurance salesmen, are 25 different personalities. The stunt, whether by discipline or con or threats or cajolery, is to get about 20 of them interested in doing their best most of the time, in the job they have already been pronounced able to do. Nobody has all 25 men doing their best most of the time, or 20 all of the time.

To bring about this end, it is good if the manager has been one of the boys, because it is easier to execute an order from a man who has himself executed. It is also good if the manager isn't one of the boys any longer. Sending a man to the minor leagues to manage for a few years gives him experience, and that's nice too. But the principal purpose of that sort of apprenticeship is to separate him from the boys, eliminating or at least diminishing the familiarity that breeds a particular species of contempt: "How can he talk to me like that, when we used to go out and drink together?" Ford and Mantle and a few of the 1954 Yankees were still around when Houk returned from the finishing school at Denver, but players like Richardson and Kubek had been his advance men, arriving in New York as witnesses to the profound respect he had earned as a manager. His accomplishments, and the three-year absence per se, had put an arm's length between Houk and his old buddies; he was one of the boys, once removed.

Leo Durocher, who is an exception to most rules, was able to lay down his glove and become an instant manager, and others have succeeded without minor-league training, but it's the hard way. The case histories of many of those who made the Indian-to-chief transition without formal preparation— Lou Boudreau, Eddie Stanky, Mel Ott, Bill Dickey— have been strangely lugubrious, for the manager, the men who played under him, or both. Hank Bauer in Baltimore is not making the fundamental error he made when he was thrust into the manager's job in Kansas City, trying to be close to his troops and getting too close. His you-can't-fire-me-I-quit decision on the next-to-last night of the 1962 season (he knew Ed Lopat would be replacing him when the season ended) was made at 2:30 A.M. in a place called Danny's Gin Mill in Detroit. Five of his more sybaritic players were with him at the time.

By no means did all the Yankees have them bad watches that they couldn't tell midnight from noon, and they did not lead the league in after-hours recreation. (The Red Sox of the early 1960s had a dynasty going in that department, while the new Los Angeles Angels showed early speed.) The Yankees didn't finish last in the revelry league, either. "We always had fun," one player said during Yogi's tenure, "but never as much as this year."

Yogi Berra, manager, first met the press at the winter meeting in San Diego in December 1963. Ralph Houk, general manager, called the boys to Yogi's suite in the El Cortez Hotel for juice, coffee, scrambled eggs and Danish. Berra, with help from Houk, fielded the questions. He had seen Mickey in Dallas, he said, and his legs seemed to be better than they'd been in a long time. Roger Maris, who had slipped to 23 home runs in 1963, probably was going to have a big year too. He seemed to have recovered from the trauma of his eminence. Yes, Yogi thought he'd follow Houk's policy of pitching Whitey every fourth day. Everything was just about as all right as it could get, it seemed. And Yogi was about as at ease in his new role as a kid at his first formal.

Well, the Yankees got by. Maris didn't have a big year, but Mantle's was big enough. They had to rush Mel Stottlemyre in from Richmond on August 11 and buy Pete Ramos on September 5, but the juggernaut rolled to one more milestone. Yogi's job, if there had been any doubts about it, seemed to have been saved. Things went wrong in the World Series against the Cardinals, but they weren't things anybody could blame a manager for. Bobby Richardson made an error to blow one game. Ford's arm went bad and he pitched only five and a third innings. Maris batted in one run in seven games. Ramos, arriving late in the season, wasn't even eligible for the Series. Still, the Yankees had Bob Gibson sweating right through the last inning. A press conference was called in the Crystal Room of the Savoy Plaza the afternoon after the Series ended, but that seemed routine. A pact-inking, presumably, and a well-done for Yogi.

The Yankee organization, however, hadn't done so well.

The Decline and Fall of the New York Yankees

Attendance was down—only a marginal 3,282, but down nevertheless—for the third championship year in a row. Out in Flushing Meadow the Mets had finished last again, but they had drawn 1,732,597 of those silly fans, more than any club in baseball except the Dodgers. Cuteness had prevailed again, and Berra's presence hadn't helped a bit.

Out in Gussie Busch's office in the Anheuser-Busch brewery in St. Louis, the cameras rolled. Johnny Keane, the Cardinal manager who had just won the World Championship for Busch, was telling him, quietly and politely, what he could do with it. During August, Busch had fired Bing Devine, whose spectacularly successful trades had put the Cardinals' team together, and made no secret of his hopes to hire Leo Durocher as Keane's successor. Bob Howsam, Devine's successor, smiled a Cheshire-cat smile as Keane acknowledged that Devine's firing was a factor in his decision to quit. Later that afternoon Keane's phone rang in the Forest Park Hotel. "They fired Yogi today," he was told.

"They can't fire you for losing a seven-game World Series," Keane said, and paused. "Can they?" The World Series, the Yankee management had said, had nothing to do with the decision. It had been made before the season was over. One of Those Things had struck again. Yogi neither winced nor cried aloud.

Three days earlier, putting his pants on in Yankee Stadium for the last time, Berra had sounded as if he had had a premonition of the imminent news. He spoke wistfully to some of the writers about the way baseball had been when he took the Yankees' $500 and left the East St. Louis sandlots. "Today you can't threaten a player," Berra had said. "You got to pat him on the back or he won't play for you. They're all college men today. If they don't like what's happening, they'll pack up and go home." And he wound up: "It was a lot better in the old days when you had to play or some one else got your job. Today there's nobody around to give them that push."

"Not the players, maybe," wrote Harold Rosenthal of the New York *Herald Tribune,* summing up for the newspaper people gathered at the Savoy Hilton for the firing ceremonies, "but somebody gave Yogi a push."

Berra wasn't at that press conference. They had talked that morning, general manager Houk said, and Yogi left to keep a golf date. "We feel this is better for all concerned," Houk said. He added that Yogi had been made a "special field consultant." The position was created, Houk said, "because we didn't want to lose Yogi." They lost him. The man who had played more games for the Yankees than anybody except Lou Gehrig became a Met coach, and any progress the management had made in humanizing itself was set all the way back to George Weiss.

But the Yankees pulled off a coup. They hired Johnny Keane. He was a manager in the Huggins-McCarthy-Houk tradition (Stengel qualifying on some points of the tradition but being a thing unto himself). Keane was about as organization-man as you can get, having spent 35 consecutive years in the Cardinals' employ. He had never played in the big league* and was well steeped in minor-league managing experience, from the deepest bushes to Triple-A, where he spent

* The theory that minor players make major managers had come into vogue in the late 1950s, as people like Bill Norman succeeded people like Jack Tighe. John Drebinger of the New York *Times* expressed the trend in verse: "We never heard of Mayo Smith/ We thought that Alston was a myth/ But now we're really over a barrel/ Who in the hell is Kerby Farrell?"

201

a decade. He was an all-business guy, long cured of the one-of-the-boys syndrome, if he ever had it. For the moment he personified success, having won a World Series with a team that shouldn't have won a pennant. Better yet, he was a sympathetic character, having turned down a fat contract on a matter of principle. That sort of thing had never interested the Yankees before, but suddenly it didn't seem such a bad idea. Tony Kubek was hurting. Maris' big season had failed to materialize again, and Mantle was struggling. Ford was on his way to the hospital for radical surgery. Bobby Richardson was thinking about retirement. And there were those attendance figures.

Keane never had a chance, and his end began on opening day, 1965, in frigid Minneapolis. Bouton, his arm hurting, threw three change-ups in a row to the Twins' pitcher, Jim Kaat, who hit the third one for a single and beat him. Bouton, useless unless he can throw hard, won four games all year. Howard made a throw to third that ripped his already injured elbow. Kubek was crippled by the dangerous spinal problem that would force his retirement. Maris chipped a bone in his hand and couldn't help. Mantle struggled on his aching legs, but needed a "caddy" so often that rookie Ross Moschitto, a .185 hitter, got into 96 games. Between them Maris and Mantle hit 27 home runs. The Yankees finished sixth. It was their first descent to the second division in 40 years, since the year of Babe Ruth's "bellyache." Attendance drooped again, almost 100,000 more. The Mets finished last again and drew 1,768,389, up a little.

During the winter the Yankee management did nothing to improve the situation, because there was nothing that could be done. The dried-up farm system yielded nothing, and no significant trade could be made, partly because the Yankees had almost nobody that anybody wanted, and partly because their competitors, finding them down after 46 years, were not about to let them up. The Yankees got Bob Friend, a 35-year-old pitcher who had had it. And to plug the shortstop hole they traded Linz for Ruben Amaro, a .240 hitter who had never made the Phillies' varsity. Amaro was a better glove man than Linz, but after the first week of the '66 season he smashed up his knee in a collision, and that was that.

Naturally, when the Yankees lost 16 of their first 20 games in 1966, Keane had to go. When the bus breaks down, shoot the driver. The Yankee apologists said Keane didn't "get along" with his men—wasn't close enough to them. This theory seemed to take substance when the charismatic Houk returned to the bench and the team spurted briefly. Then came the injuries. Maris, the bone chip removed during the winter, could swing a bat again, but in May he injured a knee. Mantle was hurt again. Ford won two games all year and planned on even more radical surgery. The Yankees finished last, for the first time in 54 years.

Harry Wolverton was sacked as Yankee manager after that disastrous 1912 season. (In 1913 Frank Chance led the team to seventh place, re-establishing his credentials as The Peerless Leader.) Last year, however, the management faced the fact that they had given Houk—and, by extension, Keane—a pretty bad bus. The management resolved to build him a new one, and, just for openers, the management replaced itself.

Some time in August 1964, the Columbia Broadcasting System bought 80 percent of the Yankee franchise for $11,-200,000. Topping and Webb each kept a 10-percent share (each worth almost two and a half times the $460,000 paid for the franchise in 1915 by Jake Ruppert and Tillinghast L'Hommedieu Huston). CBS demonstrated a hands-off policy toward its new subsidiary by keeping Topping as president. Topping and William S. Paley were old friends, a fact that may have been the genesis of the transaction but not the reason for it. As baseball men say of trades, the deal helped both clubs. The Yankees had always shown some profit; attendance had not yet dipped below the break-even point. CBS was diversifying, as giant corporations do, and the prestige of ownership of a blue-chip property in show sport certainly wouldn't hurt in show biz. Webb couldn't have cared less, but he had never taken a dynamic hand in the management of the club. Topping was in his fifties, a time when men of wealth tend to lay their burdens down and think about what to do with what they aren't going to be taking with them. "A man doesn't necessarily sell a ball club to CBS because he wants to," said Walter O'Malley, who has a tax-analyzing computer in his head. "He has to think about the value they'd put on it for inheritance purposes." Topping had been married six times and had a number of children besides Dan Topping Jr., the concessionaire who had filled in as "general manager" when Houk went back downstairs.

Webb sold his 10 percent during 1965, and Topping chucked in his hand in September 1966, when the Yankees touched bottom. Lee MacPhail was appointed general manager, promptly declared a bankruptcy of talent and announced a youth movement that was underscored by the trading of the unhappy, unhelpful Maris for ex-Met Charlie Smith. MacPhail, son of Larry MacPhail, was a Yankee organization man, having served them in several executive capacities before going to Baltimore as general manager. There was opportunity in Baltimore, and, it seemed at the time, a bright young executive could get older—and not much brighter—waiting for the autocratic George Weiss to retire. Late in 1965 the lords of baseball were in the market for a new commissioner, one who would commission wisely but not too well. They weren't going to live dangerously enough to confer the theoretical omnipotence of the office on MacPhail, the kind of executive who might take his authority at face value and *do* things. Still, there had to be somebody in the office who knew a lot about baseball, because General William D. Eckert, the compromise choice, knew only a little.* So they prevailed upon MacPhail to sit in as advisor on baseball to the czar of baseball, and he wasted a year of his time and talents. The Yankees didn't have to ask him twice.

The man who asked MacPhail was Michael Burke, who had become president of the Yankees when Topping cashed in his chips. Burke had been the CBS vice-president in charge of the Yankees ever since the sale in August 1964, but his capacity had been one of liaison or, at the most, coordination. CBS, for example, did not order the firing of Yogi Berra. The network was not participating in executive decisions about Yankee personnel at that time.

Mel Allen, though, isn't completely convinced of that. Allen doesn't know yet what hit him. Having broadcast every Yankee World Series since 1947, he "sort of took it for granted" that he was going to announce the 1964 Series. The Yankees

---

* For the record it was Larry Fox, then a reporter with the now defunct New York *World Telegram & Sun,* who uttered the classic summation of the election: "My God! They've picked the Unknown Soldier!" Many journalists of show sport have quoted the line and few have given it attribution. You may call it brain-picking, but they call it research.

hadn't picked up his option in August for broadcasting the regular '65 season games, but sometimes they hadn't gotten around to that until the Christmas party. Dan Topping had told him a couple of weeks before that there might be some changes made, but he had seemed to be talking about the future. Right now it was the Monday before the World Series and Mel Allen, who had a "principal announcer" stipulation in his contract, had to pack for the trip to St. Louis. Still, nobody had told him he *was* going to do the Series, and somebody usually had. Better check, just in case. No, the commissioner's office told him. Phil Rizzuto was doing the Series.

A "Dear Mel" letter came in November, and there was supposed to be an official announcement. Mel even sat down in the Savoy Plaza with Bob Fishel, the publicity man who doesn't forget things, to draft the announcement, only nobody ever got around to making it. But Mel Allen, like the Savoy Plaza, was being replaced. Somebody up there, at the decision level of the Yankees, or CBS, or Ballantine beer—Mel has "heard things" since then, but he still doesn't know which it was—had found something they didn't like about him, and the Voice of the Yankees had been fired.

"I suppose," Mel said later, when he stopped reeling, "that image-change bit had something to do with it." If there is any remaining validity to the word "image" after the way the commercial and political hucksters have abused it, apply it to Mel Allen's role with the Yankees. He *was* the Yankees to thousands of Yankee followers, long before they ever bought a ticket. To Yankee haters, he was the Yankee doll they could stick pins in, and did. He was the Yankees' apostle and their apologist. To the angry protests that his accounts were biased, Mel copped a plea and explained (and explained, and ex-

206

plained, the way he explained every oddity, or commonplace, until it was a bleeding thing) that "these broadcasts are intended for Yankee fans."

But he was not merely a paid cheerleader, as so many broadcasters are ("C'mon, Bucs, let's get a couple of runs this inning!"). His partisanship came naturally, because Mel Allen *was* a Yankee, pinstriped as indelibly as Joe DiMaggio, and in fact more so. Other than a deep devotion to his late mother, whom he lost the same year he lost his job, the Yankees were the focal interest of his life. He lavishly admired DiMaggio, not only as a ballplayer but as a boulevardier. The only way Mel tried to emulate him, however, was in playing center field in the New York Baseball Writers' annual game.*

In 1939, when the Yankees were about to win an unprecedented fourth-straight championship, it figured that the Breakfast of Champions would be the first sponsors of the first radio broadcasts of baseball in New York. "When Wheaties broke the local market," Mel Allen recalls, "Bill Slocum Sr., rest his soul, got me an audition at CBS. They brought Arch McDonald in from Washington, and I was supposed to go there, but they got Walter Johnson. So I assisted Arch that year, when we did the Yankee and Giant games at home." It was that way until 1946, when Mel returned from the service and began to do all the Yankee games on station WINS. He did them all from then on, until that Monday in October 1964, many, many White Owl Wallops and Ballantine Blasts later. The nasal Alabama drawl, the

---

* Mel played the game more skillfully than most of the writers, and he "hung in there," as he often counseled Yankees to do. The author once knocked him down, and he got up and doubled to right-center on the next pitch, an intended curve ball. You couldn't look it up.

involute, belabored explanations of the obvious and the qualified-to-death expressions of opinion or criticism bugged a considerable majority of a generation of listeners, some of them loyal Yankee followers. But nobody—not Ruth or George Weiss or Frank Crosetti—was as closely and long identified with the Yankees as Mel Allen. He was the 26th man.

Mel Allen made enough money in his years as a Yankee so that nobody has to run any benefits for him. He still gets work. Neither his singular devotion to his job nor the singularly personal tragedy it was to him to lose it was a sufficient reason not to fire him. In The Corporate Concept, everybody has to go sooner or later. But presumably there was a reason to fire him, and he would still like to know what it was. Bus boys are fired every day, but they are usually told by the headwaiter that they dropped too many dishes, or something.

Mel Allen doesn't know what he did—or didn't. "Dan never gave me any reasons. He said it had nothing to do with me, or my work. He said, 'You know me.' It was like it was something he didn't want to do. He said it wasn't CBS, either. Something came up later and somebody told me that there were certain words and phrases I had taken a different significance from than what other people took. But nobody ever said anything to me. I guess nobody told Yogi anything either. Wasn't he talking about a new pitching coach as late as the sixth game of the Series?"

There is the possibility that Mel's warning may have been too subtle. Among his souvenirs is a letter he received from Topping during the summer of 1964. "He was in Florida," Mel says. "He heard some of the broadcasts and he wrote to tell me how good they were. It's funny, thinking back. It wasn't his habit to write letters like that." Mel Allen may have been the only broadcaster in history to receive a vote of confidence, baseball's ominous precursor of the pink slip. How 'bout that?

Every day, in almost every way during the next two years, the Yankee machinery deteriorated into an image. Their manner of firing people, however, improved considerably. Red Barber was sacked with class. On September 26,1966, he met Mike Burke, the new Yankee president, for breakfast in the Edwardian Room of the Plaza Hotel, diagonally across the street from the Yankees' executive suite. Burke had news for Red. One of the details he had inherited from the Topping regime was the *fait accompli* that Red Barber had to go. "So I had to sit down and tell him why," Burke said.

Burke didn't want to tell anybody else why. "I promised Red," he said, "that I would not utter a word that was derogatory, so as not to inhibit him from getting another job." Burke's solicitude was sincere, but slightly overplayed. Inhibiting Red Barber from finding a job is, or ought to be, about as feasible as blacklisting Casey Stengel. There are men who attain unimpeachable stature in their profession, and if Red Barber hadn't reached that level of esteem in the business of broadcasting baseball, then its politics are even nearer the hobo-jungle plane than one is led to believe.

Barber was the greatest of the baseball announcers—or football announcers, for that matter—because he was a reporter. He told the people what happened. And because he was, in a subtle, unpedantic way, a teacher. He taught the people to understand what was happening. When he came to Brooklyn from Cincinnati in 1939, he brought with him an awareness that he would be addressing a vast, untutored audience, one almost unanimous in the opinion that giving

The Decline and Fall of the New York Yankees

Dolph Camilli a pass and pitching to Babe Phelps with first base open and one out was an act of cowardice. It was the first time big-league baseball had been broadcast in the New York area,* and the provinces of New Jersey, Westchester and Long Island abounded with teen-agers under the distinct impression that four fouls was out. Informative without being condescending (he told them why, for example, there weren't any left-handed shortstops), Red Barber disabused them of their misconceptions and a generation learned baseball.

Red also brought with him a collection of bucolic epigrams held over from his Georgia youth. If pitcher Luke Hamlin stomped and scuffed around the mound in protest over an umpire's decision, he was "hollerin' down the rain barrel." If Joe Medwick had singled, doubled and tripled in his first three trips, he was "tearin' up the pea patch." If a pitcher had two strikes and no balls on a batter, he was "in the cat-bird seat." But you're tipping your age if you remember them, because Red Barber had the gift of adjustment to his time and his environment. The cornpone stuff was fitting for 1939, when the Dodgers were still supposed to be funny and partici-pants in radio quiz shows could bring down the house with the simple statement that they lived in Brooklyn. But the team Larry MacPhail assembled won more than the pennant in

* A fan whose Atwater Kent was in good working order could catch a game from Boston, where announcer Fred Hoy had dubbed center-fielder Roger Cramer "Flit" and "The Flying Red Horse" in deference to the sponsors, or from Philadelphia, where a rookie named Byrum Saam was doing play-by-play. The games of that good old Newark team were broadcast regularly, as were those of the Giants of Jersey City, where the feats of such International League luminaries as Woody Abernathy and Smead Jolley were recounted by Joe Bolton, now the "Officer Joe" of a kids' television show.

1941. It won dignity, and Red Barber's style became appropriately sophisticated.

Red was on the payroll of the ball club, like any other broadcaster, and the sponsor paid the freight. He occasionally had to knuckle under to bureaucratic obscurantisms like the order from the front office in Brooklyn not to mention the batting average of any Dodger hitting under .250. But he always worked for the fans. There was a great exasperation, and there still is, in tuning in a game in the sixth inning and hearing 20 minutes of prattle about the color of the sky, what college Lefty Schwartz flunked out of and where tickets for future games may be bought before being apprised of the central fact: the *score*. This indifference to priorities came to Red Barber's attention early in his career, and thereafter he came to work with a three-minute egg timer, hourglass style. When the last grain of sand dropped through, Red would give the score, no matter what else was going on, and turn the glass over. Just a small, vitally important detail. But Red felt the same obligation about the large, vitally important details.

When Mel Allen turned over the microphone to Red after the first four and a half innings of that fourth game of the 1947 World Series, Bill Bevens hadn't given the Dodgers a hit. As the Dodgers came to bat in the sixth, radio listeners were startled to hear it announced that Bevens had a no-hitter going. Superstition forbade mentioning such a thing after the fifth inning, on the grounds that it would "jinx" the pitcher. "I had to make a decision," Red said. "Was I a reporter, or a dealer in superstition?" He was a reporter, as he always had been. Earlier that same season he had told the people what was happening, long before Ewell Blackwell, going for a second straight no-hitter, had Eddie Stanky bounce a single between his legs in the ninth inning. Red had been a reporter in Cincinnati on a night in June 1938 when Johnny Vander Meer had pitched the first of his two consecutive no-hitters, and he told the people what was happening.

Perhaps the highest tribute to Barber's eminence as reporter-teacher is that Vin Scully of the Dodgers, the most professional of the current generation of baseball broadcasters, gives Red grateful, unqualified credit for teaching him the fundamentals when he was a rookie in Brooklyn. And small, vitally important details, like avoiding embarrassing surprises by keeping your focus on the *ball*. If ever a recording album of excellence —as opposed to ebullience—in sports broadcasting is assembled, it should include not Red Barber's job on a Dodger game in Boston in 1950, but Scully's account of Red's job.

The Dodgers, needing a victory badly, had a lead, but the game had not gone five innings and the rain clouds were rolling inexorably in from behind left field. Once the cloudburst reached Braves Field, no more baseball would be played. If it arrived before the Braves were retired in the fifth, it would wash a "must" Dodger victory down the drain. As Red Barber followed the ball, he followed the rain. Now it was at this street, 12 blocks away, now at this one, five blocks distant. Now it was raining in left field, and the Dodgers had one more out to get. Now, Scully recalls, as enthusiastically as the rookie he was that year, Sam Jethroe hit a ground ball to PeeWee Reese. "He's up with it, and there are raindrops on the bill of his cap." Dramatic, certainly. But not the holy-cow drama, or the deep-throated hokum of Bill Stern with the ball on the one-yard line. It was the unvarnished drama that is the product of pure, meticulous, professional reporting. If the story is dramatic, it tells itself, and the reporter is merely interlocutor, as Red Barber always was. If it isn't, nothing will make it so, and Red Barber never tried. He didn't try to make the Yankees anything they weren't last year when, as Red puts it, "Reality struck."

There were reports, during the last of Red's 13 summers with the Yankees, that the image-changing bit was going to strike the broadcasting booth. *Radio Daily* said "one or two" of the Yankee broadcasting team of Barber, Phil Rizzuto, Joe Garagiola and Jerry Coleman would be dropped. The idea didn't shock Red. "In my profession," he said, "something begins to happen after you've been around for a few years. There was an accumulation of reasons why I left Brooklyn, and no really big one. I had survived a couple of power struggles in the management, and it seemed the right time to quit." It figured, in a way, that Red would get the Yankee axe. "Topping is a fellow who seems to sour on people when he gets ready to," he said. "He soured on Mel, didn't he? And I had been there longer than the others. Besides, I was high-priced. I don't know what the others made, but I was getting $50,-000."

Red heard the rumors and read the reports and made what inquiries he could. "But there was silence from Olympus," he said. "The ball club went bad, and I heard Topping was like a wild man. I suppose he had thought he could keep himself on the payroll, and his son, and everything would go right along. Then reality struck. I saw him in the stands one day, and he looked as if he'd been crying, or in a rage. I said hello to him and he just went on by, without saying a thing."

Nobody said a thing until Burke invited Red to breakfast on September 26. "I had met him for lunch at the Lambs' Club in July," Red said. "But we didn't talk about anything to do with the ball club. We just sort of looked each other over. When we met for that breakfast, I had a new blue suit on and I thought I knew what he was going to say. I thought he'd say: 'I'm a green pea on this job, and I'm calling on you to help us straighten things out. You helped build the club in Cincinnati, and you helped build up Brooklyn twice. We need your experience to tell us if we're doing the right things.'

"When we sat down, I poured a cup of coffee and had about two sips. I had a copy of that *Best Sports Stories of 1966*—I had been one of the judges, and I remarked to Burke about the way those fellows can sit in a cold press box and turn out literature.

" 'There's no use in our talking this way,' he said. 'I have to tell you we're not renewing your contract.' I asked him why, and he said, 'Lack of interest.' I don't know what it means, but I know that's the only reason I ever got."

There was a story that Red had demanded that he, as senior man, be made the captain of the broadcasting team, and that his first official act of his captaincy would be to fire one member of the team. Red heard the story. "I am a man who measures my words carefully," he said. "You may say that anyone who told you that story is a liar. There was no friction with any of the other broadcasters, as far as I know, and none with anybody in the organization, until Burke gave me the black spot."

The Old Redhead cooled off in his swimming pool at Key Biscayne, Florida, and soon recovered some part of his sense of humor—the trenchant part. He received about 300 letters, mostly from fans he had informed, instructed and entertained through the years. "I couldn't answer them all individually," he said, "so I had a card made, like a dentist moving to a new office." The card read:

"Dear ——:

"My removal from Burke's Peerage is a blessing. Your kindness is a benediction. I rest content."

The lower-left-hand corner of the card gave its origin: "The Catbird Seat."

Red Barber rests, but not content. He seethes with indignation. "Mel Allen is still waiting for them to make an announcement," he said, "and I wasn't going to wait." He stalked away from the breakfast table, back to room 4355 at the New York Hilton, called the most prominent entertainment columnist he could think of and told him he had been sacked. "I think people in the Yankee office were stunned that I made the announcement," Red said, "but I wanted everybody to know I am clean. If Mr. Burke wants to make an announcement, or if he wants to have a public debate, I am prepared. I welcome it. He says he inherited the decision, but he says he concurred in it. And he says he didn't like it. If he didn't, why did he have to do it? He had been president of the Yankees for six days. Couldn't he make his own decision?"

"I made the decision," Burke said. "I inherited it, but I agreed with it. I even sat in on the discussions. I grew up listening to Red Barber, and he was great—probably the best ever. But I believe that for every man there is a time, a time to come and a time to go. In my opinion it was Red's time to go.

"His comments are incomplete, and perhaps not entirely accurate. He did tell me at that breakfast that he expected to be made captain of the broadcasting team. But I don't think I want to say any more than that. I believe that card he sent out indicates his state of mind, and I'd rather be the bad guy in this thing than engage in the nasty kind of contest it could turn into."

"I have a record," Red Barber said, "of 37 years of fine work. I am not going to allow Mr. Burke, or anybody, to monkey with it as they did with Mel Allen." Then Red Barber, a man who measures his words carefully, said this: "The Yankees are in terrible trouble. They will be in the second division as long as you and I live. They are in terrible trouble on the field, but they are in worse trouble in the front office. Unless something changes there, nothing will get better. The club was built up by Jacob Ruppert, a man who *put in* the game. Topping and Webb never did anything but *take out,* and they thought it would last forever."

Gabe Paul, president of the Cleveland Indians, also measures his words rather well, and he may have said the same thing in other words in 1965 about the Topping-Webb regime. The idea of selling a major-league baseball team to a television network—the Yankees, of all teams—raised any number of eyebrows. Television had been figuratively taking over the game for years, but outright proprietorship was scary, even to those who had been selling it out, contract by contract.

The conflict-of-interest goblin was put to rest when a major stockholder of the Orioles divested himself of CBS stock. But some of the lords of baseball felt at the time that the game could stand a little conflict if it meant a little more interest, and Gabe Paul was one. "I voted for the sale to CBS," he said. "Frankly, I thought they might be easier to get along with than the present administration. I thought they would vote for things that would be good for the game, and not just the Yankees. I don't think CBS, from a public-relations standpoint, could afford to take positions the Yankees had taken for years. The Yankees just didn't contribute to the betterment of the game when they had great opportunities to do so."

Minnesota Twins manager Sam Mele, a journeyman with losers around the American League for a decade, took a more parochial view. "They never cried for us," he said as the Yankee star began to wane, "and you can bet your tail we're not going to cry for them."

The Yankees may be pitiable for a long time. But it will be a long time before they are pitied.

9

Wet Socks and a Sweatshirt

RED BARBER AND Mike Burke parted at the front steps of the Plaza Hotel. Red, a man with a mission, strode to the right, past the chauffeured limousines, turned left on 58th Street, then right into Fifth Avenue, disappearing past Van Cleef & Arpels, the across-the-street neighbors of the Yankee executive suite who will sell you diamond haricots for $1,900 a copy, or so. Burke watched him go, and he remembers.

"I just stood there," he said a month later. "I couldn't move. My guts felt like a laundry bag full of wet socks."

Michael Burke, six days the president of the New York Yankees, had to go back to the office on the 29th floor and think about a number of things. Things like reaching back into CBS for Howard Berk, the network's director of information service, who would take on the imposing task of implementing the "community relations" of the Yankees, an organization whose idea of relating to the community had been building VIP boxes on the third-base façade of the mezzanine, for rent at rates that liquidated the cost of the construction.*

A call by the brass of the Bronx Bombers on the Bronx borough president was the first step in a campaign that Burke hoped would "change the climate" in which the Yankees had existed. "We want to find out how we can lace ourselves more closely to the Bronx and to the New York area as a whole," Burke said. "We realize that we have been lacking in that regard. We want to convey the feeling that we are a good neighbor. In as parochial a business as baseball, identity with the community is essential."

In as parochial a business as baseball, the community— or that considerable segment of the community that cares about baseball at all—does not merely identify with the second baseman. The intrinsic psychology of being a fan, or even a follower is vicarious experience, which Webster's defines as a happening "performed or suffered by one person with results accruing to the benefit or advantage of another." The benefit can be positive or negative, because the experience may be performed *or suffered*. If my team beats yours, I am, by a transference that would be destroyed if it could be explained, somehow superior to you. I have, in the current teen-age patois, "ranked you out" simply by identifying with the winner. If Willie Mays hits a home run "for me," I stand tall because I *am,* in a small, nonsensical sense, Willie Mays.

* Inasmuch as they had to install a toilet for the convenience of the carriage trade, the management tacked on another for the adjoining press box, and this was a little victory for Lou Effrat of the New York *Times*. Up to then reporters had to use the men's room in the Stadium Club, and Effrat for several years had conducted a lonely crusade against the necessity of "putting on a coat to go to the bathroom." The comfort station is known in the trade as the Effrat Room.

219

The Decline and Fall of the New York Yankees

Fandom, however, has a masochistic alter ego, most clearly manifested in the Dodger fan of the 1930s or the Giant fan of the 1940s. If my team loses, I suffer with them. I despise their failures and deficiencies as I despise my own. But I pity them as I feel sorry for myself, and I excuse them as I make excuses for myself. They are losers because they are underprivileged, and unlucky. They have not been given the tools to do the job, and above all they have been badly used by their bosses. Given the chance, they would certainly be winners. There must be some reason for their failure, because the simple fact that they are incompetent would be tough to face.

A case study in this phenomenon was readily available to the Yankee management last fall, right in The House That Ruth Built. Suddenly a season ticket to a Giant football game, a status symbol in New York for a decade, had become an emblem of failure and an object of ridicule. Suddenly coach Allie Sherman, the Practically Peerless Leader,* had to be hustled off the field after the game by a platoon of cops lest he be strung up by his 10-year contract. But the 62,700-odd front-runners, waving bedsheet banners (in Yankee Stadium, yet) and singing songs that called for Allie's departure, weren't really manic. The fact that they were identified with a lousy team was dawning, and they were making excuses. They'll learn to love their losers and suffer along as they sing along, but it takes time when you've been spoiled.

Being a fan, or a follower, is a silly occupation but it is also a very real, very personal occupation. The average fan, alas, except for an autograph or a quick handshake at a communion

* This is a term originally applied by the peerless Red Smith to Leo Durocher.

220

breakfast, is denied the opportunity to make the identification as personal as he would like it—to touch the hem of his hero's garment or hear his voice. The voice he hears is that of his interlocutor, the broadcaster. On his car radio or his living-room television, the broadcaster is his closest, most personal association with "his" team. Whether any personal appeal of the broadcaster himself comes across is secondary, because the electronic manifestation is the average fan's greatest exposure to his team. For every minute it takes to read an account of a baseball game over the morning coffee, it takes an hour to watch it on television. For every game he sees live, the average fan takes a dozen or more through the tube. Harry Carey in St. Louis, Bob Prince in Pittsburgh or Russ Hodges in San Francisco exults with him in victory and laments with him in defeat. There is common cause, and identification. The tone of Mel Allen's voice was almost as indicative as a scoreboard.

Red Barber had, in addition to his singular skills, great personal appeal for a very long time. At a time for the changing of the New York Yankees' "image"—a word which, to his everlasting credit, Michael Burke does not include in his vocabulary—the first public act of the new, climate-changing CBS administration was the climate-chilling business of firing Red Barber. Burke, as an OSS agent during World War II and the manager of a Ringling Bros. circus that was going out of style, had taken a number of calculated risks before. But didn't this one worry him just a little?

"Sure I was worried," Burke said. "I still am. The public relations facet was carefully considered. I certainly didn't enjoy it. But it was something that had to be done."

The difficult Mike Burke had done immediately, but the

impossible was going to take a little longer. As Christmas neared, the fact that he hadn't been able to *do* very much in his first "almost 100 days" about the Yankees' plight had little dimmed his bright faith that a number of things *could* be done. Burke the phrasemaker had analyzed "the problem in the round," diagnosed its cause as "the lethargy of success" and prescribed a direct course for its cure: "You have to pay attention to your business." Burke the getter-of-things-done was paying as much as 12 hours' worth of attention a day, as many as seven days a week. And Burke the optimist, like Tom Sawyer whitewashing the fence, was exhorting his staff to recognize the excitement he had found in the bleak situation.

"There obviously was a loosening of the fabric in recent years," he said, "and we're going to have to live with a bad situation for a while. The staff will have to be intent on the job, but they don't have to wear iron pants. This is a great opportunity because the circumstance—the Yankees in depression—is unique, a once-in-a-lifetime thing. We have the opportunity to create a whole new level of excitement for Yankee fans. Almost everything has to be different, and we have to change it."

What Burke seemed to be saying is that there must be a great variation in approach between promoting a perennial winner and selling a loser (an experience he had in the 1950s in running the big-top circus, which kept returning to the vacant lot at the edge of the city and finding Levittown). "Even if we were a winner," Burke insisted, and he regularly insists on this point, "we'd still have to change every goddamn thing. Everything we're planning on would be operative and applicable if the Yankees were still champions. We're going to be a loser for a few years, and certainly we're planning promotions. But not gimmicks. You can't create or re-create an 'image' synthetically. That word itself is synthetic. You have to do something genuine."

Like, for example, what? "Well, first there's the physical problem of having a 43-year-old stadium," Burke said. "We want to open next season with a completely new look. We're painting the Stadium, inside and out, and lighting it, inside and out. We want everything about the Yankees to be as attractive as we can make it."

Such deference to the modern preoccupation with the package first and the product second seems dangerously close to image-renovating—aesthetic, if not synthetic. But if Burke is an optimist, he is a realist. "You do have to pay more attention to packaging your product these days," he said. "You have to consider the competitive forces. You can't let somebody else's game, or some other form of recreation, become more attractive than your own."

It is indicative of Burke's realistic approach that he is not wringing his hands about the architecture and location of the Stadium, the twin rationales that were issued with ever-increasing frequency as the Yankees' attendance drooped. It is a line that has been given the same unquestioning acceptance the New York press has traditionally accorded Yankee casuistry. As recently as last October as good a reporter as Leonard Koppett of the New York *Times* went for it. "The one overriding blemish" of CBS's new acquisition, he wrote, was the Stadium itself. "So magnificent when built," Koppett said, "it is now obsolete structurally, hemmed in by what many consider a declining neighborhood, choked for parking space, less accessible through deteriorating public transportation and not as attractive as the city-built Shea Stadium."

The Decline and Fall of the New York Yankees

By the same standard, St. Patrick's Cathedral is obsolete structurally, but its magnificence does not seem to have diminished. Certainly anybody building a stadium in 1972 would be unlikely to choose the neo-Gothic (if that's what it is) style that seemed such a good idea a half-century earlier. But Yankee Stadium last visited was in a considerably better state of repair than the Roman Colosseum.

The "declining neighborhood" bit is a euphemism for objection to a high incidence of Negroes (or, in the particular instance of New York, Puerto Ricans) in the vicinity. The ethnic factor usually runs in inverse proportion to paid attendance, so of course the environs of 161st Street and River Avenue in the Bronx deteriorated frightfully in 1966, when Yankee patronage sank to 1,123,648. The theory is that fans prurient in their desire to see the ol' home team are staying away in regimental numbers for fear of the mugging, raping and murdering that goes on nightly in back of the left-field stands. Somehow, however, the working press have not yet adopted the habit of coveying up in self-protection to leave Yankee Stadium after a night game, as they did at the old Polo Grounds, and still do at Comiskey Park in Chicago.*

Riding the D train on the Independent subway line, or the Jerome Avenue El was never an exhilarating experience, and the only aspect of it that seems to have become less pleasant since Lou Gehrig's time is that it now costs 20 cents instead of a nickel. In Detroit, the management would be very happy

---

* A police desk is maintained nightly at the exit of Comiskey Park, and on it is a blotter to record the horrors that are wrought in the Negro slums that surround it. A reporter once leafed through the book and found that in two weeks the constabulary had apprehended two drunks and a pickpocket.

if there were one subway line, or any other form of rapid transit, that debarked customers at the corner of Michigan and Trumbull. They have a parking problem, too, and so in some degree do nine other major-league establishments. None as severe as the Yankees', possibly. But Yankee Stadium's parking situation was just as "choked" in 1961. Still, 1,747,-736 followers battled their way in to see the M&M home-run contest. The package was the same, but the product was better.

Burke does not rule out the possibility that the Yankees may eventually become roommates with the Mets in Shea Stadium. But his belief that Yankee Stadium will not immediately become a haunted house is underlined by the fact that he has retained engineers to study the feasibility of moving the Yankees' executive offices into the Stadium. "I believe a baseball office should be in a baseball atmosphere," Burke says, which is one of the milder surprises you get out of this remarkable man. From the tips of his Italian-made shoes to the top of the wavy gray hair that cascades around his ears, Michael Burke seems to *belong* at Fifth Avenue and 57th Street, within a few long strides of the Oak Room at the Plaza. He looked like the star halfback he was at Penn. He looked like the top-grade OSS agent he was during World War II. Tall and trim at age 50, he looks good sitting on a horse in Central Park early in the morning, before most junior executives are out of their silk pajamas. If there is any validity to such a concept, Mike Burke *looks* like a hero. And in the opinion of Fred W. Friendly, news director at CBS until a political scrum early in 1966, he is one, "not because of the cloak-and-dagger stuff, but because he's a moral man." Another former associate says: "Mike's a man. He'll go to the

225

guy on the downside and give him a pat on the back. He's always been direct and straightforward. He's not an intriguer."

Directly and straightforwardly, Burke fielded the question whether previous Yankee administrations—from the president to the ticket takers—had taken themselves too seriously. "In my measure, yes," he said. "I cannot knock the successful approach of another man *in his time,* but in this time I believe we need to inculcate a sense of humor. How? By example, not by ukase. You have to communicate your own philosophy, and humor is part of my philosophy. You have to laugh. Laughter is an integral part of life, in a ball club or in a night club. We have many problems, and we will discuss them seriously, but you can break the intensity of the discussion with a quip. Losing has nothing to do with it. It is the only way I can live, in any context."

One new Yankee promotion that figured to bring a few laughs was an evening radio program in which manager Ralph Houk and some of his players, as well as other officials including Burke himself, answered phoned-in questions from fans about what was wrong with the Yankees and what they intended to do about it. "The program is consistent with our policy of being open," Burke said. "The fans have a right to know all they can about the Yankees. So let's tell them what they want to know. Let's expose ourselves."

Burke first exposed himself on Sunday afternoon, September 25, when he entered the Stadium and headed for a box next to the Yankee dugout. He was, in his first official visitation, eschewing the presidential box on the façade of the first-base mezzanine, where short days before Dan Topping had looked grimly down at what was left of his Yankees. Burke proposes to leave the VIP box to visiting dignitaries because, among other reasons, he is a fan. "I saw my first game when I was 12," he said. "Babe Ruth hit a home run. When I played ball as a teen-ager I used to pretend I was Frank Crosetti." ("I suppose I'll be the first one to get fired," Crosetti said when he was told of Burke's emulation.)

"As I approached the box," Burke recalls, "a bunch of kids 12 or 14 years old broke through the barrier and asked for my autograph. I guess they recognized me because I had been given the television-news treatment in the few days since my induction. The cops, from the Burns Detective Agency, started to chase them away and I told them to leave them alone. I guess I must have signed 30 or 40. I kept asking the kids if they didn't really want Mickey or Pepitone, but they said, 'No, we want you, Mike.'

" 'Call him Mr. Burke,' some lady said, but I said, 'No, that's all right. It's Mike.' It began to dawn on me then what a hell of an opportunity we had. Mike, instead of Mr. Burke. That was the way we wanted to be. But I saw some of the problems that afternoon, too. A couple more kids found me in the box in the second inning and I signed for them. There were a few more in the next few innings, but then I noticed the cop was chasing them away. I asked him what he was doing and he said he had a note from one of those management people telling him to keep the kids away from me. I told him to tear the goddamn thing up.

"I like crowds," Burke says, "and I like kids, especially kids who are interested in baseball. Yes, I know some people will say I'm acting on a calculated basis, but I wasn't doing anything for effect. I genuinely like doing something that gives someone a sense of pleasure.

"It happened again on my way out of the park after the

game. Kids tried to get to me and the cops pulled them off. They were just little kids, and the cops were rough. I gave them hell. I know the cops didn't think my attitude was for real, and I suppose some of our officials didn't believe it either. There was an air of consternation. The cops seemed dismayed that I didn't want to be protected.

"I suppose," Mike Burke said directly and straightforwardly, "they were used to a guy who needed that sort of thing to satisfy his own ego."

Burke seemed surprised that such tight-security policies existed in the Stadium, but they were more the rule than the exception. There is a troubled kind of man who becomes a warden as soon as somebody puts a uniform and a tin badge on him, and for years it seemed the Yankees had established some kind of scouting system to find them. A reporter attempting to do a crowd-interview story—a project that can be performed without obstruction in any other baseball park in the United States—could flash all the credentials known to his trade and still be barred from the box seats until he produced a written pass, signed by a Yankee official. Trying to get through the Stadium Club to the press box without a coat on was like trying to get past the Russian MPs at Checkpoint Charlie—or as difficult as trying to convince the Bronx borough president that you're a good neighbor when you keep your offices next door to Tiffany's and hold your press conferences at the Savoy Hilton, both a two-dollar cab ride from the Bronx County Court House.

The Yankee dreadnaught scraped the bottom that dreary, misty day last September when the turnstiles clicked only 413 times. It was a pitiful, humiliating scene in a proud old edifice that had once vibrated sympathetically to the cheers of 81,841

228

in a single afternoon. But a man with imagination could see opportunity in even such a debacle, and a man did. Leonard Koppett of the *Times* suggested that the Yankees reward the loyalty of the 413 by giving them free tickets to another game, on a better day, as the Dodger management had done in a comparable circumstance in Ebbets Field. Bob Fishel, the publicity director, relayed the suggestion to Dan Topping Jr., who was sitting in as general manager in the interregnum. "We don't do that sort of thing," Topping said.

It was the sort of occasion when Fishel would have to shrug, as he has had to shrug at a thousand suggestions and complaints, and say, as he has had to say a thousand times, "I know. But what can I do?"

Burke quickly discovered that Fishel usually does know. "Every time I think I come up with a new idea," Burke said after his first 30 days, "it seems Fishel has not only thought of it but he's prepared a sheaf of foolscap on the subject. I know his hands have been tied, but they won't be."

If Mike Burke hadn't been taken to see Babe Ruth that day in 1928, he might be leafing through foolscap at Creative Playthings or Fender Guitar. These were two of the companies he found for CBS to buy in its diversification program since 1962. They paid $14,000,000 for Fender Guitar—almost the exact price of the Yankees—and as one hootenanny led to another they had to build another factory. Burke credits Dr. Frank Stanton, CBS president, with the idea of buying the Yankees. "It was a marvelous thing for us to do," Burke says. "First, the Yankees were synonymous with quality, the best of its kind, and we [at CBS] were egotistical enough to think we were the best in our field. Secondly, baseball is a form of entertainment. Third, CBS has a stake in the success of all

229

sports. We also thought we could be constructive citizens sitting at the baseball council tables. There are 19 other businessmen sitting at those tables, and they aren't going to give CBS any special advantage. I'm going to be looking at any television deal from a Yankee perspective."

But by the time Burke took full command, the Yankees were no longer synonymous with quality. Near the end of his first 100 days, they were buying Dick Howser, a journeyman who had found ways to get on base with reasonable frequency but who couldn't play shortstop very well. Nobody knew who was on second, and Whitey Ford had his 38th birthday and another ugly surgical scar on his left shoulder. Branch Rickey used to preach the wisdom of selling or trading a player (like Dixie Walker) a year too soon rather than a year too late; Topping and Webb seemed to have unloaded their property at just about the propitious time.

"We do have a long way to go," Burke agreed over the round table he uses in lieu of a desk, "but I guess I was sired by Silky Sullivan. I like to come from behind. Hell, I *wanted* this job, very much. I can't imagine a better one. I've had fun from the first day. You have to like your job. You have to love it, and be totally absorbed in what you're doing, and I am. If somebody would pay the butcher and the baker and put my kids through school, I'd do this for nothing."

"I'm not going to disassociate myself from any decision," Burke said when asked about the few trades the Yankees had been able to make, "because in the end somebody has to say yes or no. I thought I could pull the Yankees out of this decline, but I didn't think I could do it alone. I do think I've put together a management team that can. With Houk on the field, with his great talent as a leader, and Lee MacPhail in the front office, a solid, thoroughly knowledgeable baseball man, and myself, we have a team with balance, each man with his own field of expertise.

"I'm going to throw away the old book on the Yankees," Mike Burke concluded. "If you have preconceived ideas about the Yankees, I say you should throw that book away, because we're going to write a new one. As a beginning, a preface, perhaps, the operative word to the press is going to be availability." He had already established that fact.

Mike Burke has a Navy Cross, which he earned for one of his more outstanding espionage capers in the OSS, and of course he is proud of it. It is not his only trophy. There is the Chipmunk sweatshirt he earned at the Baseball Writers' annual outing at Bear Mountain Inn in October 1966. He played first base in the baseball game, and rather well, but he didn't have to. Burke would have been awarded the sweatshirt, a symbol of a very special status in show sport, just for showing up. He was amazed to be told that Dan Topping, in almost two decades as Yankee president, had never shown up.

The Chipmunks are the New Breed of sports reporters, their outstanding characteristics being irreverence and curiosity. They interview not only the manager but the players, and they ask rather startling questions—questions that address themselves to the players as human beings rather than to the repetitious, March-to-October tedium of runs, hits and errors. Some of the Chipmunks' "offbeat" questions are asked just for the hell of it or as opening gambits to a line of questioning that might produce information more interesting than the pitcher's belief that the home run was hit off a hanging curve ball. And some of the questions are really far out.

The Decline and Fall of the New York Yankees

Burke's sweatshirt was presented by Stan Isaacs, columnist of *Newsday,* the Long Island daily that scouts the White House for talent. Though he is an aboriginal Chipmunk, Isaacs was acting ex officio; the entire spontaneous essence of the Chipmunks would be destroyed if they did anything as traditional as electing officials. Isaacs, however, was exercising the prerogative that accrues to a sort of club champion. Until somebody topped it, he had the distinction of having asked the most impertinent question in Chipmunk history. Ralph Terry, being interviewed after a signal victory for the Yankees, mentioned the fact that his wife had been feeding the new baby when he telephoned her to share the triumph.

"Breast," asked Isaacs, with pencil poised, "or bottle?"

The Chipmunks were conceived in the related beliefs that (a) since the bread-and-butter guys of the working press will never earn the considerable rewards given superannuated shortstops for prattling into a microphone, they might as well get some fun out of their ignoble toil, and that (b) if they made no attempt to relate the billion-dollar industry of show sport to the society in which it exists, they wouldn't be doing anything but writing stories about games.

And the Chipmunks were named in opprobrium. Opinion differs as to whether it was Joe Trimble of the *News* or Jimmy Cannon who dubbed them, but it could have been any one of the old-line writers whose idea of a depth question is "Who are we going to pitch tomorrow, Skipper?" (A Chipmunk does not feel "we" about the team he is covering, which is why he is a reporter rather than a writer.) Some traditionalist, in any case, observed a group of reporters chattering about an intriguing angle they had discovered and growled, "They look just like a bunch of chipmunks." There is a theory that the dental structure of Phil Pepe of the New York *World Journal Tribune* and/or Maury Allen of the New York *Post,* certified Chipmunks both, inspired the name, but this is untested.

To say that *Newsday* was the cradle of Chipmunkery would be as oversimplified as to say that the American Revolution began at Bunker Hill. It is statistically indisputable that *Newsday* sent more Chipmunks to the big league than any other publication, but Chipmunkery is much more a matter of attitude than of geography. Stan Hochman of the Philadelphia *News* is too dignified to identify, and Pete Waldmeier of the Detroit *News* would laugh at the idea, as he laughs at almost everything. But in their hearts they know they are as much Chipmunks in spirit as George Vecsey, Steve Jacobson or Bob Sales, all *Newsday* originals.* Chipmunks are as Chipmunks do.

Whatever Chipmunkery was, it was inimical to the Yankee Way. It was informal. It was nosy. It was fun. Chipmunk was a term that caught on quickly in the Yankee clubhouse as an epithet for a reporter who asked too many questions. Some of the needling—Mantle's, for one—was good-natured. But to the management, Chipmunkery, which existed for several years before it was typed and identified, represented a threat to a kind of security in which the Yankees issued only that information they deemed fit to print, and the writers settled for it. Any injury, for example, was described as "a day-to-day

* Leonard Koppett of the *Times,* in an attempt to delineate Chipmunkery for *Sporting News* in 1966, listed youth as one of seven requisites. This does not stand analysis. The author of this tome is a charter Chipmunk, and he was 40 years old at the investiture. Isaacs isn't so young, either; he just acts that way.

proposition," even though it was obvious that the injured player was *hors de combat* for two weeks. The player knew how he felt, but saying so would have violated the company line. So he didn't.

An outstanding example of the dangers of Chipmunkery took place in 1961, when Maris was hitting the home runs. He was up in the 40's, some days and games ahead of Ruth's record, when the Angels came into Yankee Stadium one night. With two outs and a runner at third, Maris pushed a bunt toward third, beating it out and batting in the "insurance" run of a 4–2 victory. What a story: A guy who had the world with a fence around it if he could hit 60 home runs sacrificed himself to help the team, just as prep-school kids used to do in those old Ralph Henry Barbour novels. Hell of a story. All it needed was a little implementation. How often, manager Houk was asked, had Maris bunted for a base hit?

"Oh, he does it a lot," Houk said. A lot? Houk sized up the reporter, one who had not been traveling with the Yankees. "He does it a lot on the road," the manager said.

Around the corner in the quiet dressing room, Roger Maris was tying his tie. Asked how many times he had bunted for a base hit during the season, Maris pondered a moment. "I think," he said, "that I did it once, in Kansas City. But I'm not sure." Chipmunkery hadn't been given its name yet, but it was becoming a problem. It was becoming tougher and tougher to manage the news.

Near the end of the 1966 season it had become impossible. Even the apologists had begun asking embarrassing questions as the Yankees dropped through the bottom of the league. With two weeks of humiliation left on the schedule, Topping threw in the towel and CBS owned the whole sticky mess. Now, less than a month later, here was Michael Burke, the new president, cavorting in a silly game with the very people who had been irreverent toward the Yankees in the waning days of their eminence. And wearing a, for Christ's sake, Chipmunk sweatshirt.

Burke's 50-year-old bones were rattled in a collision at first base with Paul Zimmerman, a large reporter who plays games with precipitous abandon. Burke's trousers split in that embarrassing area where men's trousers split, but he played on. At the end, when he peeled the sweatshirt to turn it in, Isaacs arbitrarily ruled that he could keep it. That in itself did not mean that Mike Burke was a full-fledged Chipmunk, but it did mean he qualified on at least one count: the basic unstuffiness. The new president of the New York Yankees did not take himself overly seriously. Veterans of the Stadium scene (a phrase journalists use when they are quoting themselves) could remember ushers who were more pompous. "I'm going to keep that shirt," Burke said. "I'm proud of it."

Burke's peerage had been suspect since his first press conference, which he pronounced "encouraging" because of the note of informality it sounded. "Availability," he said, "is the operative word. There was a complacency in the Yankee organization. Yes, some part of it may have 'filtered up' from the success on the field. That is only human nature.

"But I feel that if there is to be a different climate, it must come through me, and it must be genuine. I do believe that we can change that climate—not immediately, of course, but in a relatively short time. I would say that the haughty, cold, remote Yankees are a thing of the past.

"But the pride of the Yankees will exist. Not arrogant pride, but self-respect. I am immensely proud, in the best sense, of being a Yankee."

The new president of the Yankees is proud of his Chipmunk

sweatshirt, too, and this raises serious implications. Lee Mac-Phail, in his first pronunciamento after taking over as general manager, played a variation on the theme Yankee officials had been sounding since Stengel and Weiss were dispatched after the 1960 season. Winning, he said, "does not have to be a grim business."

If this is so, it is possible that losing does not have to be a grim business. It may be a very, very long time before the Yankees have a winning team again. But there could be a Yankee team that could "lace itself" to the community—one that could have fans, instead of followers, who could identify with the team, and suffer with it, and enjoy it. Maybe, just maybe, the Yankees could be incompetent but cute.

And if that ever happens, as the old reporter said when the young reporter pointed toward the sunset and asked if that was east, you got a hell of a story.

Statistics

THE STATISTICS in this appendix, many of them never before tabulated, demonstrate the Yankee domination of American League play in every critical category from 1920, the year Babe Ruth came to the team, to 1964, the year of the last Yankee pennant. Where appropriate, the tables list the 1965-66 season figures separately to show the sharp decline in the Yankees' performance from their long-maintained standards.

In all of the statistics, prior franchise records are included in the figures of the current clubs. Thus:

Baltimore includes St. Louis (1920-1953).

Kansas City includes Philadelphia (1920-1954).

Minnesota includes Washington (1920-1960).

The California Angels and the new Washington franchise entered the league in 1961, when the ten-club, 162-game schedule was begun. Because they have only been in operation for six seasons, their cumulative statistics are not comparable with those of teams in operation previously.

The statistical tables were compiled by the Elias Sports Bureau of New York.

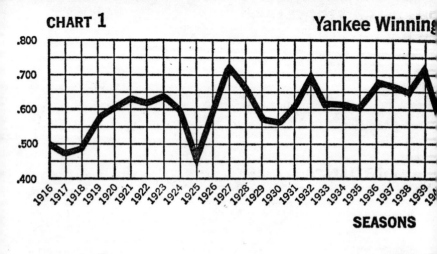

CHART 1 — Yankee Winning

SEASONS

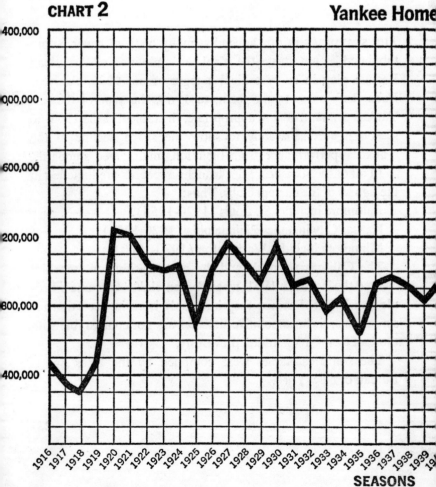

CHART 2 — Yankee Home

SEASONS

Percentage (1916–1966)

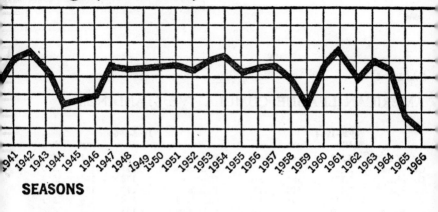

1941 1942 1943 1944 1945 1946 1947 1948 1949 1950 1951 1952 1953 1954 1955 1956 1957 1958 1959 1960 1961 1962 1963 1964 1965 1966

SEASONS

Attendance (1916–1966)

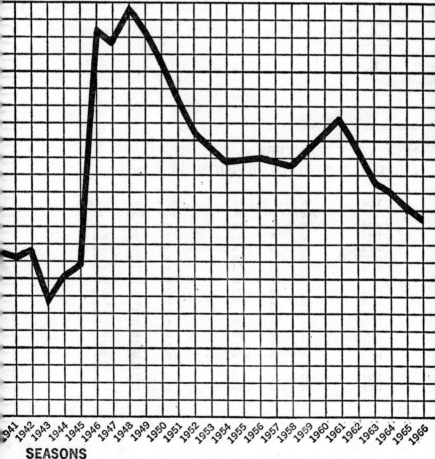

1941 1942 1943 1944 1945 1946 1947 1948 1949 1950 1951 1952 1953 1954 1955 1956 1957 1958 1959 1960 1961 1962 1963 1964 1965 1966

SEASONS

TABLE I

AMERICAN LEAGUE CUMULATIVE STANDINGS

	1920-1964				1965-1966		
	Won	*Lost*	*Pct.*		*Won*	*Lost*	*Pct.*
YANKEES	4,292	2,643	.619	Baltimore	191	131	.593
Cleveland	3,706	3,231	.534	Minnesota	191	133	.590
Detroit	3,571	3,381	.514	Chicago	178	146	.549
Chicago	3,413	3,510	.493	Detroit	177	147	.546
Boston	3,333	3,595	.481	Cleveland	168	156	.519
Minnesota	3,319	3,608	.479	California	155	169	.478
California	308	338	.477	YANKEES	147	174	.458
Baltimore	3,114	3,816	.449	Washington	141	180	.439
Kansas City	3,076	3,842	.445	Boston	134	190	.414
Washington	239	407	.370	Kansas City	133	189	.413
League	28,371	28,371		League	1,615	1,615	
Yankees	15.1%	9.3%		Yankees	9.1%	10.8%	

TABLE II

NEW YORK YANKEES vs.
FIRST AND SECOND DIVISION, 1920-1966

Year	vs. First Division			vs. Second Division		
	Won	*Lost*	*Pct.*	*Won*	*Lost*	*Pct.*
1920	37	29	.561	58	30	.659
1921	40	25	.615	58	30	.659
1922	40	26	.606	54	34	.614
1923	38	28	.576	60	26	.698
1924	30	36	.455	59	27	.686
1925	35	53	.398	34	32	.515
1926	32	34	.485	59	29	.670
1927	42	24	.636	68	20	.773
1928	41	25	.621	60	28	.682
1929	30	36	.455	58	30	.659
1930	27	39	.409	59	29	.670
1931	33	33	.500	61	26	.701
1932	40	26	.606	67	21	.761
1933	33	30	.524	58	29	.667
1934	33	33	.500	61	27	.693
1935	37	28	.569	52	32	.619

TABLE II

New York Yankees vs.
First and Second Division, 1920-1966 (*continued*)

Year	vs. First Division			vs. Second Division		
	Won	*Lost*	*Pct.*	*Won*	*Lost*	*Pct.*
1936	41	24	.631	61	27	.693
1937	41	25	.621	61	27	.693
1938	38	27	.585	61	26	.701
1939	41	22	.651	65	23	.739
1940	31	35	.470	57	31	.648
1941	38	28	.576	63	25	.716
1942	40	26	.606	63	25	.716
1943	36	30	.545	62	26	.705
1944	29	37	.439	54	34	.614
1945	28	38	.424	53	33	.616
1946	31	35	.470	56	32	.636
1947	42	24	.636	55	33	.625
1948	32	34	.485	62	26	.705
1949	36	30	.545	61	27	.693
1950	38	28	.576	60	28	.682
1951	40	26	.606	58	30	.659
1952	39	27	.591	56	32	.636
1953	35	30	.538	64	22	.744
1954	39	27	.591	64	24	.727
1955	34	32	.515	62	26	.705
1956	39	27	.591	58	30	.659
1957	40	26	.606	58	30	.659
1958	43	23	.652	49	39	.557
1959	28	38	.424	51	37	.580
1960	41	25	.621	56	32	.636
1961	45	27	.625	64	26	.711
1962	42	30	.583	54	36	.600
1963	43	28	.606	61	29	.678
1964	41	31	.569	58	32	.644
1965	34	56	.378	43	29	.597
1966	35	55	.389	35	34	.507
Totals	1728	1456	.543	2711	1361	.666

OFFENSIVE RECORDS

TABLE III

BATTING AVERAGE

	1920-1964				1965-1966		
	At Bats	Hits	Avg.		At Bats	Hits	Avg.
YANKEES	240,252	66,254	.276	Minnesota	10,878	2,738	.252
Detroit	241,251	65,975	.273	Baltimore	10,979	2,725	.248
Cleveland	239,808	65,386	.273	Boston	10,986	2,696	.245
Boston	239,113	64,100	.268	Detroit	10,873	2,661	.245
Minnesota	239,891	64,193	.268	Cleveland	10,942	2,667	.244
Chicago	238,126	63,511	.267	Chicago	10,858	2,589	.238
Kansas City	238,151	63,138	.265	Kansas City	10,722	2,552	.238
Baltimore	238,660	63,022	.264	California	10,715	2,523	.235
California	21,791	5,383	.247	YANKEES	10,800	2,540	.235
Washington	21,692	5,160	.238	Washington	10,691	2,472	.231
League	1,958,735	526,122	.269	League	108,444	26,163	.241
Yankees	12.3%	12.6%		Yankees	10.0%	9.7%	

TABLE IV

RUNS SCORED

	1920-1964		1965-1966	
	Runs			Runs
YANKEES	37,474	Minnesota		1,437
Detroit	34,146	Detroit		1,399
Cleveland	33,256	Baltimore		1,396
Boston	32,342	Boston		1,324
Minnesota	31,729	Cleveland		1,237
Kansas City	31,109	YANKEES		1,222
Chicago	30,898	Chicago		1,221
Baltimore	30,753	Kansas City		1,149
California	2,603	Washington		1,148
Washington	2,373	California		1,131
League	266,683	League		12,664
Yankees	14.1%	Yankees		9.6%

TABLE V

HOME RUNS

1920-1964		1965-1966	
	Home Runs		*Home Runs*
YANKEES	6,463	Detroit	341
Cleveland	4,526	YANKEES	311
Detroit	4,384	Cleveland	311
Kansas City	4,234	Boston	310
Boston	4,115	Baltimore	300
Baltimore	3,956	Minnesota	294
Minnesota	3,262	Washington	262
Chicago	2,886	California	214
California	523	Chicago	212
Washington	514	Kansas City	180
League	34,863	League	2,735
Yankees	18.5%	Yankees	11.4%

TABLE VI

INDIVIDUAL YANKEE BATTING RECORDS, 1920-1966 (*100 or more games*)

Player and Position	G	AB	H	HR	RBI	Avg.
Ruth, Babe—OF	2083	7217	2518	659	1975	.349
Gehrig, Lou—1B	2163	8001	2721	493	1991	.340
Johnson, Ernie—SS	159	327	107	9	37	.327
DiMaggio, Joe—OF	1736	6821	2214	361	1537	.325
Combs, Earle—OF	1454	5748	1866	58	629	.325
Pratt, Del—2B	154	574	180	4	97	.314
Dickey, Bill—C	1789	6300	1969	202	1209	.313
Meusel, Bob—OF	1294	5032	1565	146	1005	.311
Paschal, Ben—OF	346	749	232	22	134	.310
Mantle, Mickey—OF	2113	7227	2204	496	1400	.305
Chapman, Ben—OF	910	3539	1079	60	589	.305
Witt, Whitey—OF	464	1764	530	11	135	.300
Rice, Harry—OF	100	346	103	7	75	.298
Pipp, Wally—1B	817	3111	923	46	508	.297
Schang, Wally—C	529	1627	483	16	213	.297
Robertson, Gene—3B	173	560	165	1	71	.295
Skowron, Bill—1B	1087	3748	1103	165	672	.294
Lazzeri, Tony—2B	1658	6094	1784	169	1154	.293
Hill, Jesse—OF	107	392	115	4	33	.293
Silvera, Charlie—C	201	429	125	1	50	.291
Selkirk, George—OF	846	2790	810	108	576	.290
Rolfe, Red—3B	1175	4827	1394	69	497	.289
Baker, Frank—3B	163	564	162	16	107	.287
Keller, Charlie—OF	1066	3678	1053	183	723	.286
Dugan, Joe—3B	785	3043	871	22	320	.286
Reese, Jim—2B	142	433	124	6	44	.286
Berra, Yogi—C	2116	7546	2148	358	1430	.285
Woodling, Gene—OF	698	2272	648	51	336	.285
Koenig, Mark—SS	567	2233	637	15	249	.285
Miller, Elmer—OF	107	414	118	5	50	.285
Hoag, Myril—OF	471	1228	349	11	185	.284
Robinson, Aaron—C	233	743	211	29	124	.284
Hassett, Buddy—1B	132	538	153	5	48	.284
McQuinn, George—1B	238	819	232	24	121	.283
Martin, Herschel—OF	202	736	208	16	100	.283
Howard, Elston—C	1426	4845	1366	158	716	.282
Henrich, Tommy—OF	1284	4603	1297	183	795	.282
Sewell, Joe—2B	389	1511	426	19	186	.282
Byrd, Sammy—OF	564	1143	321	27	155	.281
Brown, Bobby—3B	548	1619	452	22	237	.279
Peckinpaugh, Roger—SS	288	1111	310	16	125	.279
Bauer, Hank—OF	1406	4784	1326	158	654	.277

TABLE VI

Individual Yankee Batting Records, 1920-1966 (*100 or more games*) (*continued*)

Player and Position	G	AB	H	HR	RBI	Avg.
McDougald, Gil—2B	1336	4676	1291	112	576	.276
Bodie, Ping—OF	160	558	154	7	91	.276
Lindell, John—OF	742	2568	707	63	369	.275
Johnson, Billy—3B	735	2524	694	45	388	.275
Etten, Nick—1B	568	2044	562	63	358	.275
Stirnweiss, George—2B	884	3281	899	27	253	.274
Lary, Lyn—SS	496	1718	471	21	237	.274
Rizzuto, Phil—SS	1661	5816	1588	38	563	.273
Siebern, Norm—OF	308	1002	274	29	129	.273
Rosar, Buddy—C	252	751	205	7	119	.273
Noren, Irv—OF	498	1451	394	31	198	.272
Powell, Jake—OF	272	970	264	13	125	.272
Gordon, Joe—2B	1000	3686	1000	153	617	.271
Ward, Aaron—2B	853	3047	826	45	386	.271
Lumpe, Jerry—2B	159	442	120	3	49	.271
Lewis, George—OF	107	365	99	4	61	.271
Collins, Pat—C	264	677	182	20	85	.269
Fewster, Chick—OF	131	361	97	3	29	.269
Walker, Dixie—OF	131	388	104	16	58	.268
Cooke, Dusty—OF	122	255	68	7	35	.267
Richardson, Bobby—2B	1412	5386	1432	34	389	.266
Kubek, Tony—SS	1092	4167	1109	57	373	.266
Carey, Andy—3B	688	2130	567	47	259	.266
Grimes, Oscar—3B	281	926	246	9	96	.266
Cerv, Bob—OF	379	772	205	26	118	.266
Gonzalez, Pedro—2B	101	143	38	0	6	.266
Maris, Roger—OF	850	3007	797	203	547	.265
Tresh, Tom—OF	771	2822	744	114	379	.264
Niarhos, Gus—C	153	311	82	0	27	.264
Mize, John—1B	375	870	230	44	179	.264
Clarke, Horace—2B	147	420	111	7	36	.264
Coleman, Gerry—2B	723	2119	558	16	217	.263
Lopez, Hector—OF	864	2510	658	69	322	.262
Martin, Billy—2B	527	1717	449	30	188	.262
Hemsley, Rollie—C	174	549	144	4	65	.262
Bengough, Ben—C	317	846	217	0	78	.257
Durocher, Leo—SS	210	638	164	0	63	.257
Heffner, Don—2B	161	526	135	0	60	.257
Collins, Joe—1B	908	2329	596	86	329	.256
Savage, Don—3B	105	297	76	4	27	.256
Pepitone, Joe—1B	675	2447	624	111	351	.255
Scott, Everett—SS	481	1698	431	13	173	.254
Slaughter, Enos—OF	350	663	168	16	98	.253
Stainback, Tuck—OF	211	646	163	5	47	.252
McNally, Mike—3B	202	465	117	1	45	.252
Glenn, Joe—C	138	385	97	1	56	.252
Grabowski, John—C	167	456	114	1	51	.250
Saltzgaver, Jack—3B	226	647	161	10	71	.249

245

TABLE VI

Individual Yankee Batting Records,
1920-1966 (*100 or more games*) (*continued*)

Player and Position	G	AB	H	HR	RBI	Avg.
Durst, Cedric—OF	240	485	121	6	71	.249
Jensen, Jackie—OF	108	257	64	9	32	.249
Priddy, Gerry—2B	115	363	90	3	54	.248
Dahlgren, Babe—1B	327	1143	283	27	163	.248
Metheny, Bud—OF	376	1390	344	31	156	.247
Crosetti, Frank—SS	1683	6276	1541	98	646	.246
Linz, Phil—3B	354	968	238	10	67	.246
Gibbs, Jake—C	108	264	65	5	27	.246
Blanchard, John—C	454	1063	260	64	187	.245
Mapes, Cliff—OF	317	799	196	22	119	.245
Hofmann, Fred—C	212	583	143	7	53	.245
Garback, Mike—C	149	475	116	2	59	.244
Boyer, Clete—3B	1068	3659	882	95	393	.241
Milosevich, Mike—SS	124	381	92	0	39	.241
Gazella, Mike—3B	160	352	85	0	32	.241
Miranda, Willie—SS	140	174	42	2	17	.241
Repoz, Roger—OF	126	262	63	12	37	.240
Sturm, John—1B	124	524	125	3	36	.239
Hunter, Billy—SS	137	330	79	3	31	.239
Jorgens, Arndt—C	306	738	176	4	89	.238
Throneberry, Marv—1B	141	344	82	15	44	.238
White, Roy—OF	129	358	85	7	23	.237
Wanninger, Peewee—INF	117	403	95	1	22	.236
Barker, Ray—1B	159	280	66	10	44	.236
Derry, Russ—OF	116	367	86	17	59	.234
Reed, Jack—OF	222	129	30	1	6	.233
Robinson, Eddie—1B	199	369	85	24	80	.230

DEFENSIVE RECORDS

TABLE VII

OPPONENTS' RUNS ALLOWED

1920-1964	Runs	1965-1966	Runs
California	2,701	Chicago	1,072
Washington	3,037	Baltimore	1,181
YANKEES	28,838	Minnesota	1,181
Cleveland	31,152	Cleveland	1,199
Chicago	31,502	California	1,210
Detroit	32,859	YANKEES	1,216
Minnesota	33,234	Detroit	1,300
Boston	33,439	Washington	1,380
Baltimore	34,751	Kansas City	1,403
Kansas City	35,170	Boston	1,522
League	266,683	League	12,664
Yankees	10.8%	Yankees	9.6%

TABLE VIII

ERRORS

1920-1964	Errors	1965-1966	Errors
Washington	604	Detroit	236
California	668	Baltimore	241
YANKEES	6,833	Cleveland	253
Cleveland	7,236	California	260
Chicago	7,400	Kansas City	278
Detroit	7,469	YANKEES	279
Baltimore	7,527	Washington	285
Minnesota	7,655	Chicago	289
Boston	7,656	Minnesota	312
Kansas City	7,749	Boston	317
League	60,797	League	2,750
Yankees	11.2%	Yankees	10.1%

TABLE IX

DOUBLE PLAYS

1920-1964			1965-1966	
	Double Plays			Double Plays
YANKEES	7,143		California	332
Boston	7,021		YANKEES	308
Minnesota	7,018		Chicago	305
Baltimore	6,987		Kansas City	297
Cleveland	6,944		Baltimore	294
Chicago	6,870		Washington	289
Kansas City	6,710		Boston	281
Detroit	6,531		Minnesota	278
Washington	641		Detroit	267
California	630		Cleveland	258
League	56,495		League	2,909
Yankees	12.6%		Yankees	10.6%

TABLE X

EARNED RUN AVERAGE

1930-1964			1965-1966	
	E.R.A.			E.R.A.
YANKEES	3.56		Chicago	2.85
California	3.61		Minnesota	3.12
Cleveland	3.81		Baltimore	3.15
Chicago	3.88		Cleveland	3.26
Detroit	3.97		YANKEES	3.34
Boston	4.16		California	3.37
Washington	4.17		Detroit	3.59
Minnesota	4.19		Washington	3.82
Baltimore	4.38		Kansas City	3.89
Kansas City	4.58		Boston	4.08
League	4.06		League	3.44

NOTE: *Team Earned Run Averages not available prior to 1930*

TABLE XI

INDIVIDUAL YANKEE PITCHING RECORDS, 1920-1966

(20 or More Wins)

Pitcher	G	IP	SO	W	L	ERA
Ford, Whitey	491	3127	1935	234	102	2.76
Ruffing, Red	426	3168	1540	231	124	3.48
Gomez, Lefty	367	2498	1468	189	101	3.34
Pennock, Herb	346	2189	700	162	90	3.56
Hoyt, Waite	366	2273	713	157	98	3.47
Reynolds, Allie	295	1700	967	131	60	3.30
Raschi, Vic	218	1538	832	120	50	3.47
Lopat, Eddie	217	1497	502	113	59	3.19
Chandler, Spud	211	1485	614	109	43	2.84
Shawkey, Bob	261	1613	788	106	83	3.45
Murphy, Johnny	383	989	369	93	53	3.54
Pipgras, George	247	1343	795	93	64	4.07
Turley, Bob	234	1268	909	82	52	3.62
Bonham, Ernie	158	1178	348	79	50	2.73
Terry, Ralph	210	1198	615	78	59	3.44
Byrne, Tommy	221	994	592	72	40	3.93
Mays, Carl	151	970	219	70	36	3.45
Jones, Sad Sam	202	1090	363	67	56	4.06
Donald, Atley	153	933	369	65	33	3.52
Pearson, Monte	121	826	406	63	28	3.81
Bush, Bullet Joe	115	783	297	62	38	3.44
Page, Joe	278	780	515	57	49	3.44
Borowy, Hank	107	780	340	56	30	2.75
Bouton, Jim	168	924	506	53	50	3.28
Allen, Johnny	94	616	395	50	19	3.78
Shocker, Urban	114	704	168	49	29	3.31
Hadley, Bump	140	753	309	49	31	4.28
Downing, Al	132	842	731	48	39	3.35
Ditmar, Art	168	723	301	47	32	3.24
Johnson, Henry	157	712	409	47	36	4.78
Grim, Bob	146	454	282	45	21	3.35
Larsen, Don	128	656	356	45	24	3.50
Russo, Marius	120	681	311	45	34	3.13
Stafford, Bill	163	730	408	43	35	3.48
Kucks, John	143	673	249	42	35	3.82
Stottlemyre, Mel	87	638	349	41	32	3.00
Broaca, John	99	628	245	40	27	4.04
Bevens, Floyd	96	643	289	40	36	3.08

TABLE XI

Individual Yankee Pitching Records, 1920-1966
(20 or More Wins) (continued)

Pitcher	G	IP	SO	W	L	ERA
Morgan, Tom	156	505	164	38	22	3.48
Coates, Jim	167	510	284	37	15	3.85
Wells, Edwin	107	493	171	37	20	4.58
Moore, Wilcy	171	422	139	36	21	3.31
Sturdivant, Tom	115	524	333	36	25	3.19
Sain, Johnny	130	456	200	33	20	3.32
Shantz, Bobby	138	462	272	30	18	2.73
Shea, Frank	100	483	220	29	21	3.67
Maas, Duke	96	309	145	26	12	4.22
Quinn, John Pincus	74	382	145	26	17	3.30
Collins, Harry	64	324	105	25	13	4.14
Breuer, Marv	86	484	226	25	26	4.03
Hamilton, Steve	154	270	220	23	7	2.63
Sheldon, Rollie	91	389	202	23	15	4.14
Kuzava, Bob	104	347	187	23	20	3.40
Dubiel, Walt	56	383	124	23	22	3.88
Sherid, Roy	87	418	149	23	24	4.63
Arroyo, Luis	127	200	142	22	10	3.11
Sundra, Steve	77	316	87	21	11	4.22

Index

251

Index

Index

Index

256